Bordered Bodies, Bothered Voices

Intersectionality and Theology Series

This series is a home for theologies that weave in the strands of gender, race, and class. Because weaving involves stripping the strands, this series makes room for plaiting sub- and minor- strands. Each volume of the series, as such, will exhibit the interwoven and intersectional natures of theology—theology is a weaving or intersection where words, images, schemes, stories, bodies, struggles, cultures, and more, meet and exchange. At this weaving/intersection, traditions, standards and ideals inspire, transpire, and some even expire.

SERIES EDITOR

Jione Havea

EDITORIAL ADVISORY BOARD

Kuzipa Nalwamba, World Council of Churches (Switzerland)
Mahsheed Ansari, Islamic Science and Research Academy (Australia)
Miguel De La Torre, Iliff School of Theology (USA)
Miguel M. Algranti, Universidad Favaloro (Argentina)

OTHER WORKS IN THE INTERSECTIONALITY AND THEOLOGY SERIES:

Jin Young Choi and Joerg Rieger, eds, *Faith, Class, and Labor: Intersectional Approaches in a Global Context*

Jione Havea and Monica Jyotsna Melanchthon, eds, *Bible Blindspots: Dispersion and Othering*

S. Lily Mendoza and George Zachariah, eds, *Decolonizing Ecotheology: Indigenous and Subaltern Challenges*

BORDERED BODIES, BOTHERED VOICES

Native and Migrant Theologies

EDITED BY
Jione Havea

☙PICKWICK *Publications* · Eugene, Oregon

BORDERED BODIES, BOTHERED VOICES
Native and Migrant Theologies

Intersectionality and Theology Series

Copyright © 2022 Wipf and Stock Publishers. All rights reserved. Except for brief quotations in critical publications or reviews, no part of this book may be reproduced in any manner without prior written permission from the publisher. Write: Permissions, Wipf and Stock Publishers, 199 W. 8th Ave., Suite 3, Eugene, OR 97401.

Pickwick Publications
An Imprint of Wipf and Stock Publishers
199 W. 8th Ave., Suite 3
Eugene, OR 97401

www.wipfandstock.com

PAPERBACK ISBN: 978-1-6667-0766-3
HARDCOVER ISBN: 978-1-6667-0767-0
EBOOK ISBN: 978-1-6667-0768-7

Cataloguing-in-Publication data:

Names: Havea, Jione, editor.

Title: Bordered bodies, bothered voices : native and migrant theologies / edited by Jione Havea.

Description: Eugene, OR: Pickwick Publications, 2022. | Intersectionality and Theology Series. | Includes bibliographical references and index.

Identifiers: ISBN 978-1-6667-0766-3 (paperback). | ISBN 978-1-6667-0767-0 (hardcover). | ISBN 978-1-6667-0768-7 (ebook).

Subjects: LSCH: Liberation theology. | Postcolonial theology. | Social justice—Religious aspects—Christianity.

Classification: BR1480 B73 2022 (print). | BR1480 (ebook).

03/21/22

Scripture quotations are taken from the New Revised Standard Version Bible © 1989 National Council of the Churches of Christ in the United States of America. Used by permission. All rights reserved worldwide.

Cover: Olivia Bishop, "Untitled" (Digital media, 2019). Used with the permission of the artist.

Figure 1.1: Emmanuel Garibay, "Me Lugar pa sa Mesa" (2008). Used with the permission of the artist.

Figure 1.2: Michael J Fromholtz, "The Twelve Apostles" (2011)—Own work, CC BY-SA 4.0, https://commons.wikimedia.org/w/index.php?curid=46022256

Figure 4.1: Masi (provided by author)

Figure 4.2: Stole with masi design (provided by author).

Figure 10.1: "these bodies . . . these temples" (Photo courtesy of Ian Ferguson).

Figure 10.2: "time to be bound" (Photo courtesy of Ian Ferguson)

Figure 10.3: "presenting the bound sacred" (Photo courtesy of Ian Ferguson)

Figure 15.1: Mäṉa/ Buḻ'manydji. Used with permission of the Dhamarraṉdji clan

Figure 15.2: Djambparrpuyngu bible (Photo courtesy of Michelle Cook)

Contents

Preface | ix

Acknowledgments | x

List Contributors | xi

Introduction: Our talanoa | *The authors* | xv

1. The Vein/vain(s) of Theology: Polynesia, Poets, Pigs | *Jione Havea* | 1

Part One: Noble Borders

2. Bordered Churches, Borderless Spirit | *U-Wen Low* | 23
3. *Faavae i le Atua Samoa*: A Theological Interrogation | *Faala (Sam) Amosa* | 38
4. Cultural Colonialism: A Theological Reflection | *Eseta Waqabaca-Meneilly* | 51
5. Hospitality, Othering, and the Infinity of Worlds | *Sara S. V. Bishop* | 66

Part Two: Negotiating Bodies

6. Border Crossings: Migration and Religion in Colonial Australia | *Seforosa Carroll* | 83

7. Hosting the Invader: Re-reading Rahab's Hospitality (Joshua 2) with *Ten Years* (a 2015 Hong Kong based film) | *LIM Chin Ming Stephen* | 101

8. Deleted and Reclaimed Borders: Embracing My Native Self | *Cristina Lledo Gomez* | 119

9. Second-generation Migrant Bodies: Site of Ideological Reproduction and Implications for the Body of Christ | *Joy J. Han* | 139

Part Three: Troubling voices

10. This Body | *Valentina Satvedi* | 155

11. *Kalanga*: (sh)Outing Bodily Abuse in the Bible, Society, and Churches | *Nāsili Vaka'uta* | 162

12. *Tautua Lē Pao* and Toxic Masculinity: Voicing a *Pisa* Theology | *Brian Fiu Kolia* | 173

13. Silence | *Stephen Burns* | 186

Part Four: Riotous Bodies

14. Beyond Symbolic Stripping of Women: Ezekiel 16, Draupadi, and Dalit Women in Juxtaposition | *Monica Jyotsna Melanchthon* | 203

15. *Mäna / Bul'manydji* Calls for Wounded Theologies | *Maratja Dhamarrandji* with *Jione Havea* | 224

Index | 239

Preface

THIS BOOK PASSED THROUGH several borders. It started with two symposiums in 2019 at which eleven of the authors presented and discussed earlier drafts of their essays (Aug 2–3 and Dec 7 at Pilgrim Theological College, Melbourne, Australia). Four of the presenters at the symposiums did not come through for this publication, but thanks to the Covid interruption and delay, four other contributors joined. This book came together thanks to the hard work and patience of the authors, and the support of their families and talanoa circles.

As a collective of migrant and native authors, we are grateful for the support of three bodies who gave their trust and financial support to enable the two symposiums and the editorial tasks for this publication:

- Australian Research Theology Foundation Inc. (ARTFInc), through Howard Munro and the board;
- Research Centre of Public and Contextual Theology (PACT, Charles Sturt University), through Jonathan Cole and the management team;
- Discernment and Radical Engagement (DARE) program of the Council for World Mission, through Sudipta Singh and Michael Jagessar.

Finally, we thank the administering and editing teams at Wipf and Stock for the assistance through the publication processes.

Acknowledgments

The work on this book was supported by three bodies:

Australian Research Theology Foundation Inc. (ARTFInc)

Centre for Public and Contextual Theology (PACT),
Charles Sturt University

Discernment and Radical Engagement (DARE) program,
Council for World Mission

Contributors

Faala (Sam) Amosa is from the villages of Lufilufi, Tanugamagogo and Salesatele (Samoa), a member of the Congregational Christian Church Samoa and a graduate of Malua Theological College. Faala lives with his family in Australia, where he received a PhD from the School of Theology, Charles Sturt University (2021). He engages with Samoan culture in critical ways, and he is currently working toward revising and publishing his PhD dissertation.

Sara S. V. Bishop is embodied "both-and," both Mexican-American and European-American, a US citizen who does not live in the US, a scientist who is a pastor. She lived in Australia (when she wrote this essay), an experienced world traveler, accidental diplomat, she represents three churches of two different denominations and studied with a third. Without straying into Universalism, Sara experiences Creation in a multicultural, multi-denominational, ecumenical way that leaves her forever on the fringes.

Stephen Burns hails from England and currently teaches liturgy and practical theology at Pilgrim Theological College, within the University of Divinity, Melbourne. His publications include *Christian Worship: Postcolonial Perspectives* (with Michael N. Jagessar, 2011), *Postcolonial Practice of Ministry: Leadership, Liturgy, and Interfaith Engagement* (edited with Kwok Pui-lan, 2016), *Liturgy with a Difference: Beyond Inclusion in Christian Assembly* (edited with Bryan Cones, 2019), and *Twentieth-century Anglican Theologians* (edited with Bryan Cones and James Tengatenga, 2021).

Seforosa Carroll is an Australian-Rotuman from Fiji, theologian and ordained minister of the Uniting Church in Australia. Sef is currently Programme Executive for Mission from the Margins/Ecumenical Indigenous Peoples Network, World Council of Churches (Geneva). Her areas of research are Migration, Home, and Hospitality. Sef is a research fellow with the Center for Public and Contextual Theology (PaCT), Charles Sturt University (Australia) and member of the Center of Theological Inquiry (Princeton). Sef contributed to *Theological and Hermeneutical Explorations from Australia* (2020) and *Contemporary Feminist Theologies: Power, Authority and Love* (2021).

Maratja Dhamarra̱ndji is Djambarrpuyŋu Yolŋu (indigenous elder) from Galiwin'ku (Elcho Island, East Arnhem Land) and ordained minister of the Uniting Church in Australia. He undertook theological studies at Yalga Binbi Institute (Townsville) and Nungalinya College (Darwin) and worked for over twenty years as the chief Yolŋu Bible translator. He contributed to *Indigenous Australia and the Unfinished Business of Theology: Cross-cultural Engagement* (2014) and regularly delivers cross-cultural training.

Joy J. Han is undertaking postgraduate theological studies at the University of Divinity (Melbourne, Australia). She is an Australia Awards alum, having completed studies in sociology and work in journalism in Seoul, South Korea. Her areas of interest include postcolonial theologies in the contexts of postannexational Korea and its diaspora on the unceded lands and waters of First Nations in the settler-colonised West.

Jione Havea is co-parent for a seven-year-old, migrant to the unceded Wurundjeri lands and waters, native pastor (Methodist Church in Tonga), and research fellow with Trinity Methodist Theological College (Aotearoa New Zealand) and with Centre for Public and Contextual Theology (Charles Sturt University, Australia). Jione authored *Losing Ground: Reading Ruth in the Pacific* (2021) and co-edited *Bible Blindspots: Dispersion and Otherings* (2021) with Monica J. Melanchthon.

Brian Fiu Kōlia is an ordained minister of the Congregational Christian Church Samoa who successfully completed his PhD (2021) with Whitley College, University of Divinity (Melbourne, Australia). He is an Australian-born Samoan, from the villages of Sili Savaii and Satapuala. He contributed essays to *Sea of Readings: The Bible and the South Pacific* (2018), *Vulnerability and Resilience: Body and Liberating Theologies* (2020) and *Reading Ecclesiastes from Asia and Pasifika* (2020).

LIM Chin Ming Stephen is a Lecturer in Biblical Studies at Hong Kong Sheng Kong Hui Ming Hua Theological College and an Adjunct Lecturer in Theology with the School of Theology, Charles Sturt University (Australia). His main research interests include Bible and Contextualism, Asian biblical hermeneutics, postcolonial theory, decolonial thought, and Bible in the contemporary world. His *Contextual Biblical Hermeneutics as Multicentric Dialogue: Towards a Singaporean Reading of Daniel* was published in 2019.

Cristina Lledo Gomez is a Catholic Systematic Theologian born in the Philippines and theologising from Australia. She is a Presentation Sisters Lecturer at BBI—The Australian Institute of Theological Education, and Religion and Society Research Fellow with Charles Sturt University's Public and Contextual Theology Centre (PACT). Her research areas are ecclesiology, maternal-feminist theology, and social justice issues including migration and domestic violence. Her *Church as Woman and Mother: Historical and Theological Foundations* was published in 2018.

U-Wen Low is a Chinese-Malaysian immigrant to Australia who is working through the implications of displacement and the exercise of power both for immigrants and First Nations people. He was recently a lecturer in Biblical Studies and Program Director for the Master of Theology at Alphacrucis College, residing in Melbourne, Australia. His research interests include the Book of Revelation, postcolonial criticism, performance criticism, Pentecostal theology, popular culture, and Asian hermeneutics.

Monica J. Melanchthon is a church worker (ordained minister of the Andhra Evangelical Lutheran Church, India) and theological educator. She currently teaches Hebrew Bible/Old Testament at the Pilgrim Theological College, University of Divinity (Melbourne, Australia) and has published in various academic books focusing on interpretations of Old Testament texts from the Indian context and the perspectives of the marginalized. Her current projects include a feminist commentary on 1 Kings for the Wisdom Commentary Series and an Earth Bible Commentary on Joshua 1–11.

Valentina Satvedi is a Minister in placement at Pilgrim Uniting Church in Launceston. Ordained in the Anabaptist tradition, she is current President of the Anabaptist Association of Australia and New Zealand. She pursues her interests in Pacifism, Undoing Oppressions and Reconciliation on the traditional lands of the Litarimirina people on the island lutruwita (Tasmania).

Nāsili Vakaʻuta is Principal and Ranston Lecturer in Biblical Studies, Trinity Theological College, Auckland, New Zealand. He is the author of *Reading Ezra 9–10 Tuʻa-wise: Rethinking Biblical Interpretation in Oceania* (2011), co-editor of *Bible and Art, Perspectives from Oceania* (2017), and contributed to many academic journals and book volumes such as *Bible, Borders, Belonging(s)* (2015), *Islands, Islanders and the Bible: RumInations* (2015), *Voices from the Margin* (2016), and *Land and People: Decolonizing Theologies* (2019).

Eseta Waqabaca-Meneilly is a retired clergy, Fijian woman migrant. Her hobbies include music, reading and sewing. Through sewing she has explored ways of expressing her Fijian heritage using cultural and liturgical symbols on patchwork bedspreads and liturgical stoles. She contributed to *Talanoa Ripples: Across Borders, Cultures, Disciplines* (2010) and her current research is on the relationships between Gospel narratives in John and the use of symbols and rituals in Fijian *iTaukei* (indigenous) contemporary Culture.

Introduction: Our Talanoa

The Authors

Theologies are constructed in and from lived contexts, and contexts are shaped by borders. While borders are barriers, they are also stepping-stones for crossing over and opportunities for moving further.

This collection of essays offers theological and cultural reflections from the intersections of borders (real and imagined), bodies (physical, cultural, religious, ideological, political) and voices (that endorse as well as talk back). In the following chapters—some borders are affirmed, some borders are interrogated, some borders are crossed, some borders are negotiated, and some borders are levelled into paths. And while some bodies and voices are engaged, many are not—and we humbly apologize and invite more work to be done along these limitations.

The Cover

On the cover of this book is Olivia Bishop's "Untitled" (2019), which depicts a young subject at a border. The border lines have been drawn, and they left a mark on the face of this young subject: under their—for the subject could be male, female, trans—left eye, is a cross-mark that could be a shadow of or a scar from the barbed wire. This young subject holds the barbed border with both hands, and with their left thumb tests one of the barbs—Is this sharp? Should we be afraid? The subject could also be playing with the barb—This is bearable! We are not scared! Their face is covered by their right hand, inviting viewers to imagine whether they were afraid or fearless. If not both.

The artwork by Olivia Bishop, who herself was a young migrant (at the time of creating this work) to the land now known as Australia, invites viewers and readers to see bordered bodies as troubled and marked, as well as determined and resilient. They are bordered, but they have not lost their will or their subjectivities—in spite of the marks that the borders have left upon their bodies. Along these lines, the authors in this collection embrace and engage bordered bodies and give vent to bothered voices.

The Flow

The first chapter situates the essays along the vein/vain(s) of doing theology, then the essays are divided into four overlapping clusters—Noble Borders (chapters 2–5), Negotiating Bodies (chapters 6–9), Troubling Voices (chapters 10–13), Riotous Bodies (chapters 14–15)—that express the shared drives between the authors, who engage their topics and subjects out of their own experiences as migrants and natives. This work is thus a step toward, and an invitation for more work on, migrant and native theologies.

Noble Borders

Some borders are not experienced as constricting barriers because they are seen as noble. This naïve stance is often applied to religious institutions (U-Wen Low, chap. 2), to traditional understandings of cultural values (Faala Amosa, chap. 3), to dominant cultures (Eseta Waqabaca-Meneilly, chap. 4), and to privileged teachings (Sara S. V. Bishop, chap. 5). In this cluster of essays, noble borders are engaged and interrogated. Put clearly, noble borders are not off-limits—a courageous resolve conveyed in Olivia Bishop's playful (and cheeky) subject.

In chapter 2, U-Wen Low discusses the rise of many charismatic expressions of Christianity, seemingly simultaneously and unconnected with one another, around the world during the early 20th century. Despite these parallel evolutions sharing similar beliefs and practices—and claiming to be similarly inspired by the Spirit, over time many of these expressions were gradually sublimated into and by Western Pentecostalism, itself largely derived from the Azusa Street Awakening and proselytised by missionaries with strong colonial attitudes. Using these early Pentecostal churches as a case study, U-Wen explores how newly formed bodies are naturally limited to "borders" by power-driven (colonial) mindsets, and how privileged bodies eventually come to dominate similarly inspired bodies. There is much to learn: a shared inspiration may not be sufficient for bodies to retain a unique identity as they fall under the influence of powers that seek to draw borders in order to dominate others. At the same time, hope can continue to be found as bodies connect with one another through the common inspiration of the Spirit.

In chapter 3, Faala (Sam) Amosa reflects on the motto of Samoa, *Faavae i le Atua Samoa* (Samoa is founded on God), honoured by Samoans in Samoa and Samoans in diaspora. But Samoans are not conscious about what the motto means or entails. How did *Faavae i le Atua Samoa* come about? To which deity (*atua*) does the motto refer? Who coined the phrase and how did it become the nation's motto? Prominent figures who pushed for Samoa's independence were silent on the nation's motto though they were involved in drafting the nation's constitution. Samoan and European historians, anthropologists, theologians, sociologists and political writers mention the motto, but they do not explain.

Faala's controversial argument is that *Faavae i le Atua Samoa* is anticulture. The Samoan name Atua (deity) derives from Maori religious beliefs that refer to a spirit or mana. Atua is associated with a native supernatural spirit or being. Other Pasifika islands use Atua to refer to their supreme gods and deities. In the case of Samoa, Tagaloaalagi was the supreme Atua of Samoa. In these connections, which deity is Samoan founded on, God (of White Christianity) or Atua (of Samoa)? Why did Samoans choose to worship the God of the *Papalagi* (White, European) and not continue to worship Tagaloaalagi the Atua of Samoa? How might the motto be moved to make space for both the God of the Papalagi and the Atua of Samoa? The answer to these questions comes from re-understanding "faavae" both as foundation (*faavae*) and as mobile (*faa-vae*).

In chapter 4, Eseta Waqabaca-Meneilly retells her experience as a migrant to Australia and joining the Uniting Church in Australia (UCA) which has declared itself a Multicultural Church. Eseta concludes that it is imperative that a Multicultural Church with many different languages enable communication and foster cross-cultural relationships. The language most common to all and used for this purpose is English. The English language, with its culturally stratified classes, thought patterns and frameworks, becomes the central mode of governance of the UCA. This central system places demands and expectations on the other languages and cultures to shape their cultural ways and imaginations to comply with the English language patterns and frameworks, thus giving credence to its values and structures. This centralized mode of governance system is a hallmark of cultural colonialism which is incongruent with the ideology of a multicultural church. As a result, misunderstandings and anxiety arise. This essay offers into this scenario of unrest and uncertainty the ideology of hope.

In chapter 5, Sara S. V. Bishop reflects on how living in six countries in twenty years, and spending over two years combined without more than what her family could carry in their suitcases, creates a narrative in which one pictures refugees or migrants—but in her case: expatriates, particularly diplomats who live and work at Embassies overseas in service to the government—navigating a life of always being "the other." In the world of perpetually in-between, hospitality is the bridge, and it is rarely done well, if at all, since the lens of hospitality is primarily a colonized one and has become about the host, not the guest. Sara proposes that the idea of reconciling disparate peoples can be addressed in a brief examination of lived experiences of a diplomat and Lutheran pastor, in which doors are thresholds both to keep things in as well as to keep things out, and at once persistently crossed.

Negotiating Bodies

The essays in this cluster witness to bodies constantly negotiating and relocating borders. The crux of the negotiations may be in terms of religion and coloniality (Seforosa Carroll, chap. 6), of current realities and modern culture (LIM Stephen Chin Ming, chap. 7), of suppressed identities and tongues (Cristina Lledo Gomez, chap. 8), and of assigned markers of identity (Joy J. Han, chap. 9). Naturally, bodies negotiate and relocate. And the authors in this cluster of essays, like Olivia Bishop's young subject, are not afraid of the thorns that mark their bordered subjects.

In chapter 6, Seforosa Carroll explains how migrant bodies embody and carry across borders both culture and religion, and at the same time challenge dominant religious and cultural borders by their presence. The presence of many religions in Australia is primarily a function of migration. This phenomenon is not pertinent to Australia but is reflected in many first world countries in the West. The defining characteristic of the 2015 refugee crisis in Europe was religion. This "crisis" challenged existing cultural and religious borders and gave rise to increasing nationalistic overtones. Sef accordingly explores how migrant bodies interweave, interact and intersect at, on, across and beyond borders. And how and in what ways do migrant bodies contest and re/make cultural and religious borders.

In chapter 7, LIM Stephen Chin Ming engages the fraught dynamics of what is increasingly recognized as mainlandization of Hong Kong, with

Rahab in Joshua 2 through the lens of nativism and hospitality. Stephen engaged his subject with contextual hermeneutics, understood as multicentric dialogue through three loci of enunciation. The first locus of enunciation draws from Derrida's notion of hospitality that ostensibly resists nativism of right-wing populism which has been a malady in the West for a very long time now. In order to generate a theological response, it is possible to argue that Rahab presents a model of hospitality that gravitates more to what Derrida sees as unconditional hospitality in her abundant generosity, especially her willingness to take risks on behalf of her guests at the expense of her own life. This is further emphasized in the second locus of enunciation which explores a Daoist understanding of hospitality through the legend of *Hundun* where *hundun* pays the ultimate price of his very self and identity in his act of hospitality. Both loci of enunciation emphasize in their own distinctive ways the importance of hospitality as a correction to nativism. The third locus of enunciation is drawn from a film co-directed by Zune Kwok, Fei-pang Wong, Jevons Au, Kwun-Wai Chow and Ka-leung Ng, titled *Ten Years* (2015) that reflects on the possible futures of Hong Kong after the British handover in 1997. While the previous loci of enunciation bring to the surface several ambivalences in Rahab's response, it is the third locus that compels Stephen to have a more critical analysis of the virtue of unconditional hospitality through these nativist responses.

Stephen explores the possible costs of Rahab's hospitality in the light of the evolving situation in Hong Kong where a weaker vassal is compelled to play host to a stronger Empire. This is in order to seek an(-)Other way to read this troubled instance of Rahab welcoming the enemy into her very own home so as to recover an ethic of hospitality in relation to nativism that takes into serious consideration power relations between host and guest, which would (re/)inform praxis and possibly, generate resistance.

In chapter 8, Cristina Lledo Gomez reclaims the lost borders of her "self" as a native woman from the Philippines, and as a theologian—beginning with an experience of *talanoa* and expressing feelings of being deleted and lost as a migrant and a woman of color. Internalized oppression as a result of being colonized as a people certainly contributed to these feelings of erasure and negation. It was in "being seen" as a native woman by a fellow native woman, an Australian Aboriginal woman, that enabled Cristina to begin the journey of reclaiming her native self. Discovering the *babaylan* tradition in particular, launched her into forging the beginnings of a *babayi* theology using the *babaylan* value of *kapwa*. The methodology used throughout the chapter is ethnoautobiography—an indigenous form of storytelling that restores wholeness and reconnects alienated modern selves.

In chapter 9, Joy J. Han explains how the terminology from the "three generations" analysis of migrant cohorts—such as the marker "second-generation" that is generally applied to those born in the host country to immigrant parents—serves not only to docket certain bodies but also to catalogue those bodies' sociological characteristics. Joy examines the paradoxical classification of so-called "second-generation migrant" bodies in order to show up the discursive reproduction of various historical and ideological violence, including reproductive heteronormativity and ethno-biological essentialism, upon those bodies. Particular attention is paid to the use of the terms "second-generation" and "Next Gen" within the Uniting Church in Australia (UCA). This critical examination interrogates the apparent cooptation of certain ideologies to the Body of Christ that is implied by the methodological consolidation of "second-generation Christians" as a subject of sociological interest; and show the discursive overdetermination, essentialization and resulting theological aggrandizement of "second-generation Christians" and how they negotiate postcoloniality.

Troubling Voices

While all essays in this work express troubled/bothered voices, the essays in this cluster highlight key areas of critical concern to migrants and natives. These include the hidden barriers that have been enforced by one's upbringing and heritage (Valentina Satvedi, chap. 10), by the scriptural sanctification of abuse (Nāsili Vaka'uta, chap. 11), by toxic masculinity in native cultures (Brian Fiu Kolia, chap. 12), and by the cultures of silence that bypass interrogation (Stephen Burns, chap. 13). This cluster of essays sh/outs against shitstems that facilitate and license abuse (bodies) and muteness (voices).

Chapter 10 is a poetic and artistic exploration by Valentina Satvedi that explores the intersections that bind her: born as an Asian woman into the borders of gender, religion, family, culture and tradition. Valentina walked and crossed these borders, and find the need to unbind and permeate, in order to find release, to "chrysalis" into being. Restrictive in nature, borders can be dismantled and rendered permeable, yet there is an ongoing building of borders. Such edifices arise out of deep-seated desires to overpower, overwhelm and suppress those marked as other. These actions are all deeply rooted in fear.

As a migrant, immigrant and settler with a body that was birthed in and through borders, Valentina gives voice to internalizations and socializations that continue to affect the dismantling of borders. She brings to this process the lens of an individual influenced by colonialism, raised in a patriarchal society, racialized on an ongoing basis, and continues to experience people's arrogant abilities to trespass the boundaries (compared to borders) set to protect.

In chapter 11, Nāsili Vakaʻuta rides on the wave of the #MeToo movement—a movement that has given voices to victims of sexual abuse in the hands of powerful men. Named by *Time* magazine as the 2017 Person of the Year, the movement demands close scrutiny of such abuse in all areas of life. Nāsili plays his part in this movement by calling out the complicity of religion (the church in this case), its blindness to the violence of scriptures (the Bible in this case), its validation of the "sins of the chosen" and the illusion of male innocence (e.g., Abraham, Lot), its deafness to the cries of the forgotten (e.g., Hagar, Lot's daughters, and Tamar), and above all, its failure on many fronts to be an agent for justice, freedom and transformation. Nāsili engages selected texts to expose some of the perverts of the Bible, the politics of election, and most importantly, to amplify the voices of those *across and beyond the borders* of both texts and society with particular reference to Oceania.

In chapter 12, Brian Fiu Kōlia begins with the Samoan saying *O le ala i le pule o le tautua* ("The path to authority/chiefhood is service/toil") which has been institutionalized for the Samoans in serving their elders. The reward for such hard service, is *pule* (authority) by becoming a *matai* (chief). Often, *pule* and *tautua* are stressed but not so much the *ala* (path/way). Significantly, it is in the *ala* that *tautua* (toiling) and hard work occur. In a typical Samoan setting, the men do all the heavy labor, the women perform lighter domestic duties, and *faʻafāfine* (transgender) perform the same duties as the men, but also domestic chores of women, albeit with male strength.

The brunt of *tautua* is performed by the *tauleʻaleʻa* (young untitled man). Ultimately, much of the *pule* (authority)—primarily through *matai* titles—is afforded to these young men. It is an androcentric agenda that discriminates against women and *faʻafāfine* yet plays on the masculinity of the Samoan male, propagated by expectations to perform *tautua* regardless of physical and mental health. Which begs the questions: Does *tautua* promote a cultural propaganda? Does *tautua* incite toxic masculinity? In addressing these queries, Brian proposes a *pisa* theology (a theology that talks back to tradition).

In chapter 13, Stephen Burns joins the conversation on "silence," which has received some fresh attention in contemporary theology (e.g., Sarah Maitland, A *Book of Silence* [Granta, 2008] and Diarmaid MacCulloch, *Silence: A Christian History* [Penguin, 2013]), which while touching on difficult topics (e.g. MacCulloch's short section on anti-Semitism) does not explore as it might the ambivalence of silence in relation to the "bordered bodies, bothered voices" present in this book. So, Stephen looks again at silence—sloganized ("white silence, more violence"), theorized, and enacted in solidarity and advocacy, in listening and resistance, in complicity and refusal, seeking consciousness of minorized-racialization from privileged position (white privilege, the only such kind in the collection).

Riotous Bodies

The two essays in this closing cluster draw attention to two bordered bodies that have not been appropriately engaged in the wider circles of theology—Dalit women (Monica J. Melanchthon, chap. 14) and the First Peoples of Australia (Maratja Dhamarrandji with Jione Havea, chap. 15). These two essays represent one of the riots that this collection seeks: the riot in embracing wisdom in and of stripped, humiliated, rejected and wounded bodies. Until these subjects are appropriately engaged, they continue to be riotous.

In chapter 14, Monica Jyotsna Melanchthon reads Ezekiel 16 alongside the stripping of Draupadi in the *Mahabharata*, and contemporary resonances in India evidenced particularly in the public stripping, parading, and shaming of Dalit women. This reading focuses on the manner in which borders of culture, religion and scripture are transcended for the control and the insidious traumatization of Dalit women's bodies. Draupadi was "clothed" by the divine in the *Mahabharata* but Woman-city was violated at the whim of the divine in Ezekiel 16; the upshot of Melanchthon's reading of these ancient scriptures is riotous: who will stand up for stripped and violated Dalit women in the villages and streets of India?

And in chapter 15, Maratja Dhamarrandji and Jione Havea reflect on the Yolŋu scriptures (dreamtime story, art, cooking practice) about *Mana Bul'manydji*, a wounded shark. This set of Yolŋu scriptures is presented as a theological platform for engaging with wounded bodies (including Jesus's pierced body). Maratja and Jione bring the collection to close by "calling every theology" (echoing Yothu Yindi's "calling every nation") to engage with beckoning bodies and wounded voices of First and Native peoples.

So What?

In and from their lived experiences, the authors provide platforms for outing biases against migrants and natives. This work is an attempt at doing migrant and native theologies, and an invitation for *woking* the theological trade.

1

The Vein/Vain(s) of Theologies

Poly~~nesia~~, Poets, Pigs

JIONE HAVEA

THEOLOGIES—IF THEY ARE ALIVE—WOULD have veins that, like the vascular systems in plants and animals, carry nutrition and energy to their organs and limbs. To open this metaphor up: the vascular system would also carry unhealthy and dying theological cells, toxins, and viruses, to sites where they are treated or excreted. The health of the theological vascular system is therefore critical for the survival of theologies; healthy veins feed and sustain theological bodies, but not all theological veins are healthy. To coin a phonetic play, and to echo the double-edging voice of Qoheleth, unhealthy veins are vain.[1]

The condition of theological veins, to use human imageries, is affected by the heritage and lifestyle of those theologies. Unhealthy theologies make theological veins sick(ly), and they become dysfunctional; those theologies consequently become unhealthier. Some sickly theologies die but many linger, and in both situations the diseased and the die-hard theologies haunt the theological trade.[2] At another level, not all healthy

---

1. Notwithstanding, not all theologies are healthy. Some theologies, even with healthy veins, are vain.

2. "Trade" here refers to work (theologies are done, constructed, produced, and not just thought-up or conceived through mental exercises) and exchange (theologies are

theologies foster life and serve justice; death-dealing and unjust theologies, too, haunt the theological trade.

My *talanoa* (on this native term, see below) is guilty of animating the doing (read: construction) of theologies, but it aims to invite conversations on the interflow between the veins and vain(s) of theologies. What theological veins are sick(ly) and make the doing of theologies, to borrow the words of Qoheleth, "an unhappy business that God has given to human beings to be busy with" (Eccl 1:13b NRSV)? And, flowing in the reverse direction, could what some "teachers" consider to be "vanity of vanities" (compare Eccl 1:2) be veins for healthy theologies? I engage these questions, with more energy on the second, around three affairs which teachers in the traditional theological trade see as vanities: the preference for and orientation to many-ness (Polynesia), the creative energies at the intersections of orality and oratory (Poets), and the controversies that flow in the veins of artists (Pigs).

To set up a platform for those conversations, i first muse around one of the traditional understandings of the concept of theology. My musings are carried under the wings of talanoa and framed by the keywords in the title of this book—borders, bodies, voices.

Theologies

Appropriating a theological position attributed to Anselm of Canterbury (1033–1109), i take theology/theologies (*theos* + *logos*) as a register for events in which humans use images (for Anselm's *logos*) to express and formulate understandings of godly matters (Anselm's *theos*). For the purposes of this reflection, i add the following four observations:

First, theology is a human project. Obviously. I thus expect theology to privilege human interests. However, humans come in many sizes and many shapes, out of many closets with many blind-spots, shaped by many orientations and many degrees of mobility, showcasing many shades, many colors, and many races, discriminating against other alternatives and other creatures, so that a one-size-fits-all theology is unreasonable and unfair. Humans are many, and it is only fair and just that there are many theologies.

Second, theologies are not constructed nor conveyed only in written and scripted events (for Anselm's *logos*). There are theologies in and through other platforms such as stories and storytelling (see Maratja Dhamarrandji with Jione Havea, chap. 15), dance, music, poetry (see Valentina Satvedi,

---

done through the swapping, substituting, switching, and crossing of teachings, wisdoms, traditions, scriptures, cultures, beliefs, and more).

chap. 10), art, handicraft (see Eseta Waqabaca-Meneilly, chap. 4), and so forth. In settings where writing is privileged, these alternative texts are seen as low-class. Alternative texts have something to communicate, and they even talk back against dominant literature, but they are not received in the same way as written texts are. In settings where orality is privileged, on the other hand, alternative texts are not lowered (minoritized) or hidden. In oral(izing) settings, such artistic texts are obvious and loud.

Third, i treat theologies as platforms for asserting, for testing and for interrogating *understandings* of godly matters. I use "understanding" here because that is the term commonly used to translate Anselm's motto, *fides quaerens intellectum* (faith seeking understanding). But this motto, which goes back to Augustine of Hippo (354–430), a Roman African, may also be translated as "faith seeking intelligence." With "intelligence" i problematize the default choice for "understanding" (*intellectum*) not because i want to say that faith (*fides*) is irrational but because i see theologies as platforms for *ongoing processes* of asserting, testing, and interrogating one's *conceptions* (read: theological understandings and assertions are conceived, and they are open for—by and through *intelligence*—testing and interrogation). The emphasis here is on the evolving and ongoing nature of theologies, which means that understandings will shift, and intelligence will build up (see also Joy J. Han, chap. 9).

Fourth, i look for "godly matters" (for Anselm's *theos*) beyond the shadows of the God of Christianity. I take my leave on account of the mainline trinitarian understanding according to which God—Father, Son, Holy Spirit—is a relational body (or unit). The personas of the trinitarian God relate to one another like flows in the same current—a sort of theological G(odly)-current (or G-unit). In their confluence, the trinitarian Christian G-current *draws in* other godly flows. The trinitarian God can only and truly be relational when it embraces, engages, and accommodates other godly *bodies* outside of the Christian *borders*, and when it is open to other *intelligences* concerning what it means to be godly. The trinity qua mainline Christian position thus allows me to step away from its own lines and borders, and it is at this confluence that the twist in the title to this chapter may be conceived (or understood, as in Anselm's *intellectum*): a *vein* is *vain*. Put another way, to echo the wisdom of Qoheleth, the vein that gives life to mainline Christian theologies is vanity. And also: vice versa.

These observations, in the eyes of mainline Christian theologies, are vain. But they are theological veins for asserting, testing and interrogating—which are activities favored in the circles of talanoa—theological platforms and theological positions. These theological veins are healthy in the company of liberation critics and in talanoa circles.

Liberation

Some of the therapeutic initiatives in theological and biblical studies came together in the 1960s, strongly out of Latin America and led by church and cultural critics. These initiatives birthed liberation theologies and hermeneutics which called for the emancipation of the poor and the marginalized and for closer attention to space (over against time) and context (on earth rather than in heaven, on the other side). Contextual and postcolonial criticisms followed along in the march for emancipation with chants against powers that suppress subjects based on their class, race, gender, sexuality, mobility, and other forms of subalternity.

The theological and hermeneutical march for liberation came to a fork on the road in the 1990s, mainly in response to the rising awareness of the postmodern conditions and out of respect to the tag-team of globalization and capitalism. At this fork, two communes diverted: first, a commune of liberation theologians and critics who carried the flags of identity politics (or identitarianism). This commune was devoted to being at the borders on the ground, accompanying "the poor" (initially in terms of class, gender, and race) and resisting against impoverishing and minoritizing shitstems. Second, a commune of theologians and critics who set out to chart theoretical paths for the so-called liberation turn. The first commune emphasized real subjects (interlocutors) and took advantage of the emotions of solidarity (but in some places became thin in theoretical understandings or intelligences), while the second commune surfed the waves of theoretical sophistication and convolution (but in some places became thin in engagement with real bodies). Thankfully, the diversion did not drone on. Some theologians and critics learned to participate in both communes, and this collection of essays also seeks to negotiate the diversion through the voices of natives and migrants.

An example of another project that seeks to hold the two communes together is *Voices from the Margin* edited by R. S. Sugirtharajah. The first edition of *Voices from the Margin* (1991)[3] contained essays that built upon the commitments and insights of Latin American liberation hermeneutics, that openly engaged with the contexts of readers and their communities, and that experimented with reading biblical texts in the context of other readers, other scriptures, and other faith traditions. There have since been two revised editions (1995, 2006)[4] plus a twenty fifth anniversary edition (2016), with some essays (or voices) being reprinted in all of the

---

3. Sugirtharajah, *Voices from the Margin*.
4. Inspired by the 2006 edition was Sugirtharajah, *Still at the Margins*.

editions, some voices being removed or replaced, some new voices being added,[5] and some voices shifted to other points of attention.[6] Through the four editions of *Voices from the Margin* the turn toward postcolonial criticism is strong, but the call for liberation become weaker. The postcolonial turn of the *Voices from the Margin* shows that resistance is the appropriate response to *interpreting the Bible* and *doing theology* in the spirit of liberation at contexts in which empires grab lands and colonize the minds and spirits of (native) people.[7] The postcolonial turn is a decent next step to the turns to context and liberation.

I am however disturbed by the popular assumption that contextual, liberation and postcolonial interpretations and theologies are only for people from the so-called third world (as the subtitle to *Voices from the Margin* suggest). These turns are not reserved only for interpreters and theologians from the global south, who are also expected to be interested in the survival of their churches and communities.[8] So our "badass" efforts, to borrow from Miguel A. De La Torre, are snubbed for not meeting the standards for proper academic scholarship, which is usually defined according to White and Western criteria.[9] Pushing back at such tendencies is one of the motivations for this collection of essays.

I struggle also with the tendency to overemphasize space and theory at the expense of flesh(ed) and blood(ied) bodies (see also Nāsili Vakaʻuta, chap. 11). I am reminded of a panel discussion at a Society of Biblical Literature annual conference that celebrated the 2006 edition of *Voices from the Margin*. One of the senior scholars on the panel defended the need to continue speaking of margins (as space for theoretical exploration and theological reflection) and was rattled when a lesser-known badass scholar pointed out that there are real people who live on real margins and would be offended to hear that some (unrealistic) scholars consider their (real) homes as margins. For marginalized people, margins are not

---

5. From the context of Pasifika, there was no voice in the first edition but a contribution by Leslie Boseto was included in the second edition (1995). Boseto's essay was not selected for the third edition (2006), but our region is catching up with three essays in the twenty-fifth anniversary edition (2016)!

6. Archie C. C. Lee of Hong Kong offers "The David–Bathsheba Story and the Parable of Nathan" in the first edition (1991), "The Chinese Creation Myth of Nu Kua and the Biblical Narrative in Genesis 1–11" in the second edition (1995), and "Returning to China: Biblical Interpretation in Postcolonial Hong Kong" in the third edition (2006, and reprinted in the twenty-fifth anniversary edition of 2016).

7. See Havea, *People and Land*; Havea, *Scripture and Resistance*.

8. See for example Haire, "The Centrality of Contextual Theology for Christian Existence Today."

9. See De La Torre, *Burying White Privilege*.

theoretical spaces. Rather, margins are lived spaces.[10] Along that line, the authors of the following chapters do not romanticize the reality of borders nor the experience of bodies on borders. The authors, in different ways, surf the energies of talanoa.

Talanoa[11]

The term "talanoa," used in some but not all native Pasifika languages, refers to three events—*story* (usually a combination of stories), *telling* (of story/stories), and *conversation* (musing, storyweaving). A *story* (talanoa) is lost if no one tells it and if a group does not talk about it; a *telling* (talanoa) is dry if it has no story, and it turns into scolding if there is no conversation; and a *conversation* (talanoa) withers without story and telling. As event of story-telling-and-conversation, talanoa involves (re)gathering, (re)membering and (re)purposing—i.e., *(re)storying*—and it is ongoing.

Talanoa is neither philosophy nor methodology (in the western sense), but native event-and-practice that is rooted deeply in Pasifika.[12] Pasifika breathes (because of) talanoa. Without talanoa, meanings hide and relations sag. In these regards, talanoa is an oralizing-(plat)form:

- Talanoa scripturalizes oral texts.
- Talanoa stretches orality to all aspects of living, and it is preserved in many (plat)forms including poetry, artwork, handicraft, dance, ritual, ceremony, etcetera.
- Talanoa, to borrow a postmodern image, lets authors die but awakens future generations to receive, disseminate or hide the stories, tellings and conversations.
- Talanoa weaves orality with oratory, inspiring orators to bring the past, the dead, the forgotten, together with the present and the future, into remembering and into life.
- Talanoa embraces poly/many-ness and alternatives: we need talanoa because we are many, and we protect talanoa to be—in our image—many.

10. See also Anzaldúa, *Borderlands/La Frontera*.

11. This section appropriates discussions spelled out in more detail in chapter 2 of Havea, *Losing Ground*.

12. Other native people have similar cultures and practices, but my attention in this reflection is on Pasifika. For this reason, also, i resist translating talanoa as "storytelling"—a term that has connotations in the academic and theological English-speaking worlds that oversimplify, and thus pacify, the Pasifika event-and-practice.

- Talanoa breaks social barriers so that experts, academics, and executives may humbly sit and talanoa with normal people to co-learn and inter-enlighten.

Talanoa creates events in which ongoing, churning processes (see third observation on "Theologies" section above) could take place. By foregrounding talanoa i push four of its affects upon the doing of theologies:

  i. Theologies are ongoing and open-ended. Theologies are not exercises through which one reaches conclusions with certainties, but processes of seeking to make intelligible (rational, understandable) life situations and perceptions that unfold over constantly changing contexts (see also Joy J. Han, chap. 9). In this regard, "good theologies" are restless.[13]

  ii. Consequently, theologies involve rounds and rounds of asserting, testing, and interrogating godly matters. In this connection, good theologies also reexamine and queer (see also Brian Kolia, chap. 12).

  iii. Because of their restless and queer qualities, good theologies also need to be welcoming and hospitable (see also Sara Bishop, chap. 5; LIM Chin Ming Stephen, chap. 7).

  iv. This is not to say that theologians and theologies do not also listen. As in talanoa, theologians and theologies listen when they learn to embrace silence (see also Stephen Burns, chap. 13).

Thus conceived, talanoa is among the vain/veins for doing theologies. Under the wings of talanoa, theologies become "faith seeking conception." Obviously.

Borders

Doing theologies involves crossing borders. In this assertion, "crossing" takes place in the physical and metaphorical senses of the term and "borders" are both real and ideological (see also Seforosa Carroll, chap. 6). Doing theologies involves crossing borders with body and limbs as well as with words, thoughts, teachings, talanoa, etcetera. And the borders that one crosses—in doing theologies—may be physical (like a wall or tombstone), spiritual (like a belief or commitment), scriptural (like a text or artwork), cultural (like a ritual or protocol), and so forth.

13. I am appealing here to a conversation with Gustavo Gutiérrez for whom i was a research student twice when he visited the seminary where i studied. I wanted to know what he would consider as "good theology" and his response was clear and obvious—a theology that does not feed the poor is *not* good theology.

Put another way, crossing borders is the primary call of theologies and of churches (see also U-Wen Low, chap. 2). Moreover, crossing borders is the crux of the talanoa behind and in the following chapters.

Bodies

Humans do not and cannot live alone. Humans make up one big family—even though we are not always one happy family—in the worldwide circle of life, and we are interdependent with other living creatures on earth as it is in the sea (where corals and rocks are alive) and in the underworld (where solid rocks liquefy and flow). Humans live with and thanks to other species, and to that humbling awareness i add a native Pasifika twist: humans also live and are interdependent with our dead ancestors—their memories, wisdoms, *tapu* (sanctification, protection) and *mana* (empowerment, enlightenment)—as well as with the breaths and the aspirations of unborn, future generations. In historical terms, the present is *interwoven* with the past and the future.

According to ancient Papuan wisdom, as Denis Koibur—one of my West Papuan mentors—taught me, the worlds of dead ancestors and of unborn generations are not removed from the world of living humans. On the other hand, humans live in the world of the ancestors and impact the world to come (of unborn generations). Moreover, future generations are the *roots* of the current generation. This ancient wisdom overturns the common expectation that the current generation provides the roots and nourishments for future generations. In the native Papuan understanding of the complex and delicate web of life, humans are individuals who are never alone; and unseen bodies are our roots (future generations) and comrades (ancestors). Obviously.

Bothered voices

The links between bodies are disturbed and broken by borders (which themselves are bodies) that separate them. And when bodies-that-have-become-borders stand on some of the bodies, related-or-linked-bodies have the option to assist and push back or to break the link(s), to look away, and to walk pass on the other side. The collective of voices in this book speaks against the tendencies to disconnect from and to ignore the bordered bodies.

Put another way, the bothered voices in the following chapters lay out theological veins to bodies that have been made or seen as vain (read:

vain-ed bodies). For the remainder of this chapter, i call attention to three vain-ed bodies: Poly~~nesia~~, Poets, Pigs.

Poly~~nesia~~

Tonga, my home(is)land, is grouped among the islands of "Polynesia," an inappropriate label given by European scholars who subdivided *Moana-nui-a-kiwa* (one of the native names for what is now known as the Pacific Ocean and Pacific Islands).[14] The vanities of the subregional divisions of Moana-nui-a-kiwa have been addressed by native scholars,[15] and i will not repeat that conversation here. Rather, i add my own strike—Poly~~nesia~~—so that this vain European label could become a vein for doing theologies.

With my strike, i affirm the primary connotation of *Polynésie* when it was first used by the French writer Charles de Brosses (1756)—as a reference to *all of the many islands* in Moana-nui-a-kiwa. Poly~~nesia~~ thus emphasizes our many-ness, over against our differences according to the type, size (micro) or color (mela) of island(er)s.[16] To make my strike more obvious, Poly~~nesia~~ pushes back at the drives to divide and at once *unify* which some (ancient and modern) teachers of theology undertake when they (with the rhetoric of one- and mono-ness) emphasize, for example, mono-theism and the one-ness of the deity (in the concept of trinity) and of *the* truth.

In another reflection, i used "onefication" for the *drive to unify* shared by both scholars and colonialists who put different and diverse people into one group or one category—for example: natives, pagans, savages, uncivilized, uneducated, aboriginals, migrants, etcetera—because it is easier to manage them (ideologically, emotionally, spiritually, physically) if they are seen to be one and the same.[17] Pushing back against the processes of onefication, Upolu Vaai called for "de-onefication" as a more appropriate mode for doing theology in Pasifika.[18] I too advocate de-onefication as a necessary step for decolonizing oneficating-theologies, but it is not enough to simply subvert the drive to unify. I opt for Poly~~nesia~~ because i also want to exhibit what many-ness (poly) may look like in the doing of theologies.

14. "Polynesia" is from a Greek construct that means "many islands." The other two inappropriate labels are "Melanesia" (black islands) and "Micronesia" (small islands).

15. See, e.g., Hau'ofa, "Our Sea of Islands."

16. Jules Dumont d'Urville narrowed "Polynesia" to the islands between Hawai'i, Tuvalu, Tonga, Aotearoa and Rapa Nui (based on complexion) in a lecture to the Geographical Society of Paris in 1831.

17. See Havea, "Control, Conciliation, Coalition."

18. See Vaai, "*Lagimālie*: COVID, De-Onefication of Theologies, and Eco-Relational Wellbeing."

Poly~~nesia~~ (affirmation of many-ness) is vain according to some parts of the Bible, for example, "Jesus said to him, 'I am the way, and the truth, and the life. No one comes to the Father except through me'" (John 14:6 NRSV). In this text, there are no alternatives. Jesus alone is the way, the truth, and the life. But there are other parts of the Bible which are open for many (alternatives): "I am the LORD your God, who brought you out of the land of Egypt, out of the house of slavery; you shall have no other Gods before me" (Exod 20:2–3, Deut 5:6–7). This formative text for Judaism and Christianity affirms that other Gods exist, but the LORD is the one for Israel. This stance (affirming many-ness or alternatives) is the basis for the many complaints in both the Old and New Testaments against people who turn away from the (covenant with the) God of Israel. The jealous LORD (in the Decalogue) and the exclusivist Jesus (in John) co-exist in the same Bible and Poly~~nesia~~ holds both biblical positions as supplements and extensions of one another rather than as contradictions (whereby one overtakes or usurps—the rhetoric of onefication—the other).[19] Put another way, Poly~~nesia~~ treats the Bible as an interacting (conversing, exchanging) rather than an exclusivist (colonial, displacing) scripture. In this regard, the Bible comes into the long shadow of talanoa.

Poly~~nesia~~ is a feature of life, and it is also evident in the faith and cultural traditions of humans, in the maneuvers of reason as well as in the registers of experience. In life, Poly~~nesia~~ is the way and the truth, and it is not a privilege only to the natives and living creatures of Moana-nui-a-kiwa. Poly~~nesia~~ is the way life is upon the many (is)lands of the world. Moreover, other living creatures move and survive according to Poly~~nesia~~.

In the two final sections of this chapter, i draw attention to Poly~~nesia~~ features in two of the oralizing-(plat)forms—poetry, art—that are considered vain among word/logo-centric theologians and theologies. But first, some Poly~~nesia~~ musings on oralizing-(plat)forms and alternatives.

Oralizing-(plat)forms

Orality is not limited to spoken words, in comparison to written and printed words. When i speak of orality i have in mind oralizing-(plat)forms that inspire *(re)storying*. And since some written and printed texts inspire storying, those texts are oralizing-(plat)forms also. In contrast, many spoken words do not inspire storying—those are therefore not oralizing-(plat)forms.

---

19. Because the gospel of John comes later in the biblical corpus, one could argue that one of the functions of texts and voices like that (with an exclusivist Jesus) was to shut down texts and teachings that make room for many-ness and alternatives.

In the scientific and high cultures of modernity, the arts have not received the recognition and appreciation that they deserve. In talanoa cultures, on the other hand, the arts are inspiring oralizing-(plat)forms.

Alternatives

John's Jesus (as indicated above) is not the only scripturalized Jesus available. Matthew, Mark, and Luke provide alternative depictions, which—despite biblical scholars giving them the "synoptics" label, as if they (re)present the same Jesus—have variants within and between them. Paul and other New Testament authors add their own alternatives, and Jesus becomes more Polynesia when one brings the extracanonical variants to the talanoa.

Jesus is as Polynesia as other biblical figures, from the Serpent and the Tree of Life in the garden to the tents of Hagar and Sarai, to the Crowd and the Ethiopian, to the Whore and the New Earth, and to their many cousins and descendants. The same may be said of all figures of history—their talanoa are Polynesia, and with alter-natives.

Poets and artists can help place theological subjects on oralizing-(plat)forms, so that their Polynesia-ness may be engaged. In other words, poets and artists can clear up clogged theological veins.

Poets

> Bäpa, forgive us for we were wrong
>
> Bäpa, transform us to right the wrongs
>
> We hear the cries, woes of the "Stolen Generations"
>
> Let Sovereign be theirs
>
> There's no room for less
>
> And move your Spirit among the Nation!
>
> (S. Juliette Mauaʻi, "Lord You Call Us," 2019)

S. Juliette Mauaʻi is a minister with the Uniting Church in Australia. She wrote "Lord You Call Us" at the airport, while she was waiting for her return flight to Melbourne after she attended a meeting of the Sovereignty Affirmation Task Group in Sydney (27–29 March 2019). With her permission, I cite the second verse above.

Two terms require clarifications: First, in addressing "Bäpa" ("father" in the Yolŋu and Bahasa languages), Mauaʻi signals that this is a prayer. And given that Bäpa is the title used in the Aboriginal Lord's Prayer, this prayer is directed to the God of Christians.

Second, "Stolen Generations" refers to the First Nations children of the cluster of (is)lands now known as Australia who were forcibly removed from their homes and many of whom were placed in "mission" homes, where they were washed (to rid of their blackness) and forced to assimilate to the white society (which was assumed to be superior). These whitening practices were done under the directions and blessings of the federal government's Assimilation policy (1910–1969), with the assumption that once the children assimilate then the First Nations will die out.

Assimilation

The Assimilation policy and the mission homes were the primary woes of the Stolen Generations for which Maua'i prays for forgiveness. Moreover, she prays for transformation so that she, the church to which she belongs, and her communities, can work to "right the wrongs." These wrongs were veins for white Australia and for Australian churches, but vain/vanities for First Nations.

Maua'i asks Bäpa for forgiveness not because she took part in the wrongs that made the Stolen Generations cry, but because she—a Samoan migrant to Australia—is a member of a church that benefitted from the woes of the Stolen Generations. Truth be told, *all churches* in the (is)lands now called Australia benefit from the woes of the Stolen Generations. Moreover, all churches on the (is)lands now called Australia are established on, and funded by money gained from the sale of, Stolen Lands.

Maua'i's alternative is sharp and firm: "Let Sovereign be theirs— There's no room for less." There's room for more—for confessing, for saying sorry, for talanoa, for closing the gap, for balanced reconciliation, for policy changes, for deep solidarity, for the return of Stolen Lands, for the repatriation of native minds, and for much more. But *there's no room for less* than "Sovereign be(ing) theirs."

Herein lies the lifeline in this verse: when the sovereignty of First Peoples is enabled, and Sovereign be(comes) theirs, the spirit of Bäpa will (again) move among the nation. This is to say that white Australia and white churches, since their arrival to the (is)lands now known as Australia, prevented the spirit of Bäpa from moving among the nation. The sovereignty of First Peoples was considered vain by white Australia, and this view continues to be protected and practiced in many pockets of modern Australia, but it is the vein that enables the spirit of Bäpa to move.

In light of Faala Amosa's argument for *Atua* (as used in Samoa's motto) as reference *also* for Samoa's native Gods (see chap. 3), there is room for Maua'i's Bäpa to also be in reference to the Gods of the (is)lands now called Australia. This is not a call for one-ness, according to which the Gods of Indigenous Australia are subsumed under the Christian God, but for many-ness—for many Gods. When sovereignty belongs to the First Peoples again, then the spirit of these many Gods—under the name of Bäpa—will move again in the (is)lands now known as Australia.

Oratory

In six short lines, Maua'i showed how something considered vain could actually be a vein. In Samoa, this vein feeds the tongues of effective orators (*tulāfale*). In Tusi Tamasese's 2011 movie *O Le Tulafale* (The Orator), the main character is a simple and very short villager, Saili (played by Fa'afiaula Sagote). He is a taro planter who copped ridicule and abuse because of his dwarfing size. His wife Vaaiga (played by Tausili Pushparaj) was banned from her village for marrying Saili. But when Vaaiga passed away, her brother Poto (played by Ioata Tanielu) came to "steal" her body to be mourned and buried on her family's land. This caused a stir in the village, but Poto outtalked the elders and his own family because he was a gifted orator.

Then came Saili with his daughter Litia (played by Salamasina Mataia), to fight—with words and the power of oratory—for Vaaiga's body. The movie ends with Saili and Litia at the back of a bus, with the wrapped body of Vaaiga in the aisle, in front of them. Saili had won the oratorial fight with Poto (Samoan word that means smart, wise), and he returns with Litia to bury Vaaiga at their home.

Maua'i is much taller than Saili, but she too drew upon the power of oratory. At the intersection of the talanoa of Saili with the prayer by Maua'i, i offer two observations and one plea. First, Maua'i is a real person, compared to Saili as a movie character, but her prayer emerged from a similar struggle—with abuse. In Maua'i's case, the abuse of Stolen Generations and something in the church meeting that she had just attended moved her into poetry/prayer. In both cases, of Saili and Maua'i, oratory enabled the one who was moved (read: ridiculed, irritated) to deal with their struggle with abuse.

Second, the performative aspects of orality are missing when one reads poems and verses in print or on a screen. Performance (read: oratory) here is not about entertainment but about the *affects* of one's speech/narration, and both oratory and orality interweave in talanoa. In the case of

Saili, he performed affectively in spite of his size and stature. In the case of Maua'i, her prayer affected me because i first heard it when she read it live during a Zoom meeting. This is to say that poetry is more affective when heard rather than read, and this also applies to the poem and images by Valentina Satvedi in this collection (see chap. 10).

Third, i appeal to readers to allow time and patience so that the fusion of orality with oratory could take place. It is easy to pass over a short text or verse like Maua'i's prayer, and to look down on dwarfing characters like Saili, as if those are vain. But with patient attention, one will find that such assumed vain(s) are veins. Actually. Obviously.

Pigs

Pigs are bodies—actual and metaphorical bodies—on the borders of Jewish and Christian scriptures and theologies. In the Pasifika world(views), on the other hand, pigs are culturally significant and theologically meaningful.[20] The subject for the final turn of this essay—Pigs—is vain in mainline theologies, but it is a vein in living contexts throughout Pasifika. My talanoa in this final turn unfolds over three vain/veins:

First, i draw the attention away from the border (as structure) to the bodies that are barred and trapped by borders. Theoretically, this involves standing firm at the lines of liberating criticisms with commitment to stand up for the rights as well as for the wrongs of fellow creatures.

Second, i invite engagement with native readings of Christian events. Here, i focus on works by two artists, one from north Oceania—Emmanuel Garibay of the Philippines—and one from south Oceania—Aotearoa New Zealand born Samoan artist Greg Semu.

Third, i invite readers to engage with native scriptures and native godly matters. In this final subsection, i interrogate the obviously Christian narrative that has displaced the Indigenous Australian narrative about the Sow and Piglets at what is now known as the Twelve Apostles (limestone pinnacles at Port Campbell) at the southern border of Victoria.

Bordered Bodies

Pigs (of the swine family) get a bad rap in the Bible. They are seen as defiled and defiling for the people of the good LORD (Lev 11:7), as Dalits are perceived to be in Hindu societies (see Monica J. Melanchthon, chap.

---

20. See Toap, "A Melanesian Pig Theology."

14), and several explanations have been given. One popular explanation, propagated by Mary Douglas, is that pigs do not fit neatly into the categories of purity and defilement (see Lev 11:2b–8)—pigs have divided hoofs and are cleft-footed (which should make them clean) but they do not chew the curd (thus making them unclean).[21] Pigs do not fit the taxonomy, and they are thus understood to be unclean.

A second popular explanation relates to the arid context of Palestine. Pigs cannot survive in dry contexts because they require a lot of water. It was therefore reasonable to ban them altogether so that the people would not be tempted to raise them, and consequently waste limited resources (such as water) and valuable space.[22] Moreover, in subsistence farming communities, pigs would be a nuisance. Prohibiting pigs was therefore beneficial to settled communities.

In Pasifika, we have alter-native views about pigs. In the smaller outer islands of Tonga, pigs are real bodies at real borders. These islands, some of which are the size of one or two football fields, have two fences (*'ā fonua*) that cut across the island to demarcate three spaces: space for homes at the windward end, space for plantations in the middle, and space for pigs at the leeward end of the island. The fence (*'ā ki tu'a*) that block the pigs off run into the water on both sides of the island (similar to the southern US border with Tijuana, Mexico). The pigs are blocked off because they cause damage to the home gardens and to the plantations. But when there is a significant event such as a wedding, birth, funeral or the arrival of guests, pigs are slaughtered to give the event a native and island feel. The bodies on the border give village events the feel of islandedness (or: indigeneity, authenticity), and islanders even joke that it is not a real island feast unless a pig is slaughtered, cooked and served.

In the eyes of Tongan pigs, if i may boldly imagine, it does not matter what theories of border or theories of border-crossing one constructs. What would make a difference for Tongan pigs is for Tongan people to change their eating habits and change their expectations from island feasts. Moreover, it will mean a lot for Tongan pigs if Tongan people recognize the immense sacrifice that pigs go through in order to give the island(ers) a sense of native- and real-ness. Behind this talanoa is an invitation that in the process of reflecting on borders and border crossing, that we do not overlook the bodies on the border—that is, that we do not overlook the pigs, be they actual or metaphorical.

21. Douglas, *Purity and Danger*, 10.

22. This explanation does not really work in Pasifika, where pigs can fish for food and wild pigs can find ways to survive without human intervention.

Native readings

Figure 1.1: Emmanuel Garibay, "Me Lugar pa sa Mesa" (2008)
Used with the permission of the artist

Emmanuel Garibay brings several Filipino/Filipina figures to the table (*sa mesa*) and gives political and community leaders a place at the heightened side of the table (away from the viewer). At the center of the work is a Pinocchio-like character who points at himself, and holds a dagger with the other hand, while being hugged by a winking female character holding a red telephone (see Figure 1.1). Garibay teases viewers to imagine this table as the one at The Last Supper, in which case Jesus looks like a screaming joker and any of the figures crowding the heightened side of the table could be Judas.

Under and in front of the table (closer to the viewer) are characters whom Filipino authorities see as rebels, protestors, mourners, survivors, in other words, normal people who are seen as vain. The normal people whom Garibay gathered do not have a place at the table, and this is a critical point for this work as suggested by its title—*Me Lugar pa sa Mesa*, which i hear as a request: "Place me at the table." Garibay thus haunts viewers with the faces and voices of they who do not have a place at the (Lord's) table.

Ironically, a (roasted) pig has a place on the table, and the Pinocchio Jesus is ready to stab (carve) it up. This is not a Jewish Passover table, which would be defiled by the roasted pig. Rather, this is a Filipino's table, obviously, and in my Tongan eyes it befits being announced as the Lord's table. I can easily see myself appreciating this table as a godly one.

A variant to Garibay's reading may be found in Greg Semu's *The Last Cannibal Supper* (2010).[23] At the table are Pasifika natives, men and women bearing their shoulders, chests and breasts, and Semu leaves no doubt that he was satirizing The Last Supper. On Semu's table is a pig that had been cooked in a *umu* (ground oven), and one can see that it was moist and ready to fall apart. The term "Cannibal" was used in the past in reference to the natives of Pasifika, and so Semu's works invite viewers to satirize this whitewashing label.

Both Garibay and Semu bring bodies from the border—pigs and natives—to the (Lord's) table. They provide alternative readings of a formative moment in the Christian narrative, and anyone who would approach their tables can get a full feed instead of the morsel of bread that one usually gets at Holy Communion.

An easily overlooked figure in Garibay's work is the opened mouth man wearing a worn-out V-neck T-shirt in front of the table, on the right. His left hand is raised while his right hand lazily lays a finger on his chest—the stigmata is on the back of both hands to indicate that he is the figure of Christ. Together with the normal people under the table he too asks, "Me Lugar pa sa Mesa / Place me at the table."

Native Scriptures

Postcolonial movements take the lead in reclaiming native names and narratives, in calling for reparation of native lands and enslaved bodies, and in demanding repatriation of native minds and values (see Cristina Lledo Gomez, chap. 8). I here turn to one of the tourist attractions at the hinterland of the State of Victoria (Australia).

---

23. View Semu's works at http://www.gregsemu.photography/the-last-cannibal-supper (accessed 13 April 2020).

Figure 1.2: The Twelve Apostles (2011)

By Michael J Fromholtz—Own work, CC BY-SA 4.0,
https://commons.wikimedia.org/w/index.php?curid=46022256

Even though there were only eight pinnacles (up to 2005), these limestone bodies at the southern border were renamed as if there were twelve of them—The Twelve Apostles (see Figure 1.2). The name is a clear give away that this is the doing of Christians who were most likely European and white.

Indigenous Australian Dreamtimes have a different name for these pinnacles and link them to the neighboring Mutton Bird Island—"Sow and the piglets." Mutton Bird Island is the sow, and the pinnacles are her piglets. The pinnacles are the piglets going to/coming from their mother. The assigning of a Christian name is part of the colonial legacy that approves the replacing of native narratives, and it is against such a legacy that this collection of essays come together.

So What?

What are we to do in order that we may accept pigs, and other bodies at borders, with their interests and narratives into our communes or dispersions? How may we give them a place at our tables? How may we see and accept pig(let)s as godly subjects? And how do we get to see that we are (among) the pig(let)s? (The saying "you are what you eat" is appropriate here.)

Invitation

Colonialization is a human project that wipes out native talanoa and native values, over against which it writes-in its preferred narratives and agendas. Christianity participates in this human project, under the authority of its globalized God and sanctified texts. All the authors of the following chapters are heirs to and beneficiaries of this human project.

All of the authors are also bothered by this human project and so this work brings our "bothered voices" on behalf of other Poly~~nesia~~, Poets and Pig(let)s. Our inspiration is from and for the generation of bordered bodies who, as in Olivia Bishop's "Untitled" (on the cover), have the courage to hold on to the border and test (or play with) it's barbs.

Works cited

Anzaldúa, Gloria. *Borderlands/La Frontera: The New Mestiza*. San Francisco: Aunt Lute, 2007.

De La Torre, Miguel. *Burying White Privilege: Resurrecting a Badass Christianity*. Grand Rapids: Eerdmans, 2019.

Dhamarrandji, Maratja, with Jione Havea. "Receive, Touch, Feel, and Give *Raypirri*." In *Indigenous Australia and the Unfinished Business of Theology: Cross-cultural Engagement*, edited by Jione Havea, 9–15. Postcolonialism and Religion. New York: Palgrave, 2014.

Douglas, Mary. *Purity and Danger: An Analysis of Concepts of Pollution and Taboo*. New York: Routledge, 1966.

Haire, James. "The Centrality of Contextual Theology for Christian Existence Today." In *Contextual Theology for the Twenty-First Century*, edited by Stephen B. Bevans and Katalina Tahaafe-Williams, 18–37. Missional Church, Public Theology, World Christianity 1. Eugene, OR: Pickwick Publications, 2011.

Hauʻofa, ʻEpeli. "Our Sea of Islands." *The Contemporary Pacific* 6.1 (1994) 147–161.

Havea, Jione. "Control, Ciliation, Coalition: Oecumenism in Aotearoa." In *Catholicity in Postcolonial Perspective*, edited by Stephen Burns. Lanham, MD: Lexington (forthcoming).

———. *Losing Ground: Reading Ruth in the Pacific*. London: SCM, 2021.

———, ed. *People and Land: Decolonizing Theologies*. Theology in the Age of Empire. Lanham, MD: Fortress Academic, 2020.

———, ed. *Scripture and Resistance*. Theology in the Age of Empire. Lanham, MD: Fortress Academic, 2019.

Vaai, Upolu Lumā, "*Lagimālie*: COVID, De-Onefication of Theologies, and Eco-Relational Wellbeing." In *Doing Theology in the New Normal*, edited by Jione Havea, 209–21. London: SCM, 2021.

Sugirtharajah, R. S., ed. *Still at the Margins: Biblical Scholarship Fifteen Years after "Voices from the Margin."* London: T. & T. Clark, 2008.

———, ed. *Voices from the Margin: Interpreting the Bible in the Third World.* London: SPCK, 1991.

Toap, Wesis Porop. "A Melanesian Pig Theology: An Anthropological/Theological Interpretation of a Pic Culture amongst the Woala Highlanders of Papua New Guinea." MTh thesis, Suva, Fiji: Pacific Theological College, 1998.

Part One

Noble Borders

2

Bordered Churches, Borderless Spirit

U-Wen Low

THE HISTORY OF PENTECOSTALISM, arguably one of the largest, most visible movements of "inspired" bodies in recent history, needs to be contested. Most are familiar with the "conventional" story of Pentecostalism told through predominantly Western eyes, one particular example of which states:

> The theological origins of Pentecostalism can be traced to an early twentieth century Midwestern group led by a former Methodist minister, Charles F. Parham [...] since Pentecostalism, in general, can trace its heritage to the Apostolic Faith Movement, then the Assemblies of God also owes its origin to this fellowship of believers.[1]

Whilst a true reconstruction of the story, this narrow-minded approach fails to take into account the wider history of pneumatologically inspired movements preceding or paralleling Parham, Seymour, and the Azusa Street Revival. Such an approach suggests that American Pentecostalism is the primogenitor of all Pentecostal belief around the world, and therefore is the sole proprietor of the movement, allowing it to dictate (or at least strongly influence) other movements' goals, theologies, and freedoms. This mindset

---

1. Minter, "Antecedents to the Assemblies of God," 95.

is indeed alive and well in the global Pentecostal movement, and it is intimately linked with the rise of global capitalism and the ongoing exportation of American culture,[2] making it difficult to unravel.

A postcolonial approach suggests something very different. When reading the histories of similarly inspired movements around the world, we discover that several other, similar movements sprang up contemporaneously to the Azusa Street Revival. However, as time went on, these separate bodies, though similar in origins and approach, were by and large gradually dominated and subsumed by "Western" Pentecostalism. The neo-colonial approach of Western Pentecostalism meant that these fledgling native Pentecostal approaches were first limited, then gradually absorbed into Western approaches, and so relatively few native Pentecostal movements survive today.

As Pentecostal Christianity continues to be one of the fastest-growing religious movements in the Majority World,[3] this reclamation of history becomes all the more important. The influence and control exerted by American (and Australian) Pentecostalism over other expressions is disproportionate to the size of each body, and non-Western Pentecostals deserve to be able to carve out an identity of their own without being beholden to American Pentecostalism and its own allegiances to Western culture and capitalism. Pentecostalism in the Majority World (hence known as "Native Pentecostalism") is known to be the "religion of the subalterns,"[4] in large part due to both the aspirational and pragmatic nature of Pentecostal theology, and so it is important to draw its focus away from prosperity by reminding it of its origins. In other words, Native Pentecostalism needs to redraw and redefine its borders in order to preserve some semblance of sovereignty in the face of overwhelming domination.

Perhaps most importantly, Native Pentecostal movements need to be reminded of their independence and early history in order to be able to speak to Western Pentecostals as equals rather than perceived inferiors, as brothers and sisters rather than parent and child. As Native Pentecostalism redefines its borders, this will create opportunities for the separate bodies

---

2. Hoganson, "Stuff It"; Beckert, "History of American Capitalism," 325. Beckert points out that the "territorial scope" of the United States led to its aggressive economic expansion, and that this expansion is largely built upon modern slavery and destruction of indigenous cultures.

3. By 2003, a full two-thirds of all Christians on the continent of Asia identified as Pentecostal-Charismatic; in Latin America, Pentecostal Christians comprise the largest network of associations outside the Roman Catholic Church. Hwa Yung, "Endued with Power," 64; Petersen, "A Moral Imagination," 53.

4. Pulikottil, "One God, One Spirit," 70.

of Pentecostalism to engage in a more balanced dialogue. Anderson has shown that early Pentecostal journals contained both "cultural insensitivities" and "patronising and racist attitudes"[5] that typified a neo-colonial attitude towards non-Western peoples; a strengthening of borders may well assert the rights of Native Pentecostal movements to be taken seriously by Western counterparts.

Amidst this complex problem hovers the question of the Spirit, a key distinctive amongst Pentecostal and other charismatic movements. Whilst Pentecostals have traditionally understood the Spirit as a continuation of God's salvation (as seen in Acts) empowering believers to enact God's kingdom, this is often interpreted in quite a narrow fashion.[6] However, this perspective is changing as theologians respond to Pentecostalism. Dearborn argues that part of the Spirit's work is to "cut away hegemonic structures and perspectives" and to challenge "misuses of the Word to justify social stratification."[7] Other Pentecostal theologians such as James K.A. Smith and Mike Davis have argued that Pentecostalism represents a powerful movement that combats inequality,[8] and that distinctives such as glossolalia can be seen as "an expression that resists the powers and structures of global capitalism and its unjust distribution of wealth [. . .] the language of a countercultural 'exilic' community."[9]

Helpful here too is the work of Amos Yong, who argues that the Spirit works to bring "believers into the body of Christ,"[10] and in so doing allows humans to "share in the community of the body of Christ."[11] Yong points out that baptism in the spirit "reconciles human beings across racial, ethnic, gender, and social lines,"[12] however, as we shall see, this ideal is not always reflected in reality. Nevertheless, it seems that a solution might be found in revisiting the borderless (or border-transgressing) nature of the Spirit of God.

This chapter first briefly explores concepts relating to bodies, borders, and their interactions, and subsequently goes on to use a selected case study from early Pentecostalism to explore how different bodies of Pentecostalism

5. Anderson, "The Dubious Legacy of Charles Parham"; Lindhardt, "Introduction: Presence and Impact of Pentecostal/Charismatic Christianity in Africa," 4.

6. A helpful starting point is Hollenweger's discussion of early Pentecostal doctrine regarding the Spirit. See Hollenweger, *The Pentecostals*, 321–52.

7. Dearborn, *Drinking from the Wells of New Creation*, 50.

8. Davis, "Planet of the Slums," 31–32.

9. Smith, *Thinking in Tongues*, 107.

10. Yong, *Spirit-Word-Community*, 30.

11. Studebaker, "Toward a Pneumatological Trinitarian Theology," 85.

12. Yong, *Spirit-Word-Community*, 33.

interact, how these bodies use borders to control others, and finally how these borders are shifted to allow domination by bodies with power. It will conclude by briefly discussing the role of the borderless Spirit in Pentecostal and postcolonial thought.

Bodies and Borders

To use the term "bodies" to describe anything beyond a biological construct is to commit to anthropomorphize, or at least a reconceptualize, the idea being described. Doing so reimagines the various groupings of "bodies" as "organisms,"[13] a metaphor both helpful and limiting. Thus, we can refer to a church as a "body," or organize people into disparate "bodies" whose own bodies make up a unified, whole "body." At this point, it may be helpful to briefly refer to the concept of "organicism," a philosophy which draws upon three key ideas:

- That all-natural things have organic foundations and so possess "emergent properties that cannot be predicted,"[14]
- That the entirety (the "whole") of a body is greater than the sum of its parts,[15]
- That all whole bodies are composed of interacting parts (which may themselves be whole bodies).

Without delving further into the intricacies of the philosophy, let us say that this concept suffices as a functional, helpful explanation of the ideas surrounding bodies, as it requires reasonably less explanation than certain other philosophies (such as Foucault's or Descartes'). The terminology of organicism is frequently found in other literature, and so is familiar to many.

Another helpful concept for this project is Wink's conception of "the Powers," a concept that leverages the language of the New Testament to describe collectives or entities such as institutions, organizations, and similar bodies.[16] Understanding bodies as "powers" extends the metaphor further by assigning them a spiritual dimension which allows for further interaction in a metaphysical sense. Wink's ideas assert that not all bodies have equal powers, and indeed that certain bodies are clearly privileged over others. All bodies are, of course, "embedded in multiple and overlapping

13. Horn, "Social Bodies," 18–19.
14. Towsey, "The Emergence of Subtle Organicism," 114.
15. Gilbert and Sarkar, "Embracing Complexity," 2.
16. Wink, *The Powers That Be*.

socio-political relations with other bodies politic";[17] this means that analysis of bodies must be done with an eye to their relationships with other bodies—or in other words, their borders.

Borders are a curious concept, a "paradoxical space" where two entities are both separately delineated but also intimately connected.[18] For states, borders are areas to be controlled, spaces of concern, and therefore becomes sites of both conflict and negotiation.[19] Physical borders can be designed, controlled, and challenged, and play a significant role in the lives of those who negotiate them.[20] Likewise, social groups are also "bordered" in that they are defined by their acceptance or rejection of particular norms—yet this also is a space of conflict and negotiation. At the same time, borders can also be porous and permeable, allowing for an exchange between borders.

However, borders, like bodies, are liable to become spaces for the demonstration of domination and power. Feldman presents Foucault's views quite simply: the body is "an exemplary site for the coming together of political forces and constitutes a formation of domination, a place where power is ordered and a *topos* where that ordering attains a certain visibility, a collective resonance and publicness."[21] Both bodies and borders are places of conflict, where the powers challenge each other in their quest for domination and control; it is those without power whose bodies are inevitably humiliated, subjugated, or, worst of all, completely erased.

Western and Native Pentecostalisms

As alluded to earlier, the various expressions of the Pentecostal movement and colonialism are inexplicably intertwined; in certain areas, the Pentecostal movement is a reaction to/against colonial power, and in others, it is an expression of colonial power. Nowhere is this more evident than in the battle of narratives between Native and Western Pentecostalism in Kerala, India. Of course, it must be noted that the records of Christianity in the 19th and 20th centuries in India are extraordinarily difficult to piece together; the legacy of India's colonial government means that only the "official" stories were told. Only in the 21st century are native stories beginning to surface. We still do not have a full picture, yet it is important to attempt a holistic reconstruction of events.

17. Protevi, "Bodies Politic," 37.
18. Carter and Dodds, "Borders," 22.
19. Carter and Dodds, "Borders," 22.
20. Grassiani and Swinkels, "Engaging with Borders."
21. Feldman, "Political Terror and the Technologies Ol Memory."

India: A Case Study

In 1860, forty-six years prior to the Azusa Street Revival, a brief "revival" broke out in Tirunelveli, marked by glossolalia and other traits of what Pentecostals today identify as the "baptism of the Holy Spirit."[22] In 1905, yet another revival broke out—this time, ten months before the first instance of glossolalia in Azusa Street, and located in Pune, India.[23] This revival then spread to Gujarat in 1906, and native Indian Pentecostalism was first organized as the Indian Assemblies of God in 1918, and was later known as the North India District Council of the Assemblies of God. Subsequent groups emerged in South India, specifically the Ceylon Pentecostal Mission and the Indian Pentecostal Church.[24] There were numerous revivals preceding the official "arrival" of Pentecostalism from the West in India, with the difference being that the native Indians lacked the language to "articulate it [glossolalia] as doctrine."[25]

In 1906, missionaries Alfred and Lillian Garr would arrive in Calcutta, in the east of India, where they began a prayer meeting among expatriates—fellow missionaries and Christian workers.[26] The Garrs had been among the early followers of Azusa Street, and so represented American Pentecostalism in perhaps its youngest and rawest form. They began a Pentecostal church meeting in the city in January 1907, with a congregation comprised of mostly English-speaking expatriates (and few Bengalis). Here, revival sprung up, with manifestations of the Spirit such as glossolalia, singing, and other physical movements. This was noted by both the Garrs and Moorhead, the secretary of the YMCA in Ceylon, as "the first general outpouring of the Spirit in India."[27] McGee points out the ethnocentric nature of this pronouncement, and highlights that this particular revival was met with criticism, arguments and disdain in the press—perhaps due to the fact that this revival was amongst Westerners and expatriates rather than among native Indians.[28]

The Pentecostal church in Kerala sprang from indigenous Indian origins rather than from the influence of the Garrs in a fascinating parallel development. The Keralan (Malayali) stream of Pentecostalism traces its

22. Yung, "Pentecostalism and the Asian Church," 44.
23. Satyavrata, "Contextual Perspectives on Pentecostalism as a Global Culture," 204.
24. Satyavrata, "Contextual Perspectives on Pentecostalism," 205.
25. Rapaka, "The Indian Pentecostal Church of God in Andhra Pradesh," 67–68.
26. McGee, "The Calcutta Revival of 1907," 125–26.
27. McGee, "The Calcutta Revival of 1907," 134.
28. McGee, "The Calcutta Revival of 1907."

roots back to the 1st century CE, being derived from the Syrian Christianity that was allegedly established in India by Saint Thomas. Three men, P.M. Samuel, K.E. Abraham, and K.C. Cherian, founded the South India Pentecostal Church of God in 1923, completely separate of Western Pentecostal influence.[29] Over time, they would come into contact with Western (predominantly American)-led Pentecostal movements, and, united in sharing a common inspiration, a Native Pentecostal movement, the aforementioned South India Pentecostal Church of God, was brought together with a Western Pentecostal movement, the Malankara Full Gospel Church, to form the Malankara Pentecostal Church of God.[30]

Before the merge, the South India Full Gospel Church was led by a missionary named Robert Cook. Cook, by most accounts, was a successful missionary who ministered to the Dalits (see chap. 14), India's lowest caste. Like many others of his time, however, Cook remained steadfastly (or willfully) ignorant of the Holy Spirit's movement among Indian Christians whose Christian heritage predated his own, and indeed later "portrayed himself as a bearer of light to 'dark India'" in his autobiographies.[31] As head of the Malankara Full Gospel Church, he oversaw its merge with the South India Pentecostal Church of God to become the Malankara Pentecostal Church of God. The merge occurred in 1926, with Cook becoming President and Abraham the Vice-President, and lasted just four years due to a number of different reasons, chief among which were "leadership positions, financial matters and affiliation with Western missionary societies."[32]

According to V. V. Thomas, one reason for the split was the Syrian-exclusive focus held by Abraham, himself a higher-caste Syrian who continued practicing "untouchability" toward the Dalits that the movement was attracting.[33] Pulikottil, on the other hand, points out that the native leaders were dependent upon Western financial support, yet ultimately refused to continue "under the yoke of slavery" and to continue to "drink the milk of the white cow."[34] Following this split, Abraham and other native leaders continued to remind fellow natives of the indigenous nature of Pentecostalism, asserting the early revivals throughout India as evidence

---

29. Pulikottil, "As East and West Met in God's Own Country," 10–11; Rapaka, "History of Indian Pentecostal Church," 27.

30. Rapaka, "The Indian Pentecostal Church of God in Andhra Pradesh," 74; Pulikottil, "As East and West Met in God's Own Country," 11.

31. Rapaka, "The Indian Pentecostal Church of God in Andhra Pradesh," 67.

32. Rapaka, "The Indian Pentecostal Church of God in Andhra Pradesh," 74.

33. Thomas, *Dalit Pentecostalism*.

34. Pulikottil, "As East and West Met in God's Own Country," 11.

for the movement's long history, and denying Cook's claim that he was the originator of Pentecostalism in Kerala.

Rapaka points out that Cook was symptomatic of "typical colonisers" whose Pentecostal missionary endeavors to India bore an air of superiority.[35] Despite the clear similarities between Indian native Pentecostalism and Cook's own brand of Western Pentecostalism, it seems that Cook did not see himself in any way equal to the Indians—no matter their caste. The native Indian leaders struggled to retain their distinctive Pentecostal identity and needed to form their own denomination in order to effectively do so. This was by no means an uncommon phenomenon, either; Pentecostal missionaries are noted as "carry[ing] their cultural baggage with them" across the world.[36]

Discussion

This case of Native Pentecostalism in India illuminates the complex interplay between a variety of bodies and borders, each defined in different ways. Hovering above it all is the global phenomenon of Pentecostalism, or rather the Holy Spirit—itself generally defined in complex theological terms as a body within a body.[37] The Spirit is largely recognized to be "borderless" in that it is free to go and act wherever it pleases, and ironically enough is noted by many Christians as working to "remove sociological blinders" that prevent the recognition or inclusion of others.[38] Despite the parallel growth of two Pentecostal movements in two separate countries, we see the clear development of two distinct bodies—one Indian, one colonial—and these bodies, though nearly identical in theology and motivation, are held distinct from one another by a single distinctive (border): ethnicity, or perhaps colonialism.

In this instance, the boundaries are seemingly impenetrable: the two movements, despite their similarities, are unable to overcome the border created by colonial power—a border that clearly distinguishes between different ethnicities and assigns power to those it favors. Here, Western Pentecostalism, by virtue of coming from representatives of colonial "powers," is given favor over its indigenous counterpart, and indeed expects to dominate it. Because of this, these bodies are clearly unable to

35. Rapaka, "The Indian Pentecostal Church of God in Andhra Pradesh," 67.
36. McGee, "Pentecostal Strategies for Global Mission," 156.
37. This is, of course, a broad generalization of orthodox Christian theology. For a specifically Pentecostal perspective, see Studebaker, "The Theology of Amos Yong."
38. Dearborn, *Drinking from the Wells of New*, 49.

co-operate; one body is privileged over another and so seeks to maintain a border around itself. The privileged body, Western Pentecostalism, dominates the "Other," and refuses to allow it equality—the "lesser" body goes so far as to name its domination as "slavery." Even the power of the Holy Spirit seems to be unable to overcome the invisible borders created by this sense of colonial privilege.

This becomes all the more complex when we consider the ultimate goal of both bodies as missional agencies: to bring in new converts (or new bodies) who need to first cross the "border" of being an "outsider" in order to become a Pentecostal Christian.[39] In joining these bodies, new converts are often asked to adhere to a new set of beliefs and to set aside their old identity; to be "rebirthed" into a new body of their own. This process acts as a safeguard to protect and maintain Pentecostal identity, but also acts to strongly stamp the desired distinctives or "culture" of the governing Pentecostal body upon the new convert's body—itself an act of colonization that enforces the governing body's norms. Transgression of the norms is often punished, in line with Rajaram's observation that "the colonised body is the base point at which colonial power as disciplinary mechanism *and* aesthetic spectacle becomes evident."[40]

This leaves us with an immensely complex problem which has no simple resolution. As time has gone by, Pentecostalism has continued to grow, in line with the "exports" of Western culture, particularly the alloying of capitalism with consumerism. As its borders have expanded, Pentecostalism has continued to subsume independent bodies in order to continue its growth. This is all the more difficult to challenge given Pentecostalism's lack of a systematic theology—the movement's beliefs can alter and adapt easily to suit global trends, meaning that it is in many ways more akin to a corporation than a church.

Perhaps the most challenging aspect of contemporary Western Pentecostalism's unwitting engagement with colonialism is its preservation and continued use of colonial methods and mindsets well into the twenty-first century. This is seen in the megachurch phenomenon, whereby churches actively seek to reproduce themselves and their "culture" (or at least, their ecclesial and liturgical expressions) through satellite sites planted in different locales. This process, which one sociologist has termed the "Hillsongization

---

39. This is particularly notable in Pentecostal theology, for example a Pentecostal theology of healing which creates clear borders and distinctions between the "inside / saved" and the "outside." See for example Eriksen, Blanes and MacCarthy, *Going to Pentecost*, 50.

40. Rajaram, "Dystopic Geographies of Empire," 478.

of Christianity,"[41] is particularly prone to repeating the mistakes embodied in the case study above. This idea could be extended to include the critique of the "modernist" nature of the global church, which argues that the church continues to be anchored in the modern world, particularly consumerist culture, and so is ill-adapted for postmodern thinking.

It is by no means difficult to find a broad range of criticisms levelled at Pentecostal movements like Hillsong, and in light of the case study above, many of these criticisms are both valid and concerning. Many are uncomfortable with the movement's use of technology to create "cosmopolitan spaces of community and identity formation beyond categories of ethnicity and race"[42] that "disregards cultural contexts."[43] One commentator points out that Hillsong "needs not only to produce comfortable subjects, but enthusiastic ones," and in so doing creates a pool of affective labor which is utilized to further the church's mission.[44] Others point out that Pentecostal churches tended to display "a formal ideology of sectarian self-righteousness"[45] whereby they were dismissive of other churches' work, and seem to be uninterested in cooperation with them.[46] Important too is the Pentecostal church's effect upon liturgical practice.

Each of these critiques are not unique to Hillsong but can be applied to most Pentecostal megachurches worldwide to some degree. These are hallmarks of colonial, oppressive power, which seeks to create new bodies that imitate its own whilst restricting those that do not follow the status quo. At the same time, like in many other situations, oppressive power is seductive, desirable, and so is mimicked by oppressed bodies through a process of "colonial mimicry" which gradually works to erase the distinctions between oppressed and oppressors.[47] This results in the creation of an "other" which shares the characteristics of both oppressed and oppressing bodies, but is able to transition between both; effectively being borderless.

A Shared Language: Spirit Baptism

Despite the challenges and issues discussed above, there is hope that the shared inspiration of the Spirit can assist in removing borders and allowing

41. Martí, "The Global Phenomenon of Hillsong Church," 384.
42. Klaver, "Media Technology Creating 'Sermonic Events,'" 423.
43. Klaver, "Media Technology Creating 'Sermonic Events,'" 432.
44. Wade and Hynes, "Worshipping Bodies," 177.
45. Coleman, *The Globalisation of Charismatic Christianity*, 109–10.
46. Paas, "Mission from Anywhere to Europe," 18.
47. Bhabha, *The Location of Culture*, 122.

the various bodies that compose contemporary Pentecostalism to reconcile. A helpful way forward might be to look beyond differences to re-engage with the narrative of Holy Spirit baptism. We have already discussed Amos Yong's theological assertion that the Spirit is given to humans to "share in the community of the body of Christ,"[48] perhaps with a shared reading of Luke-Acts as a starting point.[49] By recognizing that all Pentecostals (indeed, all Christians!) are unified under the Holy Spirit as a single body, yet at the same time both learning to take seriously the differences between cultural expressions, and understanding the dynamics of power between church bodies, there is indeed hope that Western Pentecostalism can correct its trajectory and learn from its past mistakes.

It is also important to recognize the increasing diversity within the Pentecostal church—in the Majority World, as well as in privileged nations like the United States and Australia. This diversity reflects the changing nature of the world, and of Pentecostalism; this represents an opportunity for a diverse array of voices to speak into the future of the movement. Rather than allowing old prejudices or mindsets to continue informing Pentecostal mindsets, church leadership needs to change to reflect the "brave new world" into which the movement speaks. Important here is the question of "language" which others in this volume have discussed: as Pentecostals share in glossolalia, they are effectively sharing in a single, unique language. This is a crucially important distinctive that is mostly agreed upon by all Pentecostals (details about particular doctrines, such as initial evidence, differ) and so has the potential to be a doctrine that advances unity by erasing particular borders (or perhaps redrawing new ones).

Unfortunately, there are significant barriers to overcome. Many of the early Pentecostal missionaries interpreted the gift of glossolalia as a removal of language barriers that would allow them to evangelize among "foreign" nations, and this mindset of benevolent colonialism continues to this day. In the 21st century Pentecostal church, Hollenweger rightly observes, many take their experience of Spirit baptism, particularly glossolalia, as a "dogmatic statement" that needs to become "normative for all other Christians"[50]—and in doing so encourage homogeneity across the church, particularly with regards to a "Pentecostal culture." This is clearly problematic, and Hollenweger proposes that the emphasis on glossolalia in Pentecostal thought be shifted away from being a "supernatural" gift toward a "human" gift akin to liturgy—with the purpose of encouraging other gifts to

48. Studebaker, "The Theology of Amos Yong," 85.
49. See Yong, *In the Days of Caesar*.
50. Hollenweger, "Rethinking Spirit Baptism," 169.

be expressed, ultimately allowing greater inclusivity within the Pentecostal church.[51] This suggestion de-emphasizes the problematic doctrine of "initial evidence" in Spirit baptism, and instead recognizes the unique complexity of the congregations who make up the church: each bring their own abilities and gifts. This allows greater diversity within the Pentecostal church whilst retaining one of its central distinctives.

The most difficult hurdle to overcome, however, remains Pentecostalism's symbiotic relationship with Western individualism and consumerism.[52] So long as Pentecostal churches continue to prioritize growth, marketing, and the self, a colonial mentality will continue to be fostered among Western Pentecostal churches. Here, perhaps we need to consider the Spirit as a "de-colonial" agent which embraces cultural identity rather than erasing it—and this may be achieved simply by hearing the stories of the Spirit moving in communities of the "Other," as this study attempts to show.[53]

It may be helpful, too, to further erase boundaries by hearing the experience of charismatic Christians in other denominations, and in so doing consider Karl Rahner's vision of a united "little flock" which acknowledges that the Spirit moves amongst all, but of its own will.[54] Rahner's acknowledgment of the Spirit's movements sparked controversy in the Catholic Church,[55] but it is a helpful reminder for all to set aside their prejudices and desires in favor of what the Spirit is doing:

> Those, therefore, who have the power to command in the Church must constantly bear in mind that not everything that takes place in the Church either is or should be the outcome of their own autocratic planning as though they belonged to a totalitarian regime. They must keep themselves constantly alive to the fact that when they permit movements "from below," this is no more than their duty.[56]

Rahner's move toward a single, distinctive body composed of individual units is admittedly utopic and perhaps naïve, yet it is no less so than what is seen in the New Testament.

---

51. Hollenweger, "Rethinking Spirit Baptism," 170.

52. For a helpful dissection of Pentecostal engagement with consumerism, see Chesnut, "Prosperous Prosperity," 215–24.

53. Yong argues that the Spirit has been "empowering resistance" among Pentecostal movements throughout history. Yong, "Many Tongues, Many Practices," 56.

54. Rahner, *The Shape of the Church to Come*, 31; 113–14.

55. Marmion, "Karl Rahner, Vatican II," 28.

56. Rahner, "Do Not Stifle the Spirit," 85.

This shared inspiration of the Spirit continues to propel Pentecostal endeavor today and will continue to do so into the future. Whether Pentecostals recognize the Spirit working among "Others" different to them, however, is the key to ensuring equality and representation within the movement.

Conclusion

Whilst Pentecostalism and Pentecostal thought remain closely linked to Western capitalism and individualism, it seems likely that the question of defining "bodies" within the movement will mostly remain an individualistic, self-centered one. However, the borderless Spirit that is central to Pentecostal theology provides a starting point for change. Looking to the future, the Pentecostal church would do well to engage with postcolonial / decolonial reading of past stories, as well as a careful re-reading of the Luke-Acts narrative that deprioritizes individual experience in favor of corporate or community praxis. Whilst my Pentecostal colleagues are undertaking a large task in building a strong foundation for the future, there is yet one more boundary that needs to be dissolved: the separation between popular or "lay" Pentecostals, particularly popular preachers, and the academy.

Works Cited

Anderson, Allan. "The Dubious Legacy of Charles Parham: Racism and Cultural Insensitivities among Pentecostals." *Pneuma* 27.1 (2005) 51–64.

Beckert, Sven. "History of American Capitalism." In *American History Now*, edited by Eric Foner and Lisa McGirr, 314–35. Critical Perspectives on the Past 79. Philadelphia: Temple University Press, 2011.

Bhabha, Homi K. *The Location of Culture*. New York: Routledge Classics, 2004.

Carter, Sean, and Klaus Dodds. "Borders." In *International Politics and Film: Space, Vision, Power*. Columbia: Columbia University Press, 2014.

Chesnut, R. Andrew. "Prosperous Prosperity: Why the Health and Wealth Gospel Is Booming across the Globe." In *Pentecostalism and Prosperity: The Socio-Economics of the Global Charismatic Movement*, edited by Katherine Attanasi and Amos Yong, 215–24. New York: Palgrave Macmillan, 2012.

Coleman, Simon. *The Globalisation of Charismatic Christianity: Spreading the Gospel of Prosperity*. Cambridge Studies in Ideology and Religion 12. Cambridge: Cambridge University Press, 2000.

Davis, Mike. "Planet of the Slums: Urban Involution and the Informal Proletariat." *New Left Review* 26 (2004) 5–34.

Dearborn, Kerry. *Drinking from the Wells of New Creation: The Holy Spirit and the Imagination in Reconciliation*. Cambridge: James Clarke, 2014.

Drane, John William. *The McDonaldization of the Church: Consumer Culture and the Church's Future*. Macon, GA: Smyth & Helwys, 2001.

Eriksen, Annelin, Ruy Llera Blanes, and Michelle MacCarthy. *Going to Pentecost: An Experimental Approach to Studies in Pentecostalism*. Ethnography, Theory, Experiment 7. New York: Berghahn, 2019.

Feldman, Allen. "Political Terror and the Technologies Ol Memory: Excuse, Sacrifice, Commodification, and Actuarial Moralities." *Radical History Review* 8 (2003) 58–73.

Gilbert, Scott F., and Sahotra Sarkar. "Embracing Complexity: Organicism for the 21st Century." *Developmental Dynamics* 219 (2000) 1–9.

Grassiani, Erella, and Michiel Swinkels. "Engaging with Borders." *Etnofoor* 26.1 (2014) 7–12.

Hoganson, Kristin. "Stuff It: Domestic Consumption and the Americanization of the World Paradigm." *Diplomatic History* 30.4 (2006) 571–94.

Hollenweger, Walter J. "Rethinking Spirit Baptism: The Natural and the Supernatural." In *Pentecostals after a Century: Global Perspective on a Movement in Transition*, edited by Allan Anderson and Walter J. Hollenweger, 164–72. Journal of Pentecostal Theology Supplement Series 15. Sheffield: Sheffield Academic, 1999.

———. *The Pentecostals: The Charismatic Movement in the Churches*. Minneapolis: Augsburg, 1972.

Horn, David G. "Social Bodies." In *Social Bodies: Science, Reproduction, and Italian Modernity*. Princeton Studies in Culture/Power/History. Princeton: Princeton University Press, 1995.

Klaver, Miranda. "Media Technology Creating 'Sermonic Events': The Hillsong Megachurch Network." *Cross Currents* 65.4 (2015) 422–33.

Lindhardt, Martin. "Introduction: Presence and Impact of Pentecostal/Charismatic Christianity in Africa." In *Pentecostalism in Africa: Presence and Impact of Pneumatic Christianity in Postcolonial Societies*, edited by Martin Lindhardt, 1–53. Global Pentecostal and Charismatic Studies 15. Leiden: Brill, 2014.

Marmion, Declan. "Karl Rahner, Vatican II, and the Shape of the Church." *Theological Studies* 78.1 (2017) 25–48.

Martí, Gerardo. "The Global Phenomenon of Hillsong Church: An Initial Assessment." *Sociology of Religion* 78.4 (2017) 377–86.

McGee, Gary B. "Pentecostal Strategies for Global Mission: A Historical Assessment." In *Called and Empowered: Global Mission in Pentecostal Perspective*, edited by Murray W. Dempster, Byron D. Klaus, and Douglas Petersen, 151–65. Grand Rapids: Baker Academic, 1991.

———. "The Calcutta Revival of 1907 and the Reformulation of Charles F. Parham's 'Bible Evidence' Doctrine." *Asian Journal of Pentecostal Studies* 6.1 (2003) 123–43.

Minter, Terry N. "Antecedents to the Assemblies of God." Regent University, 2011.

Paas, Stefan. "Mission from Anywhere to Europe: Americans, Africans, and Australians Coming to Amsterdam." *Mission Studies* 32.1 (2015) 4–31.

Petersen, Douglas. "A Moral Imagination: Pentecostals and Social Concern in Latin America." In *The Spirit in the World: Emerging Pentecostal Theologies in Global Contexts*, edited by Veli-Matti Kärkkäinen, 53–68. Grand Rapids: Eerdman's, 2009.

Protevi, John. "Bodies Politic." In *Political Affect: Connecting the Social and the Somatic*. Minneapolis: University of Minnesota Press, 2009.

Pulikottil, Paulson. "As East and West Met in God's Own Country: Encounter of Western Pentecostalism with Native Pentecostalism in Kerala." *Asian Journal of Pentecostal Studies* 5.1 (2002) 5–22.

———. "One God, One Spirit, Two Memories: A Postcolonial Reading of the Encounter Between Western Pentecostalism and Native Pentecostalism in Kerala." In *The Spirit in the World: Emerging Pentecostal Theologies in Global Contexts*, edited by Veli-Matti Kärkkäinen, 69–88. Grand Rapids: Eerdmans, 2009.

Rahner, Karl. "Do Not Stifle the Spirit." *Further Theology of the Spiritual Life 1*. Translated by David Bourke. London: Darton, Longman & Todd, 1971.

———. *The Shape of the Church to Come*. London: SPCK, 1974.

Rajaram, Prem Kumar. "Dystopic Geographies of Empire." *Alternatives: Global, Local, Political* 31.4 (2006) 475–505.

Rapaka, Yabbeju. "History of Indian Pentecostal Church of God in Andhra." *ERT* 31.1 (2007) 17–29.

———. "The Indian Pentecostal Church of God in Andhra Pradesh, 1932 to 2010: A Study of Dalit Pentecostalism." Regent University, 2011.

Satyavrata, Ivan M. "Contextual Perspectives on Pentecostalism as a Global Culture: A South Asian View." In *The Globalization of Pentecostalism: A Religion Made to Travel*, edited by Murray W. Dempster, Byron D. Klaus, and Douglas Petersen, 203–21. Oxford: Regnum, 1999.

Smith, James K. A. *Thinking in Tongues: Pentecostal Contributions to Christian Philosophy*. Pentecostal Manifestos. Grand Rapids: Eerdmans, 2010.

Studebaker, Steven M. "Toward a Pneumatological Trinitarian Theology: Amos Yong, the Spirit, and the Trinity." In *The Theology of Amos Yong and the New Face of Pentecostal Scholarship: Passion for the Spirit*, edited by Wolfgang Vondey and Martin William Mittelstadt, 83–102. Global Pentecostal and Charismatic Studies 14. Boston: Brill, 2013.

Thomas, V. V. *Dalit Pentecostalism: Spirituality of the Empowered Poor*. Bangalore: Asian Trading Corporation, 2008.

Towsey, Michael. "The Emergence of Subtle Organicism." *Journal of Futures Studies* 16.1 (2011) 109–36.

Wade, Matthew, and Maria Hynes. "Worshipping Bodies: Affective Labour in the Hillsong Church." *Geographical Research* 51.2 (2013) 173–79.

Wink, Walter W. *The Powers That Be: Theology for a New Millennium*. New York: Random House, 1998.

Yong, Amos. *In the Days of Caesar: Pentecostalism and Political Theology*. The Cadbury Lectures 2009. Grand Rapids: Eerdmans, 2010.

———. "Many Tongues, Many Practices: Pentecost and Theology of Mission at 2010." In *Mission after Christendom: Emergent Themes in Contemporary Mission*, edited by Ogbu U. Kalu, Peter Vethanayagamony, and Edmund Kee-Fook Chia, 43–58. Louisville: Westminster John Knox, 2010.

———. "Pentecostalism and the Asian Church." In *Asian and Pentecostal: The Charismatic Face of Christianity in Asia*, edited by Allan Anderson and Edmond Tang, 37–58. Regnum Studies in Mission: Asian Journal of Pentecostal Studies 3. Oxford: Regnum, 2005.

———. *Spirit-Word-Community: Theological Hermeneutics in Trinitarian Perspective*. 2002. Reprint, Eugene, OR: Wipf & Stock, 2006.

Yung, Hwa. "Endued with Power: The Pentecostal-Charismatic Renewal and the Asian Church in the Twenty-First Century." *Asian Journal of Pentecostal Studies* 6.1 (2003) 63–82.

3

Fa'avae i le Atua Samoa

A Theological Interrogation

FAALA (SAM) AMOSA

THE MOTTO OF SAMOA—*FA'AVAE i le Atua Samoa*—is meaningful to most Samoans, but many Samoans do not know its roots and implications. This essay meets these lacks for Samoans at home and in diaspora, and non-Samoans who may be interested in Samoan cultures and traditions.

There are three tasks carried out in this essay. First, to present what the motto *Fa'avae i le Atua Samoa* meant to the "fathers" of Samoa's independence. The traditional understanding of the motto—"Samoa is founded on God"—affirms Samoa to be founded on God/Atua, but which one? Second, to offer a theological interrogation of the motto. As traditionally conceived, the motto is against Samoan culture (*faaSamoa*). This claim is based on the understanding that Atua in the motto refers only to the Christian God. Third, to initiate a diasporic negotiation which holds that Atua in the motto could refer to both the Christian God and the Atua of Samoa, Tagaloaalagi. There is space for both deities to be the *fa'avae* (foundation) of Samoa.

In negotiating the motto to accommodate God and Atua as *fa'avae*, our motto could continue to be meaningful for Samoans in Samoa and in the diaspora. More importantly, the motto could thereby escape becoming a bordered or bordering body.

Faala and Fa'a-la

My name "Faala" helps in the negotiation and interrogation of the motto. I am named after my grandfather Faala Faala from the village of Lepa on the eastern side of Upolu in Samoa. Our shared name has several nuances: *fa'a* means to give and *la* means sun. "Faala" thus means to bring something out to the sun, to air it out.

With a hyphen (fa'a-la) the *la* may also refer to the sail of a canoe as in *va'a fai-la* (a va'a/boat that has pulled up its sail). The construction fa'a-la indicates movement and mobility; symbolically, it is an invitation for moving away from fixity and rigidity—the situations at which a body becomes bordered. Fa'a-la is a signpost to the reality that Samoans in Samoa symbolically live in the diaspora also. Samoans have fa'a-la (read: sailed) beyond Samoa's borders and become bordered-in by privileging the Christian God introduced from a *va'a-fai-la* over their native Atua—Tagaloaalagi.

Nuances of Faala/Fa'a-la become a "sail" in this theological interrogation, to show that there is room in *Fa'avae i le Atua Samoa* for God (of Christianity) and Atua (of *faaSamoa*) to co-exist as Samoa's *fa'avae*.

The Faala/Fa'a-la complex brings to mind scourging, burning and peeling away protection, covering or skin. The Island sun's heat can be harsh and scorching; it can burn Samoan skin as well. Some people may accordingly take this study as scorching, burning, and peeling away sanctity from Samoa's national motto—that is not my intention. I use my name to bring out the relevance of the nation's motto for all Samoans. The motto is rich in theologies and requires talanoa (see chap. 1) to negotiate meaningful conversations between Samoans in Samoa with Samoans in the diaspora.

Samoa's Motto

Samoans in Samoa and Samoans in the diaspora know our motto well. However, many do not know how the motto came about. Before the division of the Samoan Islands into the three groups of Tutuila (which became American Samoa), Sava'i and Upolu (the two main islands of Western Samoa) on the 16th of February 1900, the whole group was united under the motto *Le Faamoemoe Lelei* (Virtue is Hope).[1] After an agreement between Britain, Germany and the United States in Berlin (in 1889),[2] Germany hoisted the German Flag in *Mulinu'u* to mark the German takeover of Western Samoa on the 1st of March 1900. There was no official motto for

---

1. "Samoa I Sisifo"; see also Amosa, "A Theological Interrogation of the Motto," 60.
2. Meti, *Samoa*, 5.

Samoa under German rule. In 1914 an article in the *Thames Star Newspaper* suggested Germany's slogan "Fear of None, Favor to None, Justice to All"[3] was the unofficial motto of Samoa.

When war broke out in 1914, Britain asked New Zealand troops to land in Samoa and remove the German flag. As a result, on the 25th of January 1914 Upolu and Savai'i were placed under the League of Nations and known as [Western] Samoa.[4] At the time, Samoa still did not have an official motto but the slogan "Samoa be Courageous" was preached in church services to encourage Samoans during these difficult circumstances.[5] The slogan "Samoa be Courageous" was replaced in 1922 during a resistance movement called the *mau*. The primary objective of the *mau* was for Samoa to regain independence, have control of its affairs, and make decisions on all facets of Samoan life for the benefit of Samoans.[6] The leaders of the *mau* movement summed up their intention with "Samoa Mo Samoa" (Samoa for the Samoans).[7] The slogan became the unofficial motto for the nation and its push for independence. On the 1st of June 1962, Samoa became an independent state with the nation's motto being *Fa'avae i le Atua Samoa*. The motto identified the foundation upon which independent Samoa was being built. *Fa'avae i le Atua Samoa* was fitting at that time given the circumstances of Samoa and Samoans being bordered bodies under foreign rule.

Negotiating the Motto

Negotiating the path for *Fa'avae i le Atua Samoa* as the nation's motto started well before 1962 when the Legislative Assembly adopted it. One may even argue that *Fa'avae i le Atua Samoa* was conceived when Malietoa Vainu'upo welcomed John Williams and Christianity on 24 August 1830. Nevertheless, how did the motto come to be what it is today?

The literature on Samoan history outlines a covenant between Malietoa Vainu'upo and the Tuimanu'a Tauveve (two kings in different regions of Samoa) in 1830 shortly after the arrival of Christianity. The content of the covenant was straightforward:

> There shall be only one lotu [religion] in Samoa from Manu'a to Sava'i [...] only that which was brought by John Williams and

3. "Germany in the Pacific."
4. Fairbairn-Dunlop, *Tama'ita'i Samoa*, 3.
5. "Methodism."
6. Davidson, *Samoa Mo Samoa*, 167.
7. Davidson, *Samoa Mo Samoa*, 112.

Barff forever. Their deaths shall mark the end of human kings for Samoa, but the living and most powerful king in Heaven shall be overall bearing the good news of the death of Jesus Christ, the only son of the Almighty God.[8]

Falenaoti Iiga Pisa summed up this covenant-making event with the words "*Fa'avae i le Atua Samoa*."[9] According to Tapaleao, whether the two kings used the words is not essential. The formulation sums up the devotion of the two kings and the people of Samoa to the Christian God. Malama Meleisea reiterated the same view: "On his death in 1914 Malietoa Vainu'upo gave further testimony to his belief that the *malo* (nation, government) now belonged to *Ieova* (Jehovah)."[10] Meleisea did not comment on the motto's genesis, but he confirmed Malietoa's acceptance of the Christian God. In accepting Christianity, Malietoa took the foreign God introduced by the missionaries as Samoa's *fa'avae*.

The phrase *Fa'avae i le Atua Samoa* first appeared in public on the 1st of June 1948, when Samoa's freedom from New Zealand was confirmed and commemorated with a National Anthem called *le fu'a o le saolotoga* (the banner of freedom). Sauni Iiga Kuresa composed the anthem containing the words [*aua ete fefe o le*] *Atua o le ta fa'avae* ([do not be afraid] God is our foundation).[11] The decision to take the phrase *Fa'avae i le Atua Samoa* as the nation's motto was decided by the 2nd Legislative Assembly on the 3rd of April 1951. A week later on the 12th of April 1951, a newly developed Coat of Arms was adopted, and it displayed the motto. That Coat of Arms has the rising sun at the top of the emblem. However, on the 1st of June 1962 at the independence ceremony at *Mulinu'u* leaders of Samoa displayed a new Coat of Arms, in which a cross replaced the rising sun.[12] The adoption of the cross highlighted belief in the Christian God and the Christian influence in Samoa.

Considering all of these, the idea that Samoa was founded on God originated from a covenant between Malietoa and the Tuimanu'a in 1830. Sauni Iga Kuresa coined *Fa'avae i le Atua Samoa* after composing the national anthem for independence in 1962.[13] The 2nd Legislative Assembly adopted the motto, and it was officially displayed on the 1st of June 1962 at the independence ceremony in *Mulinu'u*.

8. Tapaleao, "Faavae I le Atua Samoa," 10.
9. Pisa, "Tala Tuu Faasolopito"; see Tapaleao, "Faavae I le Atua Samoa," 12.
10. Meleisea, *The Making of Modern Samoa*, 167.
11. Amosa, "A Theological Interrogation of Fa'avae I le Atua Samoa," 53.
12. Meleisea, *Lalaga*, 210.
13. Meti, *Samoa*, 12.

The deity referenced in the motto *Faʿavae i le Atua Samoa* was the Christian God and not Tagaloaalagi the native Atua of Samoa.[14] The establishment of Malua Theological College, the translation of the Bible from English to Samoa, the National Anthem, the Constitution and Coat of Arms, clearly attest to the Christian God being the deity in the motto.

Atua

The term Atua is sacred to Polynesians. For many Samoans, Atua is synonymous with Samoa—thus it is crucial here to delve deeper into the term. The sacredness of Atua is evident in a recent art exhibition titled "Atua sacred gods from Polynesia" at the Australian National Art Gallery. The exhibited artworks explored the depth of the concepts of gods in Polynesia.

For some of the Polynesian artist involved in the exhibition, *Atua/atua* is a potent Polynesian word similar to "divinity" in the West. *Atua* in Polynesia revolves around genealogy and lineage. An individual can trace their genealogy to *Atua*. For others, *atua* is an object with special powers; for example, chiefs had their *atua*, and so did districts and individuals. Also, *atua* is the presence of Being in an object. The artists were unanimous in saying "our sacred atuas were left abandoned when the islands accepted the Christian God [. . .] our *atua* were overlooked and discarded for Christianity."[15] Among the overlooked and discarded *Atua/atua* was Tagaloaalagi.

Tagaloaalagi

In Samoa's creation stories, there was a primeval void that gave way to natural phenomena produced in several generations by *Tagaloaalagi* (shortened as *Tagaloa*; alt. *Tangaloa*), who is known by the title of *Atua*.[16] Tagaloaalagi is Tagaloa of the Sky (lagi). An etymological study of Tagaloaalagi (alt. *Tagaloa Faatupunu'u*) describes attributes of the deity—*Taga* (alt. Tanga) means bag or sack, but it also denotes permission and freedom. The word *loa* means long, never-ending, unrestricted without barriers, borderless, limitless space. Tagaloa thus refers to a being who "holds" (or endures) extensive permission and freedom.

---

14. Tcherkezoff, "Culture, Nation, Society," 254. See also Meleisea, *Lalaga*, 70; Ernest, *Winds of Change*, 167.

15. https://nga.gov.au/atua/ the video about "Atua Sacred gods from Polynesia."

16. Lawson, *Tradition versus Democracy in the South Pacific*, 127.

Tagaloaalagi holds a significant place in Samoan mythologies.[17] Like the term *Atua/atua*, the character Tagaloaalagi is not limited to Samoa[18]— it is the name for the primary deity throughout Polynesia. Nonetheless, Samoans think that Tagaloaalagi is their deity and is honored as Atua or the Supreme God of their ancestors.[19] In a speech delivered in 2009 the previous Head of State Tuiatua Tupua Tamasese Taisi Efi, for instance, linked the origin of Samoans to Tagaloaalagi: "Tagaloa sent down his *tuli* (plover bird) to earth, and on his instructions, the *tuli* formed the image of a man from bacteria or *ilo*, man originates from *ilo* and eventually evolved from that into human form."[20]

The Samoan anthropologist Unasa Va'a also argued that every Samoan is a divine progeny of Tagaloaalagi. For Va'a, this is because Tagaloaalagi came down to earth in the form of his *suli* (progeny). Through Tagaloa's marriages with daughters of the earth, every Samoan can trace their ancestry back to Tagaloa (qua Atua).[21]

Equally, Malama Meleisea, a well-versed Samoan historian and anthropologist, noted that Tagaloa dwelt in the expanse where he made all things. Before there was any sky, sea, earth, or country, Tagaloa alone was (there); Tagaloa went to and fro in the expanse, and at the places where he stepped and stood as he roamed, there grew up a rock. He was also known by the name of Tagaloa faatupunu'u.[22]

Tagaloa existed before anything came into being. He was responsible for the creation of all things. Be that as it may, John Garrett argued that Samoans did not worship the idols and the high gods of Polynesia.[23] Holmes takes a similar line of thought to Garrett, suggesting that not all of Polynesia hold Tagaloa in the same light as Samoans.[24] Elsewhere in Polynesia, the deity had a restricted sphere of influence.[25] Against the views of Garrett and Holmes, early literature on Samoan history express otherwise, denoting the idea that Samoans dedicated prayers and food to the deity as a sign of reverence. For example, the Samoan historian Lalomilo Kamu

17. Va'a, "Samoan Custom and Human Rights," 238.
18. Gibson, *Samoa*, 41. See also Lawson, *Tradition versus Democracy in the South Pacific*, 127.
19. Meleisea, *Lalaga*, 2–7.
20. Efi, "Samoan Fragrances in Samoan Thoughts."
21. Va'a, "Samoan Custom and Human Rights," 238.
22. Meleisea, *Lalaga*, 2.
23. Garrett, *To Live Amongst the Stars*, 121.
24. Holmes, *Quest for the Real Samoa*, 62.
25. Holmes, *Quest for the Real Samoa*, 62.

argued that belief in the supernatural or Supreme Being was not foreign to the Samoan people. For Kamu, it was not even something new brought by the missionary movement.[26]

Myths relating to Atua as creator agree on one point: Tagaloaalagi (Tagaloa of the Sky) was the Supreme Being who created life and the world.[27] Samoa's belief system about Tagaloaalagi remained unchallenged until European contact in the 17th and 18th centuries. The arrival of John Williams and Christianity in August of 1830 moved the traditional understanding and belief of Samoans away from Tagaloaalagi as Atua, to the Christian God introduced by the missionaries.

Although there were conflicting narratives about Tagaloa, those did not change how Samoans perceived and worshipped their Atua. Most Samoans see the arrival of Christianity in 1830 as a blessing. I argue on the other hand that Christianity was responsible for "bothering" and "bordering" Samoan's beliefs and worldviews.

Nafanua

Samoan church historians remember Nafanua, known as a prophetess in many legends, in high esteem for her contribution to Christianity's arrival. It was Nafanua who inspired Malietoa to accept the Christian good news.

In the minds of Samoans, Nafanua is a "lesser god" called *aitu*.[28] Nafanua gained legendary status in Samoa for her renowned wisdom and as a war-goddess. The name Nafanua derives from two words *na* (hid) and *fanua* (land)—her name means "hid in the land." Nafanua was hid in the land by her mother, because she was an illegitimate child from an incestuous relationship between her and her uncle.[29]

Nafanua possessed powerful *mana* or spirit. She was sought after by high chiefs and warriors for advice. Chiefs and warriors believed that she could foretell the outcome of a war.[30] Utilizing her *mana* Nafanua gathered the four paramount chief titles of Samoa known as *papa*—they are *Tuiaana, Tuiatua, Gatoaitele,* and *Tamasoali'i*. A person who holds all four titles is known as *tafa'ifa* (literally, "four-sided"). The *tafa'ifa* connotes the

---

26. Kamu, "The Samoan Culture and the Christian Gospel," 27.

27. Kamu, "The Samoan Culture and the Christian Gospel," 27.

28. Havea, "Diaspora Contexted," 187.

29. Aiono Le Tagaloa, *The Social Status and the Economic Roles of the Female*, 2. See also Leaupepe, "Nafanua," 39–40.

30. Latai, "E au le Ina'ilau a Tama'ita'i," 9.

idea of "one supported by four" (referring to the four *papa*)³¹ and is the highest chief in Samoa.

Nafanua bestowed the first *tafa'ifa* paramount title upon Salamasina, the daughter of Tuiaana Tamalelagi and his wife Vaeotoeifaga.³² When Salamasina (*sala* means yonder and *masina* means moon) was born, Tuiatua Mata'utia's wife Sooaemalelagi adopted the girl to be her murdered husband's successor. Upon seeing Salamasina, Sooaemalelagi picked her up and said, *mavave, ua lalelei si teine e pei ole sala masina* (wow, she is beautiful like the moon yonder).³³

The four customary titles (*papa*) went to the high-ranking families of Samoa. However, one of the high-ranking families did not receive one of the four titles, and that was the Malietoa family—to which Malietoa Fitisimanu belonged. Through one of his talking chiefs (*tulafale*) named Su'a, Malietoa sought out Nafanua to appoint an *ao* (head) over his land. Nafanua responded that she had no more *ao* to give, only *i'u* (tails); but Malietoa should wait for an *ao* from above: "wait for the head of your *malo* (kingdom or government) shall come from heaven."³⁴ The arrival of Christianity to Samoa in 1830 was accepted by Malietoa Vainu'upo as fulfillment of the words of Nafanua to Malietoa Fitisimanu. In this connection, Nafanua gave Malietoa the aspiration to accept the Christian God as *ao* (head) of Samoa.

Nafanua and the arrival of Christianity are held high in the minds of Samoan Christians. At the same time, on the other hand, Nafanua was responsible for handing Samoa over to the Europeans and to their Christian God. That handing-over altered the fabric of Samoa and resulted in the imprisonment of Samoan minds and habits. How did the Christian God come to have such influence on Samoan hearts and minds, to the disregard and abandonment of Tagaloaalagi? The answer is clear: Nafanua had a role in submitting Samoa to the Christian God.

Christian God

The Christian God was foreign to Samoans before the arrival of the missionaries. In the first place, Samoans did not believe in a monotheistic God like the Europeans who brought Christianity. Samoans were polytheistic.³⁵

---

31. Meleisea, *The Making of Modern Samoa*, 11. See also Meleisea, 204; Liuaana, *Samoa Tula'i*, xvii.
32. Lawson, *Tradition Versus Democracy*, 126.
33. Masterman, *An Outline of Samoan History*, 13.
34. Efi, "Tamafaiga-Sharman."
35. Hempenstall, "On Missionaries and Cultural Change in Samoa," 244–45.

In traditional Samoan society, the highest of these gods was Tagaloa. The belief in and alliance to Tagaloa was challenged by the introduction of the Christian God to Samoa.

European sailors, whalers, merchants, beachcombers and a small number of Samoans played a part (like Nafanua) in giving Samoa over to the Christian God.[36] The foreigners were refugees, escaped convicts, seamen, and castaways from European ships who wanted to try their luck among a reportedly hostile people.[37] The escaped convicts were primarily from Australia[38] and they were known as the sailor's sect/cult. The sect played a role in Christianizing Samoa and introducing a different form of worship and deity to Tagaloaalagi. But in the eyes of the European missionaries, the sailors and their sect were blasphemous. The sailor's sect did continue to be active in Samoa well after the arrival of Christianity. From the perspective of native Samoans, the Europeans were not united.

Samoans also contributed to the spread of the sailor's sect amongst Samoans.[39] The most influential Samoan was Siovili from the village of Eva. Siovili was a sailor on trading vessels across the Pacific. Siovili picked up in Tahiti a version of Christianity. After arriving back to Samoa, he started to teach this version of Christianity to members of his *aiga* (relatives). John Williams reported that a Chief from Sava'i had confronted them while at sea saying, "that they had heard of the good news and that nearly all of Upolu and Sava'i were Christians. Williams pointed out that there was a native who had been in Tahiti and was teaching the people the most incredible nonsense. His name was Joe Vili (Siovili)."[40]

Accompanying John Williams, Charles Baff and the crew, were eight Tahitian teachers and their families, and a Samoan couple named Fauea and Puaseisei whom they picked up from Tonga. Fauea was the one who advised John Williams that on arrival he should approach Malietoa Vainu'upo. Fauea understood well: Malietoa was in power and gaining the approval of the paramount chief would be critical and helpful. Knowing the ways of Samoa and its structures, going to the central leader will ensure the acceptance and spread of Christianity in Samoa.

Notwithstanding, the claim that John Williams and the LMS were the first people to bring Christianity to Samoa has been vigorously disputed.

---

36. Dunlop, *Tama'ita'i Samoa*, 2.

37. Holmes, "Cults, Cargo and Christianity," 477. See also Gibson, *Samoa*, 68.

38. Kamu, "Samoan Culture and the Christian Gospel," 105.

39. Liuaana, *Samoa Tula'i*, 5 noted Saiva'aia from Satupaitea and Tagipo from Lufilufi as other important Samoan people in the spread of Christianity among Samoans.

40. Moyle, *The Samoan Journals of John Williams*, 109–111.

Garrett reported that when the LMS arrived in 1830, "the people had already heard about the new God, Jesus Christ... Tahitians on passing ships brought news of the *lotu Tahiti* [Tahitian religion, a reference to Christianity and later to the Congregational Church] before John Williams came."[41] In Garrett's version, Christianity was first introduced by native people.

Samoans on the other hand prefer a different version: that *papalagi* (they who burst the heavens, in reference to Europeans, White people)[42] brought "the light" and "the good news." 24 August 1830 for Samoan Christians signifies the breaking of a new morning, new age and the turning point in the country's history. Samoan oratory frequently refers to this day with awe: *E ui a i isi taeao, ae o le taeao sili lava o le taeao o le talalelei* (of all the mornings, the most crucial morning is the morning of the good news).[43] Accordingly, John Williams is remembered as the one who brought the Christian God; paramount chief Malietoa Vainu'upo is the one who accepted the new *lotu* (religion); Samoans like Nafanua, Siovili, Fauea and Puaseisei played a role in handing Samoa over to a foreign God.

Fa'avae and Fa'a-Vae

Considering the foregoing, my contention in this essay is that there is room in the motto *Fa'avae i le Atua Samoa* to hold both the Christian God and the Atua of Samoa (such as Tagaloalagi) as the nation's *fa'avae*. Since it is a convention of Pacific theologies to pay close attention to words, their roots and etymology, I appeal to this feature to make room for both God and Atua in our motto. This is a feature of our oral cultures that will, in this instance, assist in the Faala/Fa'a-la of the motto of Samoa.

The word *fa'avae* is common in Samoa. It refers to the foundation (fa'avae) of a Samoan *fale* (house). Rocks big and small make up the foundation, forming a solid and stable surface upon which the fale stands. The concrete-like surface makes the fa'avae strong and stable. The fa'avae is reliable and keeps the fale intact during winds and storms.

As a metaphor, fa'avae has several connotations and nuances that are useful for Samoans in Samoa and in the diaspora. For example, *fa'a* (give) and *vae* (feet) means that the fa'avae "gives feet" (to stand still, to stand strong). As a metaphor for "giving feet" comes the expectations of being still, static and firm. Fa'avae has always been interpreted as permanent and fixed (as in the foundation of a *fale*).

41. Garrett, *To Live Amongst the Stars*, 21.
42. Gibson, *Samoa*, 65.
43. Latai, "E Au le Ina'ilau a Tama'ita'i," 5.

I propose to push the oral feature further (as orators do) with *fa'a-vae* (the hyphen is deliberate) to suggest movement. To give feet to something is to enable it to walk, to move, to be mobile. Hence: fa'avae is about standing still (static, rigid); fa'a-vae is about movement (being in motion and flexible). Fa'avae represents a solid, firm and rigid foundation; fa'a-vae symbolizes a flexible, moving, agile and nimble foundation.

Instead of fa'avae being fixed and unmoving, fa'a-vae (with a hyphen) is flexible and open to movement and change. Fa'a-vae is forward-thinking and affirms progression; it is open to moving away and leaving behind traditional perspectives, ideas, concepts and mindsets. With respect to Christianity, the so-called traditional perspectives are foreign ways that have, in many ways, bordered Samoan bodies in Samoa and in the diaspora.

All things considered, the shift from a static and firm *fa'avae* to mobile and moving *fa'a-vae* forms a platform to escape the bordered locations, places and mindsets. These insights and attitudes have bordered and imprisoned Samoan ways and minds.

Conclusion

A theological interrogation and a diasporic negotiation of *Fa'avae i le Atua Samoa* show that, if the motto's deity is only the Christian God, the motto is anti-faaSamoa and against Samoan culture. The introduction of Christianity to Samoa brought along foreign borders and ways of thinking that have imprisoned Samoa and Samoans. This can be seen in the privileging of the Christian God, over against the traditional Atua of Samoa—Tagaloaalagi. The national anthem, the preamble of Samoa's Constitution, the transferring of authority from the Matai Samoa to the pastor, Nafanua, Malietoa Vainu'upo, Siovili, Faueau and Puaseisei contributed to the anti-Samoan culture (fa'aSamoa) represented by our motto.

Utilizing Faala/Fa'a-la invites a different way of seeing *Fa'avae i le Atua Samoa*. From a set of traditional unmoving feet (fa'avae) to a group of moveable and agile feet (fa'a-vae) come possibilities to see both the Christian God and Atua of Samoa as the nation's foundation.

Both meanings of fa'avae/fa'a-vae are relevant. Fa'avae denotes fa'aSamoa—traditional, firm and unrelenting traditions. At the same time, fa'a-vae encourages resisting imposed borders. In this dual way, Samoans will no longer be stuck as bordered bodies, but rather become fluid, agile and moving away from bordering ways and mindsets.

Works Cited

Amosa, Sam. "A Theological Interrogation of the Motto: Fa'avae ile Atua Samoa." MTh honors thesis, Charles Sturt University, 2014.

Davidson, J. W. *Samoa Mo Samoa: The Emergence of the Independent State of Western Samoa*. Melbourne: Oxford University Press, 1967.

Dunlop, Peggy. *Tama'ita'i Samoa: Their Stories*. Suva, Fiji: University of the South Pacific, 1998.

Efi, Tuiatua Tupua Tamasese Taisi. "Tamafaiga-Sharman, King or Maniac: The Emergence of Manono." *Journal of Pacific History* 30 (1995) 3–21.

———. "Samoan Fragrances in Samoan Thoughts." Paper presented at the Pacific Thoughts Symposium Mau Forum, Waitakere, Auckland, March 7, 2009.

Ernest, Manfred. *Winds of Change: Rapid Growing Religious Groups in the Pacific Islands*. Suva, Fiji: Pacific Conference of Churches, 1994.

Garrett, John. *To Live Amongst the Stars: Christian Origins of Oceania*. Suva, Fiji: Institute of Pacific Studies, 1982.

"Germany in the Pacific," *The Thames Star Newspaper*, Tuesday 1 September 1914. Wellington: Alexander Turnbull Library, New Zealand. http://natlib.govt.nz/records/15888740.

Gibson, R. P. *Samoa: 1830–1900 The Politics of a Multi-Cultural Community*. London: Oxford University Press, 1940.

Havea, Jione. "Diaspora Contexted: Talanoa, Reading, and Theologizing, as Migrants." *Journal of Black Theology* 11 (2013) 185–200.

Hempenstall, Peter. "On Missionaries and Cultural Change in Samoa." *Journal of Pacific History* 39 (2004) 244–45.

Holmes, Lowell D. "Cults, Cargo and Christianity: Samoan Response to Western Religion." *Missiology: An International Review* 4 (1980) 471–87.

Holmes, Howell. *Quest for the Real Samoa: The Mead/Freeman Controversy & Beyond*. Massachusetts: Bergin & Garvey, 1987.

Kamu, Lalomilo. "The Samoan Culture and the Christian Gospel." PhD diss., Australian National University, 1996.

Latai, Latu. "E Au le Ina'ilau a Tama'ita'i: The History of Samoan Missionary Wives in the Evangelization of Papua New Guinea from 1883 to 1975." MTh thesis, Pacific Theological College, 2005.

Lawson, Stephanie. *Tradition versus Democracy in the South Pacific: Fiji, Tonga and Western Samoa*. Cambridge Asia-Pacific Studies. Cambridge: Cambridge University Press, 1996.

Leaupepe, Malutafa. "Nafanua: A Prophetess of God the Congregational Christian Church Samoa and Hermeneutics." *Malua Journal* 1 (2013) 39–40.

Le Tagaloa, Fanaafi Aiono. *The Social Status and the Economic Roles of the Female in Traditional and Modern Samoan History*. Apia: UNESCO, 1986.

Liuaana, Featuna'i. *Samoa Tula'i: Ecclesiastical and Political face of Samoa's Independence, 1900–1962*. Apia: Malua Printing Press, 2004.

Masterman, Sylvia. *An Outline of Samoan History*. Western Samoa: Department of Education, 1958.

Meleisea, Malama. *Lalaga: A Short History of Western Samoa*. Suva, Fiji: University of the South Pacific, 1987.

———. *The Making of Modern Samoa: Traditional Authority and Colonial Administration in the Modern History of Western Samoa.* Suva, Fiji: Institute of Pacific Studies of the University of the South Pacific, 1987.

Meti, Lauofo. *Samoa: The Making of the Constitution.* Apia: National University of Samoa, 2002.

"Methodism." *Ashton Guardian Newspaper,* 15 October 1917. Wellington: Alexander Turnbill Library, New Zealand. http://natlib.govt.nz/records/15888740.

Moyle, Richard M. *The Samoan Journals of John Williams 1830–1832.* Canberra: Australian National University, 1984.

Pisa, Falenaoti Tofa Iiga. "Tala Tuu Faasolopito." Master's thesis, 1963.

"Samoa I Sisifo." http://www.hubert-herald.nl/SamoaWest.htm.

Tapaleao, Talia. "Faavae ile Atua Samoa." BD thesis, Pacific Theological College, 1991.

Tcherkezoff, Serge. "Culture, Nation, Society: Secondary Change and Fundamental Transformations in Western Samoa: Towards a Model for the Study of Cultural Dynamics." In *The Changing South Pacific: Identities and Transformations.* Edited by Serge Tcherkezoff and Francoise Douaire-Maarsaudon. Canberra: Pandanus, 2005.

Va'a, Unasa. "Samoan Custom and Human Rights: An Indigenous View." *Victoria University Wellington Law Review* 40 (2009) 237–50.

4

Cultural Colonialism

A Theological Reflection

Eseta Waqabaca-Meneilly

Because "colonialism" creates and maintains unequal relationships, "cultural colonialism" here refers to practices that promote and impose powerful cultures over against lesser "others." Cultural colonialism is where one cultural body, assisted by a cohort of associates, dominates other cultural bodies. The term is employed especially in the fields of history and postcolonial studies. It is usually used in a critical sense, often in conjunction with calls to reject such influence. Cultural colonialism in the Uniting Church in Australia (UCA), to which I belong, may be in the form of an attitude which is subtle and can be unintentional and yet it reinforces cultural domination.

Interwoven in the situation of cultural colonialism is the exercise of "power," defined by Foucault as "a certain type of relation between individuals" including the setting of strategic social positions enabling one's ability to control the environment that bears influence to those in the institution.[1] This power is woven with a conception of "truth."[2] Truth in this situation is a "system of ordered procedures for the production, regulation, distribution,

---

1. Foucault, *The Order of Things*, 4.
2. Foucault, *The Order of Things*, 6.

circulation, and operation of statements"[3] which can have a strong influence with systems of power. Therefore, inherent in systems of power is "truth" which is culturally specific and inseparable from ideologies that often coincide with various forms of domination. Domination means that there are dominated subjects or subalterns. Western philosophy has a history of not only exclusion of the "subaltern" from participating, but also does not allow them to occupy the space of fully human subjects.[4]

Cultural colonialism can be seen by the receiving culture as threat to or as enrichment of its cultural identity. It seems therefore useful to distinguish between cultural colonialism as an active or passive attitude of superiority, and the position of a culture or group that seeks to complement its own cultural production, considered partly deficient, with imported products. The receiving culture does not necessarily perceive this link, but instead passively absorbs the foreign culture through the use of its goods and services. Due to its somewhat concealed but very potent nature, this idea is described by some experts as "*banal* (causing misery or distress) *colonialism.*"[5]

Cultural colonialism and dominance can be seen in the 1930s in Australia when the Aboriginal Assimilation Policy acted as an attempt to wipe out the native Australian (first) people. The British settlers tried to biologically alter the skin colour of the Australian Indigenous people through mixed breeding with white people. The policy also attempted to forcefully conform the first people of Australia to western ideas of dress and education.

Crossing Borders from Fiji to Australia

I am a Fijian migrant to Australia. When "home" is Fiji, a far-away island in the South Pacific, there is an uncomfortable sense of exile, of not wanting to be in this new place, of not wanting to understand. What I experienced most strongly was a feeling of cultural exile. When I first came across cassava and tinned tuna, six months after leaving Fiji with my Australian husband and three young Fiji-born children, I boiled the cassava, opened the tinned tuna and threw into the fish some onion, lemon juice and chilly. Then I ate the lot with my fingers. Suddenly I found myself crying. This culturally considered "food of the poor" in Fiji became for me the link between everything that is past and present. And, that which await in the future.

3. Foucault, *The Order of Things*, 8.

4. A subaltern is someone with a low ranking in a social, political, or other hierarchy. It can also mean someone who has been marginalized or oppressed.

5. Spivak, *Death of a Discipline*, 7.

I trained as a teacher in Melbourne, Australia, in 1972 after completing secondary education in Fiji. Returning to Fiji in 1976 with my husband Chris, I taught kindergarten and pre-school teachers in conjunction with the Methodist Church of Fiji and the Fiji Education Department. I was in a team that spearheaded Pre-School Training throughout the South Pacific through the Extension Services of the University of the South Pacific. This work took me to some of the islands in the South Pacific for Pre-School student and teacher conferences and to run summer schools.

Our three children Talei, Lagi and James, now independent adults, were all born in Fiji and have strong affiliation with, and pride in, their Fijian roots and heritage. Until 2003 when I became a student candidate at the United Faculty of Theology in Melbourne (now Pilgrim), I continued in kindergarten/primary school teaching. I became a Uniting Church Minister of the Word in 2006 and, due to family reasons, retired in 2014. My husband and I with three granddaughters in our permanent care now live by the beach in beautiful Rosebud.

Fiji, Land of the *Masi*

Fiji consists of a group of about three hundred islands whose people are deeply attached to the spirit of the land and keenly aware that the life pulse moves through all people and all things around them. The spiritual depth and measure of the Fijian is evidenced by the love and respect they have for their land and culture. Their love for religious and spiritual life is evidenced by their endless involvement in their church.

This spirituality is part of the traditional nurturing which forms the network of consciousness throughout the islands uniting men and women, young and old, to the ancestor gods who are still very much a part of Fijian life. The sacred, living nature of the land of Fiji is seen in many ancient crafts such as pottery, wood-cutting, house building, weaving, fishing, and the making of *masi*, also known traditionally as the cloth of the gods, *na masi-kalou*.

Figure 4.1: *Masi* (provided)

It is the craft and art of *masi* that I talanoa (story, telling story, story-weaving) around in this essay. The product known in Fiji as *masi* is better known throughout the world as bark-cloth or *tapa*. Made from the inner bark of a tall, slender tree (paper mulberry) also called *masi* and grown on land which is considered sacred, the *masi* cloth is far more than a nicely-designed wall hanging that a visitor sees in a handicraft centre (see Figure 4.1).

Masi contains the spirit of the land from which it comes. It also contains the tree that it was once a part of, and, very importantly, the stories of the women who beat the bark and decorate it. Very much an integral part of every aspect of traditional life, from the cradle mat to the grave, *masi* continues to be part of contemporary Fijian life and culture as the country and her people move more and more into the world of technology, urbanisation, and the influence of western civilization. Even in the diaspora, *masi* is still important in the Fijian identity (or *iTaukei*).

After I became an ordained minister of the Word in 2007, I decided to make liturgical stoles for myself based on *masi* designs including Fijian cultural symbols and liturgical motifs (see Figure 4.2). The *masi* designs, cultural and liturgical symbols in the stoles become an expression of that which will always be a part of me. The liturgical stoles are an expression of the links between my old roots and the new, representing both the influence of the missionaries in the introduction of Christianity to the Fijian culture, and my new direction in life as a mother, grandmother, and minister in the

UCA. The work in the stoles is an expression of the things I have come to experience, appreciate, and honour about life.

Figure 4.2: Stole with *masi* design (provided)

Masi in Diaspora

It will be wrong for me to uproot the *masi* tree from Fiji and plant it in Australia, the current residence for my Australian husband, three Fiji-born children, five grandchildren and me. There is not in Melbourne, or anywhere in Australia, the right kind of soil or weather. The masi tree will die. It will be a cruel thing to do. Like the land, the tree must be left behind. To leave behind something that is sacred and gives identity creates grief. What does one do when one has to leave behind something that is sacred, makes meaning, and much loved? Where does a stranger go in a strange land?

I take us now to the talanoa of the Bible, in particular the Old Testament. In Genesis, Abraham is described as "a stranger or a sojourner"; in Exodus, Moses is described as a "stranger in a strange land"; in Jeremiah, the Israelites are described as "living among strangers." This message and experience of diaspora transcend time and space.

When a land that is much loved is left behind, the soul experiences chaos, darkness, grief. In the new place—everything becomes different: the sun does not shine as warmly, the rain is cold, the food is strange. In Fiji my husband's first placement as a Methodist Church minister was in Dilkusha, an Indian circuit. The staple diet of the Indians in Fiji is rice and/or roti eaten with curry. So, my three very young children—the second was born when we were in Dilkusha—grew up on this Indian diet.

When we arrived in Australia and settled in a North-Central small country town called St. Arnaud, in the state of Victoria, where my husband was placed as a Uniting Church minister, for the first few months I cooked curry a few times a week so my children could eat some familiar taste while getting used to new tastes of food in this new land. One day a friend gave me broccoli, a green, tree-like vegetable I had never seen before. I threw this new vegetable into the curry pot. When we sat at the table and I dished out the food, I couldn't see any broccoli. It had completely disintegrated into the curry. Now, broccoli is one of my favorite vegetables and I know how to cook it just right.

I also realized in this new place that I could not use any of the things that gave me identity—the *sulu* (wrap around sarong), *salusalu* (lei, garland), my language. There were no other Fijians in that town. I could not spread out my mats made from the pandanus leaves, or *masi* cloths. I could use these if I really wanted to, but the occasions never seemed to be right. Also, underlying my hesitancy were the questions—Would they understand? Would they laugh at me? I did not want people who did not understand my culture to make fun of things which I am proud of and are sacred to me. Thus, most of these items stayed in their boxes.

Although I was happy in St. Arnaud and love my husband and children dearly, there was constant unrest within me. I couldn't define this unrest until, six months later, I first came across *tavioka* (cassava) and tinned tuna as explained above. I ate this meal not with a knife and fork but using my fingers in the way I know best. It suddenly became clear to me that what I was missing most was my Fijian cultural identity. All of it; the unspoken language, the fish in *lolo* (coconut milk), the feel of *voivoi* (pandanus leaf) under my feet, in my hand, the *salusalu*-making (lei) in celebration of my children's birthdays.

I slowly started to learn to improvise using whatever was around to make *salusalu*. Chris and I would give Fijian items to friends at weddings or birthdays, explaining what these were and how they would be used in a Fijian household. I joined craft groups, including the Country Women's Association (C.W.A), the biggest women's craft group in Australia.

In our fifth and final year at St. Arnaud, I put some of my craft work into the Wimmera Valley C.W.A. competition. Of the three items I put in, one achieved first prize, another second prize, and the third a third prize. I finally felt at home. I have a place in this new setting and a part to play. I learnt to see and appreciate its landscapes, its peoples, their gifts, their peculiarities. Chris and I offered friendship and hospitality to many and received back much more.

My experience raises the question of how to honestly confess that we are created as one in the midst of our cultural and spiritual differences? We are peculiar kinds of people without common language, single color or cultural identity, and yet we are all related by the blood of Jesus Christ. Such an understanding of one peoplehood is a radical departure from traditional and prevailing experiences of race relations and cultural colonialism.

People in a new land seek reconciliation with it. The church has a role for this. Writing our talanoa in essays for *Bordered Bodies* gives us a chance to share the things we carry in our soul, things that are better to be put out there and shared with those who are of similar sentiments, things that will help healing and reconciliation to take place. Healing and reconciliation can come about through acknowledgment of chaos, darkness, grief.

Cultural Diversity versus Cultural Colonialism

One of the reasons often given for opposing any form of cultural colonialism, voluntarily or otherwise, is the preservation of cultural diversity. This goal is analogous to the preservation of ecological diversity. For example, the deliberate reintroduction of programs allowing the First Peoples of Australia their cultural use of bush medicine and the chance to relearn some existing languages as some are now lost.[6]

Cultural diversity helps to preserve human historical heritage and knowledge and, just as important, makes available more ways of solving problems and responding to catastrophic disasters, natural or otherwise. Successful multicultural societies discern these aspects of culture and allow

---

6. I have been "treated" in such a program in a "culture clinic" on a visit to Yirrkala in 2007. These clinics are set up, some with federal financial assistance as the one in Yirrkala, to bring back to recorded existence some cultural memories.

them to grow and flourish. Diversity is not seen as a threat to the stability or economy but rather, as nurturing prosperity. Prosperity is the fruit of good-will, good intentions and hard work.

History shows that bridging cultural gaps successfully and serving diverse cultures and peoples adequately and appropriately require structures, laws, and institutions that transcend culture. Furthermore, the history of a number of ongoing experiments in multiculturalism suggests that workable, even if not perfected, integrative models exist. Some things that have become extinct in the culture of the First Peoples, for example language, community ways of living, artwork on a variety of media (bark, rock, wood), may never be resurrected. But some things that are even vaguely remembered can be brought back, for example the treatment of illnesses using bush medicine, the use of nature for cosmetics and art paintings, body paintings as part of the talanoa of the dance, the natural cycle of land produce and expectations of the seasons.

The Uniting Church in Australia (UCA) declared itself a Multicultural Church (1985), and this cannot only be a gathering of the cultures of Second Peoples. It must include the First Peoples. The declaration contained in all Acknowledgment to Country of the First Peoples of Australia, the longest living culture in the world, that they are the God-given custodians of the land now known as Australia, means that First Peoples are the Sovereign Peoples of Australia and of the UCA.[7] Unless the First Peoples are named as sovereign the declaration that the UCA is a Multicultural Church will lack something, and this will be the missing link in all the good things the UCA is doing. Accordingly, for the remainder of this reflection, I refer to the First Peoples as Sovereign Peoples.

To connect with this missing link, I invite HOPE. We can claim the ideology of hope to de-stabilize the continuing reign of cultural colonialism of the federal government of Australia and encourage the return to Sovereign Peoples of some culture lost. The Sovereign Peoples continue to carry the deep pain of being disowned on their land. The mantra of "We are a Multicultural Church" and yet the Sovereign Peoples are not given the acknowledgment that they are sovereign custodians of the land puts them in the category of Second Peoples.

---

7. I take my example of "Sovereign" from the name "iTaukei" that all indigenous Fijians call themselves as custodians/owners of Fijian lands. iTaukei means Sovereign.

Hope

This essay stitches the talanoa of my loss, my longing, and more than those, my healing and reconciliation. In this I remember that God cares more about how we behave than the land we possess or the roots we leave behind. As a people of God, we have no place anywhere, so we carry our identity in our songs and dances, our craft, our history, our talanoa of the things we remember.

In the wilderness, God directs us to face with courage and humility the things that give us chaos and darkness, and at the same time to embrace and make friends with the part of ourselves that is vulnerable and grieving. We need to listen for what the prophet Elijah experiences as "the still, small voice of God," the self-murmuring conversation in our most wounded places that yearn for goodness and ache for forgiveness. To be open to grief is also to be dedicated to the healing of it. The most freeing aspect for me is the realization that as I stop to acknowledge my chaos and grief, I also acknowledge the loving grace of Christ that is mine for the taking and with which I can construct my own forgiveness.

As a people of a nation or group of islands as Fiji is, one needs land, yes, but as a people of faith, one does not. Moses, the most central figure of the exodus, taking God's people to the new land and freedom under God's instructions, never set foot on this promised land, only saw it from a distance before he died. But David and Solomon, who sat on the land and were its greatest leaders, were not morally attentive and were, sometimes, a disappointment to God.

The lesson of the New Testament is that physical land, political power, even the temple in Jerusalem, were not the end for God's people. The only thing that is the end for God's people is obedience to God's Word. What can we learn from that time that is relevant today? First, I must acknowledge my roots, my ancestors. I must know my cultural background and talanoa if I want to go courageously and confidently into the future. *Masi*-making, pottery, wood-cutting, fishing, the chiefly hierarchy, stole-making are all in my Fijian culture. With this knowledge I can travel bravely and confidently into the future.

In this new land I find memories and remnants of my family home; bark paintings of the Sovereign Peoples, mats and baskets made from reeds and pandanus, seed and shell jewelry, different earth colors used as paint and dyes, sacred places, the honoring of the wisdom of the elders, the honoring of cemeteries and ancestors, the honoring of the *vanua* (land). In spirituality I can find my talanoa (history) and therefore my connections and relationships with the different peoples of Australia. In both, I find myself.

Wherever I travel I carry with me my culture, my history, my roots. In this I shall find my freedom, my peace, my home.

By the rivers of Babylon—there we sat down and there we wept when we remembered Zion. Psalm 137 gives us hope, precisely because it captures this truth of faith. As history suggests, in moments of chaos, some people will get angry and blame God, some will try and smash babies against rocks, drown newly born baby boys in the Nile, run vehicles into buildings and crowds, turn away people on boats or randomly shoot children in a classroom. But others will find new ways to reach out to God by cradling, feeding, even nurturing the babies of their enemies, or holding out their arms, some even giving up their lives to stop the chaos and destruction. Some will search among the ruins, ashes, and debris, and in there find hope.

In the relationship between humans and God, we have enormous power for we make the choices. We are the ones who choose how to behave. We, even in exile, can save ourselves from the feeling of exile. We can choose to belong. Humans, made by God in God's image, find God in the depth of grief. And God once again reaches out. With God in this new place, we seek to redeem ourselves and creation through forgiveness.

We try new roads; we find new ways to do what we can. The acceptance of chaos moves us out of our feeling of exile into freedom. All lands are different from any other. But every land has in it the good and the beautiful, also the bad and the ugly. It is the interaction of our differences that in our society gives us balance in religion, faith, and community. These are the differences that exist between different cultures, and the differences that will help us discover a piece of ourselves in a land and a culture that are new and strange.

Hope is a desire and expectation for a particular thing to happen, a wish, an aspiration, an expectation, a longing and yearning, an optimism, a promise, a light at the end of the tunnel. Hope is searching for the lost, loving the rejected, naming the nameless, accepting the ugly, teaching the lame to dance, the voiceless to sing, the mountain to move. Hope is God's gift to earth in the form of a baby born in a manger whose first visitors were shepherds, sheep, cows, and asses. Hope is making the impossible possible.

Hope is an ideology the UCA can share with its members. We are all made in the image of God, to look and behave like God and be custodians of God's creation. But we cannot be custodians of creation if we are fighting against each other: race against race, white against black, black against white, man against woman, straight against gay. We easily define people, mainly at first sight, to be part of an "other" group and immediately have fears and negative thoughts about them. We categorize. Moreover, all the reasons we give for othering, such as "Asian migrants and Pacific Islander workers are taking our jobs" come after the initial negative judgment which takes place subconsciously. We judge first ("they are lazy people") and give reasons later.

Pacific Islanders are known for the "coconut time" syndrome, the coconut will fall when it is ready, when it is the right time. The sensible thing therefore is not to stand or sit under a coconut tree! The invitation of HOPE in this scenario is to cross borders and sit in a place that is both unknown and chaotic or known and peaceful, and "wait for time" which will arrive when it is ready. Another example is the Bamboo time of Asia. When some of the very tall bamboo is planted, nothing seems to happen for five or six years. Then suddenly, when the bamboo knows it is time, it begins to grow up to the height of 18–25 meters.

Another globally known example is birth time, where birth happens when everything is in place (align) and creation gives out the message that now is the time. Some of the Parables of Jesus, along with other stories from the Scriptures, Hebrew and Christian, point to God's use of such ways and such concepts of time (Matt 24:6, 36; 1 Tim. 4:1; 2 Pet. 3:3–4).

This "waiting for time" is known in Greek as *kairos* or maturity (coconut), height (bamboo) or alignment (birth) time. It is God's-time. This "waiting for time" becomes a time for honoring and planning, but mainly, waiting. It is a different time from *chronos*, another concept of time that is simply "clock time." Kairos is a call to faithfulness in action, a trust in waiting for maturing and harvesting. Kairos belongs to God's activity, not human beings' *chronos*.

Hope is crossing borders and hospitalities. Hospitality is not merely visiting but respectfully staying, seeking out "the other" and accepting their contribution in the form it is offered. Hope is crossing over into the unknown and listening to the voices and cultural norms that belong in that place. Crossing borders is where altruism begins.

HOPE for the Multicultural Church

The UCA refers to cultural colonizers in its membership as "the dominant voices." All Second Peoples cross borders as either migrants or cultural colonizers/dominant voices. There is not much difference between these, except that migrants have respect.

There is HOPE for the UCA if we start with respect. Those who arrive in Australia as exiles are different again. Most carry fear, mainly of being sent back to the life and death situation they have escaped. We can learn from one another. Multiculturalism is living in understanding of the many parts that we are, and reconciliation of these parts when disagreements occur. If it is reconciliation we seek, we must learn to sit and listen with respect to all the voices. We must listen also to the still, small voices in the silences. We may, in these silences, also hear God listening and speaking.

Not speaking into a conversation or discussion cannot be assumed to mean assent. This can also mean dissent, or the silence of the borders or the bordered![8] If people do not feel they are respected, valued, heard and/or understood, they will not contribute or learn to belong in the most inclusive of ways. Their true faithfulness and insights will not find voice and will therefore not find place. Reconciliation then becomes marginalized. A voice is a contribution the UCA looks for in all its members but sometimes does not know how to ask for or find it. Listening with respect is a good start when trying to hear bordered voices.

The chasm between Sovereign and Second Peoples of Australia remains the nation's greatest shame. The first 150 years of British colonialism in Australia was, for the Sovereign Peoples and as history records (1788–1938), a period of dispossession, physical ill-treatment, social disruption, population decline, economic exploitation, discrimination, and cultural devastation. "The Stolen Generation"[9] is a part of this legacy. For the Sovereign Peoples, this was the beginning of loss from their homelands followed by dispossession from family, culture, and life as they knew it.

The ripple effects of this era, of communities torn apart for no reason other than race, continues today. For the Sovereign Peoples, that intergenerational trauma is compounded by continuing experiences of racism, exclusion, and disadvantage. Julia Gillard refers to these factors as increasing "the risk of mental illness, substance abuse and suicide."[10] The number of

---

8. "Space for Grace", a UCA documentary from the Cross-Cultural Reference Committee written by Tony Floyd and Amelia Koh-Butler (available from Assembly.uca.org.au).

9. The Stolen Generations (also known as Stolen Children) were the children of Sovereign Peoples who were removed from their families by the Australian federal and state government agencies and church missions, under acts of their respective parliaments. The removal of those referred to as "half-caste" children were conducted in the period between 1905 and 1967, although in some places mixed-race children were still being taken into the 1970s. Official government estimates are that in certain regions between one in ten and one in three Indigenous Australian children were forcibly taken from their families and communities between 1910 and 1970.

10. Julia Gillard, former Prime Minister of Australia (2010–2013) and Chair of "Beyond Blue," a major funder of mental health research in Australia with a focus on depression, anxiety, and suicide.

Sovereign Peoples children in care has doubled since Kevin Rudd's apology to the Stolen Generation in 2008.[11]

It is time for us to honestly face our past. It is time for the UCA to break through borders of cultural colonialism that keep the "other" away. It is time for Second Peoples, which includes first, second and third generation migrants, to sit and talk and ask questions. We sit with Sovereign Peoples and respectfully listen and learn as they tell us stories about dreamtimes, koalas and kookaburras, sea and river colors, contours and plains, and the land that gives them life. Listening to and learning the story of the "other" must become an intentional part of our life.

Multiculturalism is not a partnership between Sovereign and Second Peoples. It is a covenant, an agreement to a relationship, between God and God's people. The UCA has tried a few ways of relationship and reconciliation with its bordered bodies from other cultures. It has stood in solidarity with Uniting Aboriginal and Islander Christian Congress (UAICC, formed in 1985 by the Sovereign Peoples members of UCA as a separate body of Assembly).[12] In terms of multiculturalism, some important areas the UCA has been active in is to:

---

11. Kevin Rudd, former Prime Minister of Australia (2007–2010), moved a motion of Apology to the Sovereign Peoples. Rudd became the first Australian Prime Minister to publicly apologize to the Stolen Generations on behalf of the Australian federal government. The number of Sovereign Peoples in government care rose from 52.5% in 2014 to 59.4% in 2018 (Australian Institute of Health and Welfare, 2019).

12. Some activities which the UCA has actively participated in relating to the UAICC include:
– 1985: Declared itself as a Multicultural Church, rejoicing in its diversity of races, cultures, and languages as God's gracious gifts;
– 1985: After the above declaration, the Sovereign Peoples members of the UCA formed the Uniting Aboriginal Islander Christian Congress (UAICC) to be a recognized body of the UCA;
– 1988: the UAICC invited members of the UCA to join in a solemn act of covenanting before God;
– 1994: the UCA accepted the 1988 UAICC invitation (above) to enter into a covenant relationship for a destiny together for a fuller expression of our reconciliation in Christ;
– 2009: added a preamble to the UCA Constitution which includes: "The (Sovereign) Peoples had already encountered the Creator God before the arrival of the colonizers; the Spirit was already on the land revealing God to the people through law, custom and ceremony. The same love and grace that was finally and fully revealed in Jesus Christ sustained the (Sovereign) Peoples and gave them particular insights into God's way."
– 2012 Assembly: UCA members walked silently from the Assembly to the Parliament House of South Australia to hold a vigil of public act of worship of lament in protest to the federal "Stronger Futures" legislation following from the earlier "Intervention" legislation which saw an increase in (Sovereign) Peoples youth imprisonment and suicides. This is an example of the silent and not so silent protests the UCA has

1. Intentionally seek membership of UCA members who may contribute as voices from "other" cultures;
2. Set up "Uniting World" as a contact between UCA and "other" church partners;
3. Set up "Reference Committee for Multi/Cross-cultural Ministry" as contact between UCA and "other language" congregations and ministries;
4. Give independence to each language group to plan and run its conferences and worship services in their native language;
5. Have important documents translated into migrant languages.

We continue to find ways of reaching out to bordered bodies. We offer what we can. We manifest altruism: we walk the second mile, give the shirt off our back, rejoice with those who rejoice, mourn with those who mourn, speak up for those who cannot speak, become eyes for those who cannot see and legs for those who cannot walk, defend the rights of the poor and needy, and, simply, do to others what we would have them do to us.[13]

> A Living Hope
> entered through
> bordered wires
>
> Released by God
> now with us
> in the mires
>
> And glory shone around.

---

participated in to show solidarity for its UAICC members and Sovereign Peoples.

13. In the TV Channel 9 news at 6 pm on Sunday January 26, 2020, I watched the Sovereign Peoples' protest against "Australia Day." They were joined by many Second Peoples. The interviewer questioned random members of the protest group, all of whom said, "Australia Day" (January 26th) was wrong. There were a number of Second Peoples, many with strong migrant accents and a few with true-blue Ossie accent. But all shared a similar view: "we agree with the Aboriginal peoples of Australia . . . what happened to them was wrong . . . the colonial celebration of Australia day is wrong . . . we are here to give a voice of solidarity . . . they need our 'other' voices . . . it is their land we live on, we honour that."

Works Cited

Bird, Carmel, ed. *The Stolen Children: Their Stories*. Melbourne: Random House Australia, 1998.

Bos, Robert, Norman Habel, Shirley Wurst, eds. *Rainbow Spirit Theology—Towards an Australian Aboriginal Theology: By the Rainbow Spirit Elders*. Adelaide: ATF, 2007.

Derwerse, Rosemary. *Building Bridges: Living God's Gift across Cultures*. National Library of Australia, 2014.

Feiler, Bruce. *Where God Was Born: A Journey by Land to the Roots of Religion*. New York: HarperCollins, 2005.

Foucault, Michel. *The Order of Things: An Archaeology of the Human Sciences*. New York: Pantheon, 1970.

Habel, Norman C. *Reconciliation: Searching for Australia's Soul*. Eugene, OR: Wipf & Stock, 1999.

Heinrichs, Steve, ed. *Wrongs to Rights: How Churches Can Engage The United Nations Declaration on the Rights of Indigenous Peoples*. Altona, Manitoba: Mennonite Church Canada, 2016.

Koh-Butler, Amelia, Tony Floyd. "*Space for Grace—Living in the 'Grace Margin' in Respectful, Empowering, and Inclusive Decision-making.*" Further contribution about processes and timelines in building conversations and decision-making for the ASC, Assembly and the Councils and communities of the UCA: Epiphany 2015.

Seruvakula, Semi B. *Na Bula Vakavanua*. Suva, Fiji: Institute of Pacific Studies, University of the South Pacific, 2000.

Spicer, Catherine and Rondo B. B. Me. *Fiji Masi: An Ancient Art in the New Millenium*. Burleigh Heads, Qld: Catherine Spicer and Rondo B.B. Me, 2004.

Spivak, Gayatri C. *Death of a Discipline*. The Wellek Library Lectures. New York: Columbia University Press, 1966.

Uniting Church in Australia. *Constitution and Regulations*. The Uniting Church Assembly, 2012.

5

Hospitality, Othering, and the Infinity of Worlds

Sara S. V. Bishop

My home is both an intensely private place and a public location where we cultivate, nurture, and grow relationships. As the spouse of an accredited diplomat, representation of our country is our duty and responsibility. Actual diplomacy doesn't take place in the office; it takes place after hours at cocktail parties, receptions, dinners, and outings that bring a realization that the other is a real person with loves and hates, problems and solutions that mirror our own. This relationship between others is the bridge that allows us to make connections and be willing to work on problems together.[1] However, I immediately acknowledge that in spite of being a female child of both Mexican-American and Euro-American heritage, I am a child of exceptional privilege. I have the privilege of a passport (US), an education (Master's degree), an income (at all!), and the freedom to travel. I also experience a peculiar hybrid reality, living in neither my own culture nor the culture of my host country, but in a third-culture gray area of both. The benefits are clear: income, community, travel, and parties; but it is also deeply challenging and disorienting. Maintaining one's sense of self is ar-

---

1. Bishop, "Living the Hospitable Life," ¶5.

duous. We must be resilient and resourceful, but the opportunities to live a life hospitably are unique.

At this juncture, I offer some working definitions: in art, *negative space* is the space between or around subjects in a piece. Architecturally, it is the space between floors and walls, which is extensively used, but not seen. Biologically, an *interstitial space* is similar, surrounding tissue cells and providing a micro-environment for bodily function. Theologically, *liminal space* currently means between what was and what is next, a place of transition, a season of waiting, and not knowing. All three spatial concepts—negative space, interstitial space, liminal space—will be used interchangeably to avoid preferencing any one discipline and to emphasize the reality and flexibility of the space and mindset.

In terms of mindset, *kenosis* is defined as a divine self-emptying, pouring out, and Creation itself is a manifestation of God's ultimate gift. All that we see is a mirror of the love that the Creator has for Creation. The theologies of kenosis and Ubuntu bring together what hospitality is *meant* to mean, rather than how we tend to practice it. Gabriel Setoloane explains, "it is as if each person were a magnet, creating together a complex field. Within that field, any change in the degree of magnetism, any movement of one, affects the magnetization of all."[2] Kenosis is the magnetization and hospitality is the magnetism. Serendipitously, biophilia is the direct object of both. Biophilia is defined as the innate tendency to focus on life and lifelike processes.[3]

Drawing from the above definitions, I take these three concepts as the backbone of hospitality: 1. the both-and as well as neither-nor; 2. the negative, interstitial or liminal space; and 3. the self-emptying, interconnected biophilia and kenosis of Ubuntu.

Hospitality

In the creation of community, the *previously present* communities are neither replaced, adapted, nor evolved; a *new* community is created. There is a pre-existing negative space between the two communities. This is a useful space, but it should not be con-fused with the spaces on either edge. For example, the wolf, a North American predator, exists in a dynamic in which the interstitial space holds a key role. It is an active player in the life of several packs. In this place, young wolves can disperse from the natal pack and in that space find others, mates, or travel through it to new territories. This

2. Battle, *Reconciliation*, 51.
3. Wilson, *Biophilia*, 1.

is done without risking death that would be entailed in an established pack's territory. The pack mitigates the risk of injury or death to its own individuals by honoring this negative space. The seeming emptiness is in fact both inhabited and is an actor in the dramas. Hospitality is interstitial space to do important things that ensure survival.

Veli-Mati Kärkkäinen states that there are three stages in the process towards flourishing: separation, liminal period, and re-assimilation.[4] This assumption unwittingly perpetuates a widely held binary and Western view that the center is of more value, and that the margins, or liminal spaces, are not home, but places from which to get away, as if the center were fixed and static. Not only does the interstitial space between known and unknown have creative possibility, but this space is not limited by the cultural unconscious of the center. This concept of "integration being synonymous with flourishing" also presumes that liminality cannot last forever. Throughout the New Testament, we are confronted with Jesus deliberately avoiding the center, and looking to the margins. Jesus didn't come from Jerusalem, where the Messiah *ought* to have come from, but from Nazareth. Jesus wasn't the son of a prominent rabbi or scribe or Pharisee, but of a carpenter. The Bible makes the experience of marginality normative for the people of God. For the Israelites and early Christians, understanding themselves as aliens and sojourners was a reminder of their dependence on God.[5]

Divine hospitality is the Holy Spirit's invitation to relational engagement,[6] right relationship between one's self, others, and God. By showing us what that is and how it looks, Divine hospitality inspires vulnerability and openness. Gratitude is the recognition of all that holds us in the web of life and all that has made it possible to have that life that we have and the moment that we are experiencing.[7] Divine hospitality is nothing less than a manifestation of this gratitude, and a sharing of *imago Dei,* seating deep in the center of Godly Creation, a "hermeneutic of hopefulness."[8] Regardless of reward, there is a willingness to risk. There are likely to be far fewer rewards than risks, particularly if you are an inhabitant of the interstitial space. Like Creation, God's own image, hospitality doesn't look for a return on investment. The economic lens is a symptom of a much deeper injury to Creation, a humanism, which in the West recognizes truth as somehow

---

4. Kärkkäinen, *A Constructive Christian Theology,* vol. 3, 440.
5. Pohl, *Making Room,* 105.
6. Kärkkäinen, *A Christian Theology in the Pluralistic World,* 508.
7. Bstan-'dzin-rgya-mtsho, *The Book of Joy,* 242.
8. Kärkkäinen, *A Christian Theology in the Pluralistic World,* 373.

based on materialism,[9] an economy of things, benefit to the human species, rather than an interdependency and mutual support.

Hospitality is, above all else, a lifestyle and way of living. Bishop Desmond Tutu explains it as Ubuntu, "that a person is human precisely in being enveloped in the community of other human beings, in being caught up in the bustle of life. To be is to participate in that interdependence"[10] regardless of where we are in terms of the center. As Martin Luther puts it, "the divinity of the triune God consists in that God gives himself [sic] in terms of the Word, justice, truth, wisdom, love, goodness, eternal life and so forth."[11] Kindness, freely given; caring, given instinctively; tenderness, offered unawares. These are the hermeneutic of hopefulness that hospitality entails, and are, in themselves, their own reward. Hospitality is an awareness of others placed into one's life and living in the tension *between* the borders of both lives, as a lifestyle, not an attention to detail. In the language of biophilia, Ortega y Casset makes a statement that exudes hospitality, "Prepare an attention of a different and superior kind, an attention that does not consist of riveting itself on the presumed but consists precisely in *not* presuming anything and avoiding inattentiveness."[12] Living it well will impact *all* other aspects of one's life. It is the intentional, responsible, and caring act of being with those who are strangers, enemies, distressed, with human and non-human companions in Creation, with oneself, without regard for reciprocation. The Holy Spirit is the spirit of *koinonia,* the eternal bond of love, and as such is the source for this kind of anthropology of the Other.

Hospitality embodies *philoxenia,* love of the other, friend, stranger, even enemy. In such hospitality, one is born into the very life of God and having this life brings knowledge of God.[13] As a result, we are bound by love to share it, regardless, purely for the joy of it. In this way, it is a spiritual gift. It is a transition from "you to our" that is naturally resisted, particularly with the Western mindset of "individual as ideal." This resistance comes from traditionally empowered individuals or societies because giving is viewed as a reduction, rather than as an expansion. For this reason, hospitality may be dressed up as service, in which a specific program is planned and defined, but the people are interchangeable. It may be given a dress of mission, where overt or covert proselytization of the "right" way to be Christian is presented, not as a gift but as instruction in correct

---

9. Battle, *Reconciliation,* 36.
10. Battle, *Reconciliation,* 39.
11. Kärkkäinen, *A Christian Theology in the Pluralistic World,* 83.
12. Wilson, *Biophilia,* 103.
13. Lucien, *Living the Hospitable God,* 53.

practice. Witness and charity are just as easily co-opted, taking the receiver *and* the giver out of the equation, made easily interchangeable because it fits into a Western worldview of either-or.

Discussion of hospitality generally includes what one receives from the acts and actions of hospitality. This discussion disregards the acts of opening, of trust, and conscious absence of expectation of compensation with friendship or good food or some other tangible or intangible reward. Hospitality is living in right relationship. Customs shift, cultural allowances differ, and local hospitality traditions change. What I assume is based solely on *my* experience, any study that *I've* done, or the presence of a translator or an emissary present because of *me*. Hospitality is a companion in that transition from "you" to "our."[14] The focus on acts, rather than a persistent state of being, detracts from the *agape*, unconditional God love, nature of hospitality. Much of what is written on hospitality is from an active advocacy position. Entire books on Christian hospitality are written from the point of view of benevolence, commitment, and giving. The "how" of Christian hospitality is primarily focused into the context of one, usually Christian, going out and giving, doing, or helping, which maintains a hierarchy in which Christian is the head. This language is flawed, and hospitality is thus treated as a set of motions, or a piece of theater, or a deed. In this definition, it is a one-time act *even if* it is an act that is repeated on a regular basis. While it may include service, true hospitality is not about providing a service. The gifts that hospitality gives include sacrifice, self-giving, discipleship, and turning to others.[15] Succinctly, hospitality is radical and fringe. Transformative hospitality still finds its most effective location on the edges of society, where it is offered by those who have a sense of their own alien status.[16] This was brought home for us as a family as we moved every few years. Hospitality is the opening of liminal space. It is where love flows freely in both directions, and frankly, beyond, because it creates and cements interconnected relationships, strengthening the magnetism of bringing together. Hospitality is often presented as a spiritual gift (1 Peter 4:9, NIV), as service,[17] as witness or mission,[18] and, "In 3 John 5:8, hospitality is not presented as a work of charity but also as a participation in the ministry of the Word."[19] However, the importance of hospitality which

---

14. Bishop, "Living with Church Hospitality," ¶2.
15. Kärkkäinen, *A Constructive Christian Theology*, vol. 2, 312.
16. Pohl, *Making Room*, 124.
17. Kärkkäinen, *A Constructive Christian Theology*, vol. 2, 312.
18. Yong, *Hospitality and the Other*, loc 3299 & loc 3809.
19. Lucien, *Living the Hospitable God*, 64.

occurs in negative spaces is uniquely visible to those for whom the liminal, interstitial, and in-between spaces are home.

The previous ways of defining hospitality are flawed and are better defined as acts of tolerance. "A primary difference between tolerance and hospitality is that tolerance attempts to remake or reshape the other into an acceptable, that is familiar or similar, image, while hospitality *requires* acknowledging that the other, the stranger, really is different."[20] It is rare for strangers to cross the interstitial space, physically, emotionally, or spiritually, let alone also perceive fellow travelers in that space as equals. It presupposes that we instinctively recognize our common humanity in its myriad variations[21] first and foremost, rather than recognizing the differences in skin tone, language, dress, or culture. Boundary lines have become indistinct. Now the world is interstitial. The international blurs into the national. We do not quite know who is us, and who is them, particularly as neither race nor language can define nationality any longer.[22]

Mestizaje

"Mestizaje means 'mixing' and refers to the mixing of ethnic and cultural groups in Mexican history. However, like Mexican ideas of racial identification, the concept of mestizaje is a fluid one, ever changing in its relation to social, political, and philosophical ideas about the nation and national identity."[23] Mestizaje is Othering from both directions. I am a person who has always been both/and: both of Mexican and white European heritage; both in possession of a United States passport and a citizen of the world; both a scientist and a pastor; both spiritual and not religious. I am the spouse of a diplomat, which involves a lot of social and public activities, and an unrepentant introvert. My home is both a welcoming space for *anyone* who enters it, human or four-legged, and an intensely personal space.[24] Conventionally speaking, I don't fit properly anywhere. Practically speaking, I am comfortable virtually everywhere. Being presumed as an outsider makes the liminal space my comfort zone. My lack of externally imposed, comfortably defined identity results in my presence in the margin, and it is less unique than the center would prefer.

20. Kärkkäinen, *A Constructive Christian Theology*, vol. 2, 331.
21. Lucien, *Living the Hospitable God*, 68.
22. Kärkkäinen, *A Constructive Christian Theology*, vol. 3, 439.
23. Muscato, *History, Culture and People*, 6.
24. Bishop, "Living in A Church Bubble," ¶3.

Systematization of knowledge of all kinds, including theology and Biblical studies, is rooted in a Western worldview. Western scholars began to codify the languages, cultures, religions, and histories, including those of the many different nations that they chose to call Asia or the Orient. At the same time, these scholars developed scientific views of historical criticism and theological discourse that served to make normative the western "worldview" and *remain* the standard of excellence in the academy and academic publishing, although they are historically and culturally limited to one phase of history in one part of the world.[25] Those receiving training in the Euro-American contexts are taught western methods, and use interpretative lenses that begin with a hierarchy of values determined by those who benefited from colonial power.[26] The long-term effect is the inherent suspicion of other knowledge, ideas, and world views that are only now being seriously questioned from the margins, and replaced from the center. When we decolonize our minds, we begin thinking from the margins, rather than from the center.[27]

Decolonization, where a colonized people redefine themselves as a people and reassert their distinct identity, is by no means an easy effort. It is not only limited to those cultures invaded everywhere, epitomized in the Northern and Western hemispheres in the Native American or indigenous Australians in the Southern and Eastern hemispheres. This colonization effect is also felt in the resultant culture, the now-United States citizenry or Australians et al, with their native, immigrant, and colonial grafts. Recognition of the very existence of the effect of colonization is heavily fraught with fragility, bitterness, and naked fear of losing that sense and definition of self. The post-colonialist critique persistently reminds us that colonialism goes beyond the issues of racial discrimination, economic poverty, and political marginalization, although those are symptoms.[28] As a result, there are people and places that are on the boundaries of the usual, the edges of normal, the blurry side of comfortable, which is deeply disturbing to the dominant culture. Most cultures exist in that non-dominant space, and dominant culture knows it is outnumbered. The only option to survive, let alone thrive, was to be vulnerable and accept how we were seen by others, negative baggage and misconceptions included. This is a key step in decolonizing one's mind. One does not have to understand how one is seen; just acknowledge.

---

25. Russell, *Just Hospitality*, loc 562.
26. Russell, *Just Hospitality*, loc 732.
27. Russell, *Just Hospitality*, loc 1482.
28. Kärkkäinen, *A Constructive Christian Theology*, vol. 3, 445.

As a family, we have been serving in the U.S. Foreign Service Department of State for twenty years. As part of our service to the US government, we were not only representing a dominant world power, but were always going into spaces that the dominant culture considered to be hardship, unusual, or marginal. In those places we found rich histories, cultures and worldviews. My husband and I served in the U.S. military prior to that, and have worked under various administrations, all over the world. How we are perceived has changed several times.

Acceptance that others' views of oneself change depending on context, is a troubling one. The Western-Euro-American view teaches that there is one "me," and all comprehension radiates out from this understanding. The sense of oneself is as an individual and therefore unique and important. This sense of specialness of self permeates relationships. Individual and collective identity are constructed in a complex, planetary society where both individuals and groups are given increasing power to autonomously define themselves. We are simultaneously exposed to stronger pressures to conform to systemic regulations, to incorporate into our behavioral patterns, the deep cognitive and motivations structures that anonymous (read Western Euro-American?) apparatuses impose on us through the hidden encoding of information flow.[29] Individuals find themselves enmeshed in multiple bonds of belonging which we enter or leave far more often and more rapidly than we did in the past. We are migrant animals in the labyrinth of the world metropolises, in an infinity of worlds.[30] The result is a world of non-persons, marginalized ones, or Others, who understand the deeply disturbing part of this formula; we must accept that *we* are the strangers, and that perceptions of us as such, and assumptions and preconceptions that go with it, are valid definitions of our being. Even more bewildering, these views change repeatedly, depending on context or time. The final challenge is that this is flexible, not static. There cannot be an underlying anthropology of the Other as non-person, upon which to impose an identity. That must be let go in order to *own* otherness and live in the negative space so shunned by the center. Othering is key in Ubuntu, but turned on its head. Ubuntu derives from the proverbial Xhosa expression *Ubuntu ungamntu ngabanya abantu*. Roughly translated, it means "each individual's humanity is ideally expressed in relationship to others" or "a person depends on other people to be a person,"[31] and this relationship, of and with others, is key in hospitality.

---

29. Melucci in Webner 2015, 79–80.
30. Werbner, *Debating Cultural Hybridity*, 81.
31. Battle, *Reconciliation*, 39.

Othering occurs whether you are living in the centered set looking outward, or in the interstitial spaces. Hospitality is a vaccine against Othering. Hospitality is not limited to simple interactions, nor it is acts of entertaining, gifting, or charity. Hospitality breaks open identity and plurality, unity and diversity, the familiar and the strange. It creates a sense of being at home in the world and being a pilgrim in a strange land, negotiating a common world and honoring that plurality *at the same time*. These are thresholds, of varying types, which allow people, as individuals or groups or cultures, to enter away from a center into their margins and be comfortable there. The environment of vulnerability builds true community,[32] in the same way that God became Creation *for* and *with* humanity. This gracing relationship[33] is not determined by outside definitions, expectations, or anticipations; it simply *is*. While it isn't specified directly, each party begins as Other by the contrasting party, but then transforms into *us*. Members of both enter from a margin away from their center. Coming together in good faith, this is done not as Other but in hospitably as Us. Once we are us, we put non-self ahead of self. We do so without compromising self; in fact, we strengthen self in doing so. We are not buying into either-or but have instead become both-and more. A border "is a place of encounter, and is by nature, permeable. It is not like medieval armor, but rather like skin. Our skin does set a limit to where our bodies begin and end,"[34] but it lets things through, protects, and if it were ever to vanish or be closed off, we would die.

As mestizaje, practically speaking, I am comfortable virtually everywhere. Being presumed as an outsider makes the liminal space my comfort zone. My lack of externally imposed, comfortably defined identity results in my presence in the margin, and this is less unique than the center would prefer. I firmly believe that *most* of us are citizens of the margins, even the language used to describe it subscribes unconsciously to the language of dominance. Rather than being an occasion for the celebration of diversity, hybridity usually leads to marginality which comes in many forms, from social to cultural to economic and beyond.[35] It is a factor in being seen or heard, paradoxically, it also results in a freedom to do those things that are common and comfortable in the *spaces between*, but are surprising and radical otherwise. "Identity is both a system and a process. The field is defined

---

32. Battle, *Reconciliation*, 40.
33. Kärkkäinen, *A Christian Theology in the Pluralistic World*, 7.
34. Cruz, *Towards a Theology of Migration*, 32.
35. Kärkkäinen, *A Constructive Christian Theology*, vol. 3, 440.

by a set of relationships, and it simultaneously is both able to intervene, and to act upon itself or to restructure itself."[36]

Creation

The Gospel, we may reflect, is often counter-cultural. We are called to empathize with the most unloved,[37] those furthest away from the center. Interconnected relationships are more easily visible from the liminal space because the full web of relationships is visible and engaged; they have to be, to survive in the space. There *are* top-down relationships, but the hoarding of power is less effective in the interstitial space because it impedes function. We are required to engage compassion and empathy on a higher level. We are not to feel them as reaction, we are to predict and anticipate the need for these responses and take steps to shield others from that need. Compassion is not simply a feeling; it is primarily a *capacity* to enter into the joys and sorrows of another. The referent of compassion is always "other."[38] In doing so, we will appropriately interact with ourselves, our neighbors, and God.

Both Bishop Tutu and His Holiness the Dalai Lama emphasize that this compassionate concern for others is instinctual and that we are hardwired to connect and care,[39] something that E. O. Wilson, American biologist, naturalist, and writer, calls "Biophilia."[40] Connecting Ubuntu (needing people to be a person), kenosis (self-emptying), and biophilia (love of life) uses the language of several disciplines and connects touchstones from several cultures. This speaks to the universality of the idea, which reiterates Bishop Tutu's belief that the "staggering result of kenosis is that Creation is the outpouring of God's love."[41] This results in a church that thrives on difference, diversity, and plurality. It envisions not so much a 'melting pot' but a mosaic society.[42] We ourselves are mosaics of self. Without the ability to respond to self and the world, change our faces, voices, languages, and relationships, we lack compassion for ourselves and for others. Without compassion, humility, and hope, it is impossible to adapt towards that image of God that we are made to be. The image of God is Creation in interconnected, interactive, supportive, and symbiotic relationship.

36. Werbner, *Debating Cultural Hybridity*, 85.
37. Newlands, *Hospitable God*, 1295.
38. Lucien, *Living the Hospitable God*, 59–60.
39. Dali Lama XVI and Tutu, *The Book of Joy*, 274.
40. Wilson, *Biophilia*, 1.
41. Battle, *Reconciliation*, 45.
42. Cruz, *Towards a Theology of Migration*, 95.

What is seen in the other when viewed through Ubuntu is *imago Dei*, God's wonderfully distinctive creation in the other, the divine life of that person.[43] Bishop Desmond Tutu's theology of Ubuntu is relevant in a discussion of hospitality, particularly in connection to Creation writ large because of the distinctiveness that other creatures bring to relationships. If the theology asserts that persons who are ends in themselves only through the discovery of who they are in other,[44] expanding the definition of others to include non-human creatures reaches deeper into the divine. In the end, this compassionate, hospitable being *is* the image of God, and it is felt deeply when interacting with such beings. In *The Book of Joy*, Archbishop Tutu says, "Becoming an oasis of peace, a pool of serenity that ripples out to all of those around us. When we have a generous spirit, we are easy to be with. We radiate happiness, and our very company can bring joy to others."[45]

There is an integral connection to Creation, living in right relationship is both a hospitable manner and being a citizen of liminal space with all creatures. Creation recognizes this resonance of peace and serenity, compassion and hospitality, which do not always exist well in colonized, confined spaces. In the Western view, there is little tangible return on investment for living hospitably within creation. Of course, there are connections, and ways of interacting with creation; however, in a postcolonial worldview, these tend towards economic, political, and binary. False dichotomies do exist in other contexts, and care of Creation can exist in the Western Euro-American context, it is just more difficult. Creation is a liminal space; in fact, we use language like we want to *get away* and *get back to* nature. "To explore and affiliate with life is a deep and complicated process in human development. To an extent still undervalued in philosophy and religion, our existence still depends on this propensity, our spirit is woven from it, our hope rests on its currents."[46] To subscribe to the postcolonial view is akin to forgetting natal language; it is actively contributing to the loss of that relationship with Life. The hospitality of Creation is not binary; wolves are both apex predator providing balance and sustenance for a huge chain of species, and an animal dangerous to the slow, awkward species of *Homo sapiens*. Creation is so multilayered that it crosses into complex mathematics. It is like the Trinity in a dynamic, lively, non-binary way and this approach replaces the derivationist, subordinationist, and hierarchical ways of conceiving the Triune God. It is a

---

43. Battle, *Reconciliation*, 46.
44. Battle, *Reconciliation*, 43.
45. Dali Lama XVI and Tutu, *The Book of Joy*, 274.
46. Wilson, *Biophilia*, 1.

relational pattern of mutual giving and receiving, in which we are defined by our relationships with each other.

Conclusion

Jesus crossed thresholds. Jesus both accepted Roman authority and was a Jewish citizen, of this world *and* not of this world. His humanness was endangered by living in that interstitial space, but he did not just invite people into that space with him, he brought them in. Always, Jesus was walking in the margins, looking outward at the other rather than inward to the privileged. In doing so, he humanized those in the liminal spaces, in a way that taught hospitality as a way of embracing difference for no other reason than to be loving. Hospitality resists boundaries that endanger persons by denying their humanness.[47] Most ironically, it is now being addressed as if it were a new concept.

"The remarkable rediscovery in mainline Euro-American theology of cosmic and creational pneumatology, coupled with a pantheistic way of conceiving God-world relationship, received a lot of support from eco-Feminists, science-religion advocates, theologians of First Nations, as well as in accounts of the Spirit in the global south."[48] Such a statement is rife with dominant postcolonial language, and is downright self-congratulatory. The reality of thresholds is that they were not "lost" to its inhabitants. It was simply not recognized within Western spaces, and then the claim of rediscovery is re-appropriation, or claim, of sorts. Thresholds are interconnected relationships which are required for thriving in *both* spaces, particularly as they are homogenized into the postcolonial world. We struggle to maintain individual, cultural identity, and yet the dominant cultures of the world chip away and draw these identities into their own power structure. The view of power as a finite, and carefully husbanded, never-shared commodity, is less useful in a space where all empowering comes from interconnected relationships, and one cannot risk being oppressively dominant without risking the whole. Jesus' kenosis preaches that power is not something to be retained or withheld; it is essentially about relationships and giving of self. It is neither power over, power against, nor power for, but power *with*.[49] The liminal place of marginality is where God is to be found.[50] This is not limited to Jesus. The Spirit also does not

---

47. Pohl, *Making Room*, 64.
48. Kärkkäinen, *A Constructive Christian Theology* 2016, 50.
49. Lucien, *Living the Hospitable God*, 57–58.
50. Kärkkäinen, *A Constructive Christian Theology*, vol. 3, 441.

call attention to herself; She empowers, and bears witness to Christ[51] and Creator, while working endlessly in the interstitial spaces. Hospitality is always between Others, and the resulting, "Us-ness."

I used a small example from the wolves. I will end with one as well, albeit a little tongue in cheek, because it both anthropomorphizes wolves and has a decided bias in favor of dogs: Over evolutionary time, the friendliest of wolves (and possibly the most intelligent) learned that wagging their tails and delivering slippers was an easier way to earn a living than hunting caribou in the wilds. An original wolf might say to the dog, "You have lost your freedom. Your obsequiousness is humiliating to the family Canidae." The dog might reply, "I am much less warlike, far more altruistic, and besides, it's a wonderful standard of living."[52] This unwittingly, again, buys into the binary of civilization being better, and therefore wild is worse, or harder; however, I suggest that this is using the wrong lens. As recently as January 2020, scientists published a study in which wolf puppies played fetch. "The discovery comes as a surprise because it had been hypothesized that the cognitive abilities necessary to understand cues given by a human, such as those required for a game of fetch, arose in dogs only after humans domesticated them at least 15,000 years ago."[53] If it is true that a growing child can be especially sustained by learning to receive and extend affection through developing close ties to nature and life,[54] it is not illogical to hope that the *candid* child of God could, and would, do the same.

In a way, we all must embrace our mestizaje-ness, the mixing of who we are; what we perceive, and what others perceive. I am always surprised at how people react to me, particularly when it is in a context that I am "costumed" for, like a ball, or formal dinner, or the beach. The filters we put on ourselves and others are based on what we see, and they limit our willingness. And then someone says something that makes you realize, this person is like me, they're both-and also. Comradeship commences. Or, the something they say takes your breath away with the unconscious othering that puts you back into your liminal space, watching a drama from the outside, looking for the eyes that are doing the same, and then reaching out from that space in welcome, regardless.

Hospitality, that gift of Grace, is a negative space in the sense that it is defined by the spaces on either side, like the space between God's finger and Adam's in Michelangelo's *Creation of Adam* in the Sistine Chapel. It is

---

51. Kärkkäinen, *A Constructive Christian Theology*, vol. 4, 188.
52. Kellert, *The Biophilia Hypothesis*, 258.
53. Hansen Wheat and Temrin, "Intrinsic Ball Retrieving," 1.
54. Kellert, *Kinship to Mastery*, loc 1188.

full of potential and nuance. Colonization and Othering cannot contain it. As most of the world does not function in dominant space, but within dominant structures, we welcome, with joy, creatures, human and non-human to share the joy of our day as we find it. Those who exist in the margins, those who cross them as hybrids or mestizaje, are ambassadors and translators for a shared joy in living. In God's New Creation, margins will no longer exist for we will all be a part of the family. The liminal place of marginality is where God is to be found.[55]

Works Cited

Battle, Michael. *Reconciliation: The Ubuntu Theology of Desmond Tutu*. Cleveland: Pilgrim, 1997.

Bishop, Sara S. V. "Living in a Church Bubble." Blogpost, 16 June 2019. https://medium.com/@saravillarrealbishop/living-in-a-church-bubble-b7276f976186.

———. "Living the Hospitable Life." Blogpost, 10 August 2019. https://medium.com/@saravillarrealbishop/living-the-hospitable-life-e5aa21e95bea.

———. "Living with Church Hospitality." Blogpost, 14 October 2019. https://medium.com/@saravillarrealbishop/living-with-church-hospitality-78d1145afdc7.

Cruz, Gemma Tulud. *Towards a Theology of Migration: Social Justice and Religious Experience*. Content and Context in Theological Ethics. New York: Palgrave, 2014.

Dalai Lama XIV, and Desmond Tutu. *The Book of Joy: Lasting Happiness in a Changing World*. New York: Penguin, 2016.

Hansen Wheat, Christina, and Hans Temrin. "Intrinsic Ball Retrieving in Wolf Puppies Suggest Standing Ancestral Variation for Human-Directed Play." *iScience* 23/2 (2020) 1–5. https://www.cell.com/iscience/fulltext/S2589-0042(19)30557-7?_returnURL=https%3A%2F%2Flinkinghub.elsevier.com%2Fretrieve%2Fpii%2FS2589004219305577%3Fshowall%3Dtrue).

Kärkkäinen, Veli-Matti. *A Christian Theology in the Pluralistic World: A Global Introduction*. Grand Rapids: Eerdmans, 2019.

———. *A Constructive Christian Theology for the Pluralistic World*. Vol. 1: *Christ and Reconciliation*. Grand Rapids: Eerdmans, 2013.

———. *A Constructive Christian Theology for the Pluralistic World*. Vol. 2: *Trinity and Revelation*. Grand Rapids: Eerdmans, 2014.

———. *A Constructive Christian Theology for the Pluralistic World*. Vol. 3: *Creation and Humanity*. Grand Rapids: Eerdmans, 2015.

———. *A Constructive Christian Theology for the Pluralistic World: Spirit and Salvation*. Vol. 4: Grand Rapids: Eerdmans, 2016.

Kellert, Stephen. *The Biophilia Hypothesis*. Washington, DC: Island, 1993.

———. *Kinship to Mastery: Biophilia in Human Evolution and Development*. Washington, DC: Island, 1997.

Lucien, Richard. *Living the Hospitable God*. Mahwah, NJ: Paulist, 2000.

Muscato, Christopher. *History, Culture and People of the Americas*. 2009. https://study.com/academy/lesson/mestizaje-definition-history.html.

---

55. Kärkkäinen, *A Constructive Christian Theology* 2015, 441.

Newlands, George, and Allen Smith. *Hospitable God: The Transformative Dream*. New York: Routledge, 1999.

Pohl, Christine D. *Making Room: Recovering Hospitality as a Christian Tradition*. Grand Rapids: Eerdmans, 1999.

Russell, Letty M. *Just Hospitality: God's Welcome in a World of Difference*. Louisville: Westminster John Knox, 2009.

Werbner, Prina, and Tariq Madood, eds. *Debating Cultural Hybridity*. London: Zed, 2015

Wilson, E. O. *Biophilia*. Cambridge: Harvard University Press. 1984.

Yong, Amos. *Hospitality and the Other: Pentecost, Christian Practice and the Neighbor*. Maryknoll, NY: Orbis, 2008.

Part Two

Negotiating Bodies

6

Border Crossings

*Migration and Religion in
Colonial Australia*

SEFOROSA CARROLL

Migration is one journey amongst a number of journeys that involve the crossing of borders: the migrant like the exile and the nomad crosses borders and breaks barriers of thought and experience.[1]

The questioning of boundaries, and the movement across borders, leads to an expansion of vision and an ability to see more.[2]

THE MOVEMENTS OF RELIGIONS and migrants are historically intertwined. Across the globe migrants have resettled and adapted their faiths and practices to living in their host societies. Although "nation states have long sought to foster or impose religious homogeneity to unite their citizenry, diverse processes of international migration have sustained religious pluralism."[3] Australia is an interesting study in this regard, particularly

---

1. Ahmed, *Strange Encounters*, 85.
2. Ibid.
3. De Wind, "Foreword," vii.

as the founding undergirding ideology for more than three quarters of a century was to keep the non-European other out.

White Australia's roots lie in a history of invasion, occupation of space resulting in the exclusion of the "other" according to race. The "other" has been expanded to include the refugees, asylum seekers and Muslims who are seen as a threat to national identity and social cohesion.[4] Australia is a country shaped by anxiety, geographical isolation, insecurity and obsessive border control. This past continues to haunt the Australian imagination and has often played a part in the shaping of immigration policies and national consciousness. Against the backdrop of this history, it is intriguing that more than a century later Australia is a culturally and religiously diverse country. This radical change has been a result of the changes in Australia's immigration policy which has consequently changed and affected the Australian landscape and culture.

Colonial Australia

Borders or boundaries exist all around us. A border is simply by definition, a line or boundary (invisible and visible) that divides one entity from another. These "lines" serve to define, enclose, give meaning, protect, include and exclude. Borders are forms of identification. Gloria Anzaldúa maintains that "borders are set up to define the places that are safe and unsafe, to distinguish *us* from *them*."[5] Borders are literal, real and metaphorical and are varied in their manifestations and practice. Kwok Pui-Lan explains:

> the border may be physical and geographical, as millions have left their country of origin to become immigrants, refugees, expatriates, diasporans, and people in exile. The border may be cultural, linguistic, and political ... The border maybe religious and civilizational, conjured as the "Islamic world," "Hindu civilization" or "East–Asian culture." The border has been mapped out frequently in terms of the body and body politic ... The border may also be imaginary when we play with the notions of the "in-between space," the "third space," the "imaginary homeland," and other similar constructs.[6]

---

4. Zhou, "Australians Accepting of Migrants but Negative towards Islam."
5. Anzaldúa, *Borderlands*, 95.
6. Kwok, "A Theology of Border Passage," 104.

Nations are, as Benedict Anderson defines, "imagined political communities."[7] Nations are formed by borders. Borders in turn form a body of people, notions of nationhood and citizenship. Ironically, although borders are technically at the peripheries of a nation, the theoretical work that borders produce is actually central to the country. Sutapa Chattopadhyay describes border making or "mapping as an enterprise of the state that desensitizes landscapes; though maps are mute they communicate histories of colonial territorial control and iteratively reproduce boundary marking practices towards the maintenance of the hegemony of empires."[8] The border site is thereby "representative of complex nation-building processes, and nationalist practices that can have material manifestations."[9] Nations are not just bordered by or formed by lines on a map, they are given legitimacy through narratives constituted through language, a process J.M. Arthur calls "imaginative construction." Imaginative construction is a mapping process that intentionally "constructs a relation between an occupying culture and the place it has occupied. These constructions weave the assumptions, hopes, imaginings, of the place into the colonialists' experience of Australia."[10]

These narratives have to do with ideas that "construct and inform our value-systems and belongings."[11] Arthur is concerned with language and its relationship with space/place: how "the place 'Australia' is imagined and understood by non-indigenous 'Australians'—those members of the occupying society in the dominant language of that society—through their words."[12] Her study of "Australian English" (the settler's language) explores the relationship between the settler/colonialist, their imagination and their relationship to place. Arthur explores how language was used to consolidate and legitimize colonial belonging in Australia.[13] She examines the colonizing process of imagining and its impact on place through the projection of words. Arthur demonstrates that words can be used to convey ownership. She skillfully demonstrates how place is changed both through the colonizer's relationship with place and the image projected by the colonizer onto place.[14] In Australia's case, "English became a language

7. Anderson, *Imagined Communities*, 5.
8. Chattopadhyay, "Borders Re/make Bodies," 158.
9. Chattopadhyay, "Borders Re/make Bodies," 157–158.
10. Arthur, *The Default Country*, 7.
11. Duggan, *Ghost Nation*, xi.
12. Arthur, *The Default Country*, 8.
13. Arthur, *The Default Country*, 8.
14. Arthur, *The Default Country*, 7.

that did not return home but found a new home; it was used for relocating the community within a colonized territory, for attaching the exiles to the place and imagining it as, making it, home."[15]

But colonial history in Australia is part of a broader narrative. Borders played an important role in the colonial world. Colonial powers established borders to mark their territories or moved existing borders to suit their interests. Within the confines of their established and protected borders, the "colonial powers ruled supreme, as they not only pursued their economic benefit but promoted their political influence, cultural and religious values as well as their legal systems."[16] To justify their colonial objectives "Europeans developed a very broad legal vocabulary to accompany their empires."[17]

The international law of colonialism known as the Doctrine of Discovery, for example, was a narrative providing a Christian framework justifying the crossing of borders to promote Christian domination, European culture and seizure of lands. The Doctrine, a series of papal bulls originating from Spain and Portugal in the 1430s established spiritual, political and legal justification legitimizing European explorers to conquer the lands inhabited by non-Christians.[18] Each colonial power found ways to utilize the papal bulls for their benefit. The Doctrine contains key concepts such as *terra nullius*, pre-emption, first discovery, and civilization—all of which were bound and validated by Christian underpinnings. Andrew Fitzmaurice contends that the "Doctrine was used to denigrate and subjugate Indigenous nations and peoples; steal their lands, assets, and rights; and it has impacted them from the onset of colonization until today."[19]

Theological Explorations

This essay explores the notion of border in the real, imagined and metaphorical senses by exploring the interrelationship between borders, bodies, migration and religion in the Australian context. Borders have impact on bodies and likewise bodies have impact on borders. The presence of migrant bodies often troubles the concept of "border" as a defining social entity. These identities (borders, nations, nationality, and citizenship) often become agitated and change despite resistance from the dominant society. This essay argues

---

15. Arthur, *The Default Country*, 3.
16. Rieger, *Across Borders*, 245.
17. Fitzmaurice, "On Nobody's Land," 37.
18. "Upstander Project."
19. Fitzmaurice, "On Nobody's Land," 38.

that migrants, as they cross borders, their bodies (particularly if these bodies are religiously marked) also contest and shift borders.[20]

Douglas Ezzy et al. in their study on Australia's growing religious plurality observe that the revitalization of religion in the Australian context "may be experienced as destabilizing of traditional cultural practices and social structures."[21] The changes experienced through the "increasing numbers of those who do not identify with a religion (the 'nones'), and the growth of religious minorities, including Islam, Buddhism, Hinduism, and Sikhism"[22] are often understood as problematic for social cohesion. The authors maintain that the "pursuit of social stability and cohesion has often been associated with the maintenance of privilege and forms of social exclusion" and "social policies that pursue social cohesion tend to defend existing structures of privilege."[23] The authors thereby argue for a reconsideration of social cohesion as an analytical concept and policy that is constructed on "a set of relational practices that are democratic, participatory, and egalitarian, whether these be in everyday life, or in legal or political decision making."[24]

The premise of this essay is that the presence of religious migrant bodies reshapes the contexts in which they (re)settle despite being displaced and bordered out. Martha Frederiks argues that research has largely focused on and shown how "migration affects and transforms the beliefs, practices, and community formation of people who migrate" but "relatively little attention has been paid thus far to the fact that migration also impacts the religious traditions and beliefs and practices of 'non-migrants.'"[25] Yet, Frederiks states "in many areas, migration has profoundly changed the religious landscape, both in terms of multi-religious diversity and in terms of intra-religious diversity."[26] Australia is a case in point. Sociologist

20. The ongoing furor over the burqa and burkini is an example of how both particular religious bodies cause discomfort and yet at the same time contest and even shift borders. The burkini was invented by an Australian Muslim woman and is becoming an accepted dress code on Australian beaches. This is a significant move in Australia given that the beach is a national image of *white* Australian identity. In the case of the Cronulla beach riots in 2005, the beach became the site in which claims to home, by way of naming Australian Values were being reinstated. Lebanese Muslims were seen as a threat to Australia's social cohesion. On a national scale, Cronulla epitomized the struggle to secure home; a struggle over identity and Australianness, and over place and belonging.

21. Ezzy et al., "Religious Diversity in Australia," 2.
22. Ezzy et al., "Religious Diversity in Australia," 1.
23. Ezzy et al., "Religious Diversity in Australia," 5.
24. Ezzy et al., "Religious Diversity in Australia," 6.
25. Frederiks, "Religion, Migration, and Identity," 22.
26. Ibid.

of religion, Garry Bouma asserts that "as a result of migration, Australia has become a nation of many religions; it has become religiously plural."[27] Migration has relativized religion in the Australian context.

This essay will discuss the ways borders have operated in Australia to keep others out and the ways religious bodies have contested these borders and transformed the Australian landscape. Secondly, the essay argues that as borders are manifestations of power, borders are also a convenient strategy for identifying and subverting power. Thirdly, the essay explores how and in what ways borders and border crossings can open up new ways of seeing and being in the context of cultural and religious diversity. Migration as Ahmed states "is one journey amongst a number of journeys that involve the crossing of borders: the migrant like the exile and the nomad cross borders and breaks barriers of thought and experience."[28] These explorations will inform a closing section on border crossing.

Borders and Religious Bodies

Borders and their relationship to bodies is a recurring theme in the Australian experience of invasion, settlement, nationhood, and migration in both a literal and metaphorical sense. From time-to-time, borders have been relaxed and extended to accommodate bodies of difference. At other times borders have been placed to exclude certain bodies. Arguably, Australia is a country changed by the presence of bodies from other cultures and religions. The shifting patterns of immigration policy have altered the cultural and religious landscape in unexpected and unforeseen ways despite Australia's carefully planned social engineering to keep Australia "white" and nominally Christian. However, the real question remains whether the agitation of the borders by migrant bodies has been enough to bring about transformational change at the core.

With regard to nation building David Dutton states that "Australia took a path of gradual change within the overarching bonds of Empire which refined and supplemented rather than replaced and transformed."[29] Borders existed and still exist in Australia to keep "certain others" or "bodies" out. Although this has been the case, cultural and religious bodies have by their very presence been able to change the Australian landscape despite being bordered out.

---

27. Bouma, ed., *Many Religions, All Australian*, 9.
28. Ahmed, *Strange Encounters*, 80.
29. Dutton, *One of Us?*, 155.

White Australia

Australia's borders have been defined around a particular identity and culture (whiteness) and redefined through subsequent waves of migration and immigration policies. The overriding view of what it means to be Australian and be "one of us" was shaped by a particular pattern of immigration policy. That posture is driven by particular concerns—the most notable of which was the desire to keep Australia "white."

The Australian Commonwealth in 1901 was instituted from a commitment to create a particular kind of society. The White Australia policy, a physical manifestation of Alfred Deakin's statement, became a successful tool, in effect, a household code through which to keep the inhabitants of Australia "White." It became the foundational means by which Australia understood itself, its relationship with the "other" and in broader terms, how it has bordered itself as host for many cultures and religions. Federation embodied the hope and vision of a nation that would be exclusively White. For much of its history the Australian immigration program had been carefully controlled to minimize difference, with preference always being given to British migrants. The point is well made by James Jupp who argued that Australia is a product of conscious social engineering, with the objective of creating a particular kind of society whereby the population was carefully controlled through philosophies and policies of immigration.[30]

The motivation behind the White Australia policy was "the desire of Australians to build a strong and prosperous society founded upon the principle of racial and cultural homogeneity."[31] The ideology underlying this racial preference was argued on the basis of maintaining white Australia's racial unity and racial purity.[32] Andrew Markus contends that "fundamental to understanding the White Australia policy is the reality that it was targeted at both immigrant groups and Aboriginal peoples."[33] There was a strong objection to mixed breeding or blood. David Dutton argues that "the White Australia policy was intended to prevent the contamination of the nation's stock, or blood, or racial health, with inferior blood, since that would lead to a deterioration of the quality of the nation's citizens and civilisation."[34]

---

30. Jupp, *From White Australia to Womera*, 5.
31. Tavan, *The Long Slow Death of White Australia*, 11.
32. Dutton, *One of Us?*, 33.
33. Markus, "Of Continuities and Discontinuities," 178.
34. Dutton, *One of Us?*, 33.

The *Migration Act* in 1958 required officers of the Immigration department to judge the degree of "blood" in the veins of applicants for settlement. It was left to the discretion of immigration officials to determine whether the applicant was granted entry or not. According to Jupp, "it was claimed by ministers and their apologists that to bring into Australia anyone who looked different would provoke social unrest in a totally homogenous white British society."[35]

This desire for homogeneity fed the fear of external invasion and threat into a perceived need to people Australia's vast empty spaces, and the necessity of building economic strength and prosperity. That fear of invasion has further informed a deep-seated concern for security which lies within the emerging core imaginary. It was severely tested through the bombing of Darwin in 1942 which alerted Australia to its level of vulnerability through being an isolated outpost of western civilization on the edge of the teeming Asian masses to the north. It was no accident that Arthur Calwell, the first minister for immigration (1945–1949), pioneered the phrase "Populate or Perish." Anthony Burke has subsequently argued that Australia's obsessive insistence on security has dominated and distorted Australia's foreign policy and national life, from Cook's first voyage to the Asian crisis, and with reference to terrorism.[36]

Borders and Power

In the discussions on contemporary Australia questions and issues discussed tend to be associated with identity and citizenship and the level of sustainable diversity. One of the effects of this tendency has been the establishment of what Miriam Dixson has called the core imaginary Australian.[37] Dixson draws on a particular cultural period whereby talk of what it means to be Australian is affected by understandings of race and blood. For Dixson, however, recognition and celebration of difference must be tied to some form of solidarity or belongingness which is dependent on a "holding core."[38] Dixson argues for a maintenance of unity based on the adherence to formative influences. Using the analogy of child and parent, Dixson argues that a "holding core," like a parent or early significant figures, can either succeed or fail in containing the "anxieties" of a child.[39] Dixson believes

---

35. Jupp, *From White Australia to Womera*, 9.
36. Burke, *In Fear of Security*, 32.
37. Dixson, *The Imaginary Australian*, 18–28.
38. Dixson, *The Imaginary Australian*, 158–61.
39. Dixson, *The Imaginary Australian*, 21.

that the "holding core" or role of the "parent" lies in the Anglo-Celtic core culture. Herein lies the core imaginary Australian.

That expression of the Australian national imaginary is powerful. The ensuing years have born witness to an increasing level of cultural diversity and polylinguality but the core imaginary remains strong. James Forrest and Kevin Dunn believe that "contemporary Australian society and polity is often characterized as increasingly multicultural, but still struggling to disengage from a legacy of Anglo privilege and cultural dominance."[40] It is a characteristic of a self-confessed multicultural society for there to be religious diversity. It is arguably the case that the very notion of multiculturalism should now not simply be confined to a plurality of cultures. It is indeed currently being challenged, broadened and revised to include religious diversity;[41] there is now an acceptance of how religion is part of a person's identity and "remains an important part of ethnic identity retention."[42] It was expected that "Christianity could remain a significant part of the glue, which held the nation together" through the waves of migration prior to the 1970s.[43] Ghassan Hage[44] and Sophie Sutherland[45] have, nevertheless, separately concluded, that this kind of religious diversity has been overshadowed by the preoccupation of a national identity which assumed a white, Christian core.

This basic core imaginary had been under some pressure for a period of time well before the shift in immigration policy in 1973. That was the year when the potential for a radically different kind of diversity established in religious and cultural membership would emerge. Prior to this period of change, the rhetoric of "whiteness" was redefined as initial steps away from a policy, which looked to Britain for immigrants who could be "one of us" were made towards other European migrants. The immediate postwar immigration embraced substantial waves of people from countries with languages other than English during this period. The overwhelming majority nevertheless were from religious groups already well established.[46] The profile of Catholics became more European (Italian) and not just Irish; the

40. Forrest and Kevin Dunn, "'Core' Culture Hegemony and Multiculturalism," 208.

41. See Bouma and Ling, "Religious Resurgence and Diversity and Social Cohesion in Australia"; Cahill et al., *Religion, Cultural Diversity and Safeguarding Australia*; Fozdar, "Social Cohesion and Skilled Muslim Refugees in Australia"; Jupp, "Preface: A New Era in Australian Multiculturalism."

42. McCallum, "Religion and Social Cohesion," 942.

43. Hughes, "Social Capital and Religion in Contemporary Australia," 133.

44. Hage, *White Nation*; Hage, *Against Paranoid Nationalism*.

45. Sunderland, "Post-secular Nation."

46. Bouma, *Many Religions*, 2.

level of Greek migration led to the growth of Orthodox Christianity. The implied understanding was that "Australia is [still] a multicultural society with predominantly Christian affiliations."[47]

Religious Diversity and Migration

The changing religious profile in Australia is intimately tied to the practice of immigration and citizenship which initially privileged Anglo-Celtic migrants. The Christian faith was the assumed religion or faith. Religion, namely Christianity has played a major role in the formation of Australian society. Manning Clark, in the first of his six-volume *A history of Australia*,[48] argued that forces of Enlightenment, Roman Catholicism, and Protestantism were indeed instrumental in the formation of Australian society. From the perspective of its settlement the most obvious practical consequence was the importing of a denominational pattern from the other side of the world.

Bouma is right to highlight how religion is a function of migration—but there is a further consideration. The denominational pattern is in many cases tied to ethnicity and culture—and a matter of timing. In 1901 the census recorded 39.7% Anglicans, 22.7% Catholic and 33.33% other Christians. In the 1947 Census Anglicans were 39%, Catholic 20.9% and other Christians 28.1%. These churches were essentially mono-ethnic, as Ian Breward observed:

> In the brief two centuries of Christian presence on this ancient continent the churches have, like migrant churches elsewhere, reproduced the familiar and the secure. When so much else was unsettling and different, the churches provided a piece of surrogate homeland. Until the 1960s, all the major denominations were immediately recognizable to migrants. Colonial origins have been enduring.[49]

The abolition of the White Australia policy profoundly affected the landscape and nature of this country. The current multicultural landscape is essentially an outworking of the changing shifts in migration policy. The changes in the social, cultural and ethnic landscape are clearly visible in Australia. A case in point is Sydney to which the term "Australia's largest ethniCITY" has been applied.[50] Graeme Hugo makes the point that

47. Healey, ed., *Religions in Australia*, 1.
48. Clark, *A history of Australia*.
49. Breward, *A history of the Australian churches*, 218.
50. Burnley, "Sydney's changing peoples," 37.

the "major change in Sydney's population over the last two decades has not been in number but in a massive increase in its diversity."[51] This observation is supported by the 2001 census which recorded 249 different countries of birth and 251 ancestries in Sydney. More than half of Sydney's population were immigrants or children of an immigrant. The 2016 Census of Population and Housing showed that 26% of the population were overseas-born, and that 45% had at least one overseas-born parent in comparison to fifty years ago when Australia's overseas born population was only 18% of the total population.[52]

In opening its borders to migration from all parts of the world Australia now hosts a diversity of peoples, their cultures and religions. The arrival of migrants from Asia, the Middle East and Africa has meant that diversity can no longer be limited to culture and ethnicity. There are now shifts of religious identification.[53] The diversity of the settlement of people of other faiths was an unforeseen and unaccounted aspect of migration. The Australian religious landscape had altered yet again from the post war period of settlement. The 2016 census reveals that Australia is now home to more than 300 languages, over 100 religions and more than 300 different ancestries.[54]

Theological Dilemma

The dilemma facing contemporary theologians is whether Dixson's core imaginary Australian creates sufficient space for the other/alien now present in Australian society? Gary Bouma would argue as indeed Jupp that this process has not been thought through. The focus was on who is allowed in and how they may become "one of us." Lopez argued that "several of the significant developments that contributed to the establishment of multiculturalism in public policy did not originate in attempts to create a multicultural society."[55] There was no attention to settlement processes or to the possibility of pluralism. It was assumed people would adhere to Dixson's core-imaginary Australian.

Contrary to the belief of sociologists in the 1960s, "God is not dead"; religion is thriving, and it is not likely to go away.[56] This claim coincides

51. Hugo, "Australian demographic change," 3.
52. Australian Bureau of Statistics, "Cultural Diversity."
53. Bouma, *Australian soul*, 52.
54. Australian Bureau of Statistics, "Cultural Diversity: Who we are now."
55. Lopez, *The origins of multiculturalism in Australian politics*, 458.
56. See Bouma, *Being faithful in diversity*; Bouma et al., eds., *Freedom of religion and belief in 21st Century Australia*; Cahill et al., *Religion, cultural diversity and safeguarding*

with the emergence of the worldwide return of God, fundamentalism and globalism which has pushed religion back into the public sphere. The presence of other religions revitalized interest in religion in the public space. That presence has become more visible. It is represented in architecture, clothing, and consumer goods. The reason for such was not simply numbers but the gradual emergence of other religious buildings. It is now not uncommon to find the suburban landscape of Sydney dispersed with mosques, temples, and churches, alongside each other. The variety of restaurants and shops that span the countries and cultures of the earth are part of Australia's changing landscape.

Christianity is now one of many religions in the public sphere and with the influx of cultures and religions, the meaning and understanding of religion has acquired a broader and wider meaning. At least until the 1960s, the term religion in Australia was synonymous with Christianity. This change has also posed a challenge (and an opportunity) for the Christian churches in Australia as the practical effect of the multicultural policies and sociological shifts has been to make the Christian church more culturally diverse and to relocate them in a recognizably multifaith society. The church now finds itself in an increasing secularized and pluralistic society.

The public forum in which the Christian faith is now expressed is characterized by religious pluralism. According to Bouma, this state of affairs is the "new normal." The very existence of this pluralism—not to mention its extent—offers a profound challenge to Christian faith and practice. It raises the need to rethink Christian identity, particularly with how evangelism is understood and how mission is practiced. It is asking us to think about—to be self-reflexive—on how our understandings of theology, both explicit and implicit, are heard beyond the walls of the church.

It is a "new normal" that has the capacity to take disciples of the Christian faith outside their comfort zone. There are analogies elsewhere which can help reinforce that point. Writing on the history of the churches in Europe and North America, Luke Bretherton observes that they have always had cultural priority.[57] In Australia, the Anglo-Celtic denominations have played a formative role in the construction of the Australian imaginary and a civil religion for social occasions like state funerals and ANZAC Day observances. Such is the momentum of that past religious institution in a country that Sophie Sunderland is wary of granting legitimacy to the claim that Australia may now be a post-secular society. She argues that Australian spirituality privileges a "secular, white, Judeo-Christian culture" which, in turn, supports

---

Australia.

57. Bretherton, "Inter-faith Relations as Hospitable Politics."

a default nominal Christianity.[58] Bretherton observes that "churches are not struggling to make sense of their new situation, because they have established institutions, educational and representational processes and wide-ranging relational networks."[59] Churches have long become accustomed to being the host. They are less used to being the guest or participating in the transformative blurring of those two seeming opposites.

Border Crossing

In the growing multicultural, multireligious environment, the church is faced with a challenging task. It is also a product of history and culture. Part of its task is to recognize the borders that exist within that prevent it from welcoming the other, the stranger, and to create welcoming spaces to which the stranger can be welcomed. Religious diversity is an additional dimension that presents both challenge and opportunity for churches. The dilemma is that Christianity has had a long exclusivist history of the religious other. It has often viewed the religious other in terms of being heathen, pagan, and requiring evangelization and conversion. It has operated with a salvific purpose where the finality of Christ tolerates no rival. The theological task is in part, as Francis Nichols argues,

> to examine the historical roots of the problem Christianity has had with the stranger. Christianity must come to terms with its past if it is to have the resources to face its future. It must recall the times it has closed itself to the stranger and the times it has opened up. The church must try to understand what enabled it to grow in dialogue with the other, and how its hostility to strangers has stifled its own life.[60]

Although borders are manifestations of power and exclusion, they can also be subverted and used as a convenient strategy for identifying and subverting power. Borders expose dominant realities and provide a "vantage point from which to examine and critique" dominant narratives.[61] Joerg Rieger asserts that "without border thinking and a self critical stance, we have no choice but to perpetuate the status quo."[62] Border crossing requires thinking (analysis) and movement which I identify as awareness that comes

58. Sunderland, "Post-secular Nation."
59. Bretherton, "Inter-faith Relations as Hospitable Politics."
60. Nichols, "Christianity and the Stranger," 7.
61. Premnath, "Introduction," 2.
62. Rieger, *Across Borders*, 302.

from self-critique. This awareness leads to border crossing in the form of welcome and hospitality to the other.

Borders seemingly denote an end and at the same time also signal a space or horizon of new possibilities. Yves Cattin makes the point that the border or frontier is both a limit as well as a crossing point.[63] Cattin maintains that the frontier and the bridge are markers of the human condition. It is part of the human condition "to set up limits, to build walls, to establish frontiers." These frontiers or limits are needed to establish identity and "cultivate a humanity." But Cattin adds that these limits, these frontiers that we build, should always open to an "elsewhere" to which we can go, and which can come to us.[64] This frontier or limit should serve also as a bridge to offer hospitality and to welcome otherness. It is when the frontier becomes fixed, impermeable, and tightly defined that they become barriers.

In developing his concept of the border, Justo Gonzalez makes a distinction between the border and the frontier. For Cattin the frontier serves the same purpose as Gonzalez's border, but it must be understood as both a limit and a crossing point. According to Gonzalez, both the frontier and the border are growing edges. The distinction between them is that at the frontier growth or encounter takes place by conquest, by pushing the adversary back. On the border, growth takes place by encounter and mutual enrichment. Gonzalez contends that traditionally the history of Christian mission has been read in terms of frontier rather than border. He asserts that "a true border, a true place of encounter, is by nature permeable."[65] Understood in this way the border can be a place where meaning and identity can be negotiated and created.[66] The border becomes a space of new articulations and transformations.

Border thinking according to Walter Mignolo is a conceptualization of the experience of living in the border conscious of the multiple ways coloniality intersects within a matrix of domination.[67] Mignolo's work is rooted in the border and in the subaltern. Although Mignolo's interest is not in crossing borders but inhabiting and dwelling in the border, his

---

63. Cattin, "Human Beings Cross Frontiers," 11.

64. Cattin, "Human Beings Cross Frontiers," 8.

65. Gonzalez, *Santa biblica*, 80.

66. See Tanner, *Theories of Culture* 133–75. The border or the boundary is a space where meaning and identity can be negotiated. With regard to Christian identity, Tanner argues that this is "constituted most fundamentally by a community of argument concerning the meaning of true discipleship" and "the shared sense of the importance of working it out." This sense of "working it out" relies on the fluidity of the borders or boundaries that form one's sense of identity.

67. Mignolo, *Local Histories/Global Designs*.

insights provide an important framing for border crossing. Border thinking enables us to do the necessary analysis (thinking) of how coloniality, empire, imperialism, or privilege manifest and affect our lives as well as the ways we may be complicit (knowingly or unknowingly) in perpetuating the oppression of others. As Rieger points out, using the example of the concept of multiculturalism on offer in the diversity of menus in mall food halls—those who consume these foods are rarely aware of the relations or history between the West and these countries, the stories of the people who live there and the reasons for their migration.[68]

Border thinking begins the process of border crossing. Border thinking is a process of awakening and conscientization of the different kinds of borders that exist and our place or position within them. Border thinking leads us to border crossing with integrity and authenticity aware of the different ways oppressions intersect and our place and complicity within it. Border thinking embodies theory and practice that challenge us to think from, in and beyond the borders.

Border crossing as a methodology, strategy and metaphor has become a very useful and effective strategy for crosscultural hermeneutics and theology. It has become especially useful for those in diaspora who have had to negotiate multiple identities and live within a number of contexts or communities. D.N. Premnath, drawing on the work of Henry Giroux, argues for a pedagogy of border crossing: the "basic premise of border pedagogy is that the process of learning entails crossing borders."[69] He explains border pedagogy as a process that

> enables learners to identify and engage these borders. By negotiating these multiple borders, learners, in effect, are generating multiple references of meaning, knowledge, social relations, and values. As learners cross borders, alternative forms of knowledge emerge and the dominant definitions of reality come under closer scrutiny. Border pedagogy results in reshaping and reconfiguring boundaries.[70]

Border crossing, Thomas Thangaraj suggests, is a way of translating theology into theological practice. Reflecting and drawing from his own theological journey, Thangaraj argues that when we cross boundaries, whether cultural, linguistic, religious, or musical, we are engaged in theological practice.[71] Border crossing opens up new horizons and ways of

68. Rieger, *Across Borders*, 265.
69. Premnath, "Introduction," 6.
70. Premnath, "Introduction," 6.
71. Thangaraj, "Let God Be God."

seeing and being. As Ahmed reminds us: "it is the questioning of boundaries, and the movement across borders, that leads to an expansion of vision and an ability to see more."[72] The "act of border crossing opens up new locations for conversation and new alliances."[73]

As the church of Christ, we are called to bear witness in this here and now, we are encouraged to overcome the limitations and often paralysis of our own borders that keep us stranded, and to move toward the limit, the border, to encounter the other for Christ's sake. This will require crossing and recrossing theological borders that exclude the cultural and religious other and making the necessary ontological shifts.

Works Cited

Ahmed, Sara. *Strange Encounters: Embodied Others in Post-Coloniality*. Transformations. London: Routledge, 2000.

Anderson, Benedict. *Imagined Communities: Reflections on the Origin and Spread of Nationalism*. Rev. ed. London: Verso, 1983.

Anzaldúa, Gloria. *Borderlands, La Frontera: The New Mestiza*. 2nd rev. ed. San Francisco: Aunt Lute, 1999.

Arthur, J. M. *The Default Country: A Lexical Cartography of Twentieth Century Australia*. Sydney: UNSW Press, 2003.

Australian Bureau of Statistics. "Cultural Diversity: Who We Are Now." (2016). https://www.abs.gov.au/ausstats/abs@.nsf/Latestproducts/2024.0Main%20Features22016?opendocument&tabname=Summary&prodno=2024.0&issue=2016&num=&view.

Bouma, Gary. *Australian Soul: Religion and Spirituality in the Twenty-First Century*. Cambridge: Cambridge University Press, 2006.

———. *Being Faithful in Diversity*. Adelaide: ATF Press, 2011.

———, ed.. *Many Religions, All Australian: Religious Settlement, Identity and Cultural Diversity*. Adelaide: Open Book, 1996.

Bouma, Gary, Desmond Cahill, Hass Dellal, and Athalia Zwartz, eds. *Freedom of Religion and Belief in 21st Century Australia*. Canberra: Australian Human Rights Commission, 2011.

Bouma, Gary, and Rod Ling. "Religious Resurgence and Diversity and Social Cohesion in Australia." In *Social Cohesion in Australia*, edited by James Jupp and John Nieuwenhuysen, 80–89. Melbourne: Cambridge University Press, 2007.

Bretherton, Luke. "Inter-Faith Relations as Hospitable Politics." (2010). http://www.abc.net.au/religion/articles/2010/12/08/3087748.htm (accessed 23 April 2011).

---

72. Ahmed, *Strange Encounters*, 85.
73. Premnath, "Introduction," 1.

Breward, Ian. *A History of the Australian Churches*. St Leonards, NSW: Allen & Unwin 1993.

Burke, Anthony. *In Fear of Security: Australia's Invasion Anxiety*. Melbourne: Pluto, 2001.

Burnley, Ian. "Sydney's Changing Peoples: Local Expressions of Diversity and Difference." In *Talking About Sydney: Population, Community and Culture in Contemporary Sydney*, edited by Robert freestone, Bill Randolph, and Caroline Butler-Bowdon, 37–49. Sydney: University of New South Wales Press, 2006.

Cahill, Desmond, Gary Bouma, Hass Dellal, and Michael Leahy, eds. *Religion, Cultural Diversity and Safeguarding Australia*. Canberra: Commonwealth of Australia, 2004.

Cattin, Yves. "Human Beings Cross Frontiers." *Concilium* 2 (1999) 3–17.

Chattopadhyay, Sutapa. "Borders Re/Make Bodies and Bodies Are Made to Make Borders: Storying Migrant Trajectories." *ACME: An International Journal for Critical Geographies* 18.1 (2019) 149–72. https://acme-journal.org/index.php/acme/article/view/1428/1325.

Clark, Manning. *A History of Australia*. Vol. 1. 6 vols. Melbourne: University of Melbourne, 1963.

DeWind, Josh. "Foreword." In *Intersections of Religion and Migration: Issues at the Global Crossroads*, edited by Jennifer B. Saunders, Elena Fiddian-Qasmiyeh and Susanna Snyder, vii–x. New York: Palgrave Macmillan, 2016.

Dixson, Miriam. *The Imaginary Australian: Anglo-Celts and Identity—1788 to the Present*. Sydney: University of New South Wales Press, 1999.

Duggan, Laurie. *Ghost Nation: Imagined Space and Australian Visual Culture*. St Lucia: University of Queensland Press, 2001.

Dutton, David. *One of Us? A Century of Australian Citizenship*. Australia: University of New South Wales, 2002.

Ezzy, Douglas, Garry Bouma, Greg Barton, Anna Halafoff, Rebecca Banham, Robert Jackson, and Lori Beaman. "Religious Diversity in Australia: Rethinking Social Cohesion." *Religions* 11.92 (18 February 2020). https://doi.org/10.3390/rel11020092.

Fitzmaurice, Andrew. "On Nobody's Land: Understanding Terra Nullius." In *Yours, Mine, Ours: Unravelling the Doctrine of Discovery*, edited by Cheryl Woelk and Steve Heinrichs, 35–37. Canada: Mennonite Church Canada, 2016.

Forrest, James, and Kevin Dunn. "'Core' Culture Hegemony and Multiculturalism." *Ethnicities* 6.2 (2006) 203–30. https://doi.org/DOI:10.1177/1468796806063753. http://etn.sagepub.com.

Fozdar, Farida. "Social Cohesion and Skilled Muslim Refugees in Australia: Employment, Social Capital and Discrimination." *Journal of Sociology* 48.2 (2011) 167–86. https://doi.org/10.1177/1440783311413482; http://jos.sagepub.com/content/48/2/167.

Frederiks, Martha. "Religion, Migration, and Identity: A Conceptual and Theoretical Exploration." In *Religion, Migration and Identity: Methodological and Theological Explorations*, edited by Martha Frederiks and Dorottya Nagy, 9–30. Theology and Mission in World Christianity 2. Leiden: Brill, 2016.

Gonzalez, Justo L. *Santa Biblica: The Bible through Hispanic Eyes*. Nashville: Abingdon, 1990.

Hage, Ghassan. *Against Paranoid Nationalism: Searching for Hope in a Shrinking Society*. Annandale, NSW: Pluto, 2003.

———. *White Nation: Fantasies of White Supremacy in a Multicultural Society.* Annandale, NSW: Pluto, 1998.
Healey, Kaye, ed. *Religions in Australia: Issues for the Nineties.* Balmain, NSW: Spinney, 1998.
Hughes, Philip. "Social Capital and Religion in Contemporary Australia." In *Spirit of Australia Ii,* edited by Brian Howe and Philip Hughes, 131–44. Adelaide: ATF, 2003.
Hugo, Graeme. "Australian Demographic Change and Its Implications for Sydney." In *Talking About Sydney: Population, Community and Culture in Contemporary Sydney,* edited by Robert Freeston, Bill Randolph and Caroline Butler-Bowdon, 3–24. Sydney: University of New South Wales Press, 1993.
Jupp, James. *From White Australia to Woomera: The Story of Australian Immigration.* Cambridge: Cambridge University Press, 2002.
———. "Preface: A New Era in Australian Multiculturalism." *Journal of Intercultural Studies* 32.6 (2011) 577–78. https://doi.org/10.1080/07256868.2011.618103.
Kwok, Pui-Lan. "A Theology of Border Passage." In *Border Crossings: Cross-Cultural Hermeneutics,* edited by D. N Premnath, 103–17. Maryknoll, NY: Orbis, 2007.
Lopez, Mark. *The Origins of Multiculturalism in Australian Politics, 1945–1972.* Melbourne: Melbourne University Press 2000.
Markus, Andrew. "Of Continuities and Discontinuities: Reflections on a Century of Australian Immigration Control." In *Legacies of White Australia: Race, Culture and Nation,* edited by Laksiri Jayasuriya, David Walker and Jan Gothard, 175–89. Contemporary Issues. Crawley, WA: University of Western Australia Press, 2003.
McCallum, John. "Religion and Social Cohesion." In *The Australian People: An Encyclopedia of the Nation, Its People and Their Origins,* edited by James Jupp, 938–42. North Ryde, NSW: Angus & Robertson, 1988.
Mignolo, Walter. *Local Histories/Global Designs: Coloniality, Subaltern Knowledges, and Border Thinking.* Princeton Studies in Culture/Power/History. Princeton: Princeton University Press, 2000.
Nichols, Francis. "Christianity and the Stranger." In *Christianity and the Stranger: Historical Essays,* edited by Francis Nichols, 1–15. South Florida-Rochester-Saint Louis Studies on Religion and the Social Order 12. Atlanta: Scholars, 1995.
Premnath, D. N. "Introduction." In *Border Crossings: Cross-Cultural Hermeneutics,* edited by D. N. Premnath, 1–12. Maryknoll, NY: Orbis, 2007.
Rieger, Joerg. *Across Borders: Latin Perspectives in the Americas Reshaping Religion, Theology and Life.* Kindle ed. Lanham, MD: Lexington, 2013.
Sunderland, Sophie. "Post-Secular Nation: Or How "Australian Spirituality" Privileges a Secular, White, Judaeo-Chriatian Culture." *Transforming Cultures eJournal* 2.1 (Novermber 2007) 57–77. http://epress.lib.uts.edu.au/journals/index.php/TfC/article/view/596/543.
Tavan, Gwenda. *The Long Slow Death of White Australia.* Melbourne: Scribe, 2005.
Thangaraj, M. Thomas. "Let God Be God: Crossing Boundaries as a Theological Practice." In *Border Crossings: Cross Cultural Hermeneutics,* edited by D. N. Premnath, 89–102. Maryknoll, NY: Orbis, 2007.
"Upstander Project." https://upstanderproject.org/firstlight/doctrine.
Zhou, Naaman. "Australians Accepting of Migrants but Negative Towards Islam, Poll Finds." *The Guardian* (2019). https://www.theguardian.com/world/2019/may/04/australians-accepting-of-migrants-but-negative-towards-islam-poll-finds.

7

Hosting the Invader

*Re-reading Rahab's Hospitality (Joshua 2) with
Ten Years (a 2015 Hong Kong based film)*

LIM CHIN MING STEPHEN

Introduction

THE WORLD IS WITNESSING the rise of nativism, even in the West which was believed to have moved into a cosmopolitan phase of development that embraces multiculturalism. It is not helped by an influenza pandemic that has forced countries into a semi-isolationist mode, catalyzing the fomenting of anger among the locals against foreigners which invokes again the specter of stranger danger. This is by no means a new phenomenon—Jacques Derrida, to whom I appeal in this essay, started writing about the need to address such nativist tendencies in the early 2000s.

In this essay, I choose to read against the grain of perceptible moves against nativism within scholarly discussions largely sparked by right wing populism in many quarters of the West. To do so, I explore the hospitality of a fairly marginal figure in the Bible called Rahab in conversation with the *mainlandisation* of Hong Kong over the last two decades. My interest here is not so much to give a fine analysis of nativism and its discontents but rather to see how the seeming contradiction between hospitality and nativism could help me read differently the story of Rahab who plays host(ess) to two spies from a people with every intent of conquering her homeland.

Hong Kong: In Between East and West

According to Iam-chong Ip, Hong Kong has long been a city which receives immigrants not only from mainland China but also Taiwan, Southeast Asia and as far as Pakistan and India.[1] A discernible local identity could be traced to the 1970s during the tumultuous period of decolonisation across the world. By the time Hong Kong had to be handed over to mainland China, the moves by the British colonial authority in the previous two decades—ranging from political reform that facilitated some form of quasi-democracy to restructuring civil service in order to admit non-white people into senior positions to the massive strides of development in local cultural industries among many other things—provided a fertile environment for a nativist identity to emerge. Coupled with Chairman Mao's political transformation of China, which was closely followed by Premier Deng's open-door policies, many Hong Kongers no longer find China a familiar, or even desirable origin to return to.

Today, Hong Kong faces the reality of what is increasingly recognized as progressive *mainlandisation* of its political, cultural, and social landscapes. While some see it as inevitable especially the older generations, we have found in the recent past that the younger generations are more than aware of its effects. Triggered by an extradition bill (in 2019) that now lies in the dustbin of history, hopefully never recovered, thousands upon thousands, waves upon waves of Hong Kongers took to the streets in protest of what has already congealed into the status quo. At the point of writing, the protests have been largely laid to rest because of a combination of factors ranging from increased police enforcement, the Covid pandemic, and the national security law passed on 30 June 2020 that is yet another important chapter in the mainlandisation of Hong Kong.

Taking into consideration that Hong Kong is a relatively powerless vassal before the great imperium of mainland China, I read the story of Rahab as one who is arguably in a similar situation. She is also trapped between her city, her people, her culture, and what she recognizes as a strong conquering army of the Israelites led by YHWH himself. On the surface, her act of hospitality facilitates the invasion of Canaan and is placed strategically in the book of Joshua to welcome the Israelite conquest. Therefore,

---

1. Ip, "Political De-institutionalization," 462–63.

the key question I ask is how we could read this story in between the topoi of hospitality and nativism.

The approach I adopt is contextual hermeneutics as multicentric dialogue,[2] and here I engage three loci of enunciation. As highlighted earlier, Hong Kong lies at the intersection of its western and Chinese discursive influences with a fairly distinct local culture. In this light, the first locus is drawn from the West through the (re)situating of Rahab as an extension of what Jacques Derrida argues as an aporia between conditional and unconditional hospitality. The second locus is a regional perspective in East Asia where I explore a Daoist understanding of hospitality through the legend of *hundun* that upholds hospitality as an act that is not self-conscious of its own virtue. The third locus is from Hong Kong itself, where I engage with perspectives drawn from a 2015 film co-directed by Kwok Zune, Wong Fei-pang, Jevons Au, Chow Kwun-Wai and Ng Ka-leung, entitled *Ten Years* that reflects on the possible futures of Hong Kong after British handover in 1997. Here I explore the possible costs of Rahab's hospitality in the light of this evolving situation in Hong Kong where a weaker vassal is compelled to play host to a stronger Empire. In bringing these three interlocuters together, I seek an(-)Other way to read this troubled instance of Rahab welcoming the enemy into her very own home so as to recover an ethic of hospitality in relation to nativism that takes context into serious consideration, which would (re/)inform praxis and possibly generate resistance.

Hospitality and Nativism: Never the Twain Shall Meet?

Nativism in Hong Kong

In one of the most recent analysis, John Lowe and Stephen Ortmann (2020) characterize nativism in Hong Kong through Han-Georg Betz's (2019) facets of nativism: economic nativism, welfare chauvinism and symbolic nativism. They pick up on one common discourse that caricatures mainland Chinese as "locusts" to illustrate the feature of economic nativism which is how migrant labor not only suppresses wages and competes with the locals for jobs, but also how local resources have to be channeled to these people. Based on a popular campaign against pregnant Chinese mothers coming into Hong Kong to take advantage of the cheaper and more efficient healthcare system, they show how the locals are afraid that their social benefits

---

2. Lim, *Contextual Hermeneutics as Multicentric Dialogue*.

funded by their own taxes are now being channeled to these immigrants which could be dubbed as welfare chauvinism.[3]

Of most relevance to this essay is the third form called symbolic nativism. Betz defines it as "centred on the defence of the fundamental traditions, values and historically evolved institutional arrangements that define a particular community, its culture and identity."[4] In Lowe and Ortmann's analysis of graffiti that have sprouted up for the 5 years since the Umbrella movement in 2015, they argue that the rift between Hong Kong Chinese and mainland Chinese have become increasingly palpable. The former sees itself as progressive but thinks of the latter as symbol of a colonial past that it wants to forget. It would seem to fall in line with Betz's own assertion that central to symbolic nativism "is the notion that certain cultures are incompatible with each other."[5]

If we were to take Lowe and Ortmann's analysis at face value, it is highly suggestive in surfacing the issues of discrimination against foreigners driven by not only a selfish sense of self-preservation, but also a kind of mindset of superiority that denigrates the Other in colonial-like fashion. Perhaps the issue here is the application of right-wing populism in the West, borrowing Walter Mignolo (2000), used as a "global design" that emanates from a "local history" which I discuss further in the conclusion. However, before going any deeper into this, there is need to address from the standpoint of the foreigners/guests, the polar response to nativism: hospitality.

Hospitality as a Corrective for Nativism

While Derrida wrote at a time where right-wing populism of the West has not gained as much salience as it had in the 2010s, it is difficult to miss that the key target for his conceptions of hospitality is the stranger in their midst. In negotiating the difficult bind that positions the local and the foreigner as almost mutually exclusive entities, he posits what he sees as the aporia between unconditional and conditional hospitality that is largely derived from the Hebrew Bible, Stoicism and Pauline Christianity.[6]

Unconditional hospitality, which I think of as "ideal," in Derrida's conception is an im-possible standard that is summed up by David Shepherd as, "*performance* constituted of risk-taking and vulnerability; a radical *gift* of excess, a moment of *divine* madness, an ethical performance which is

---

3. Lowe and Ortmann, "Unmasking Nativism in Asia's World City," 404.
4. Betz, "Facets of Nativism," 123.
5. Betz, "Facets of Nativism," 126.
6. La Caze, "Not Just Visitors," 316.

always pushing the boundaries, seeking to break through the encirclements and conditions placed upon it."[7]

In this light, unconditional hospitality receives the Other without reservation, or having even "enjoin[ed] him to state and to guarantee his identity, as you would a witness before a court."[8] In fact, absolute hospitality does not ask the guests for "either reciprocity (entering into a pact) or even their names."[9] The result as Marguerite La Caze mentions, even though Derrida thinks of the status of the foreigner differently, be it visitor, immigrant or refugee, is ultimately based on these "terms" of unconditionality.[10] Such hospitality is extended without discrimination. Conditional hospitality on the other hand is entangled with the laws of the land, especially in terms of citizenship and rights. It is highly discerning, evaluating the foreigner on various grounds especially economic and political. Its language is of control and mastery.

That being said, Derrida recognizes the im-possibility of unconditional hospitality because it is still reliant on conditional hospitality. As La Caze argues, unconditional hospitality is not so much an "ideal" but a means for the laws of hospitality to "be transformed and improved" and also to "temper [the latter's] irresponsibility."[11] While La Caze recognizes that the visitor "can always become an invader or colonist,"[12] there is little discussion as to what that means and its implications on current conceptions of hospitality. It seems to me that by couching unconditional hospitality as the check and balance for conditional hospitality, the former *is* being upheld as an ethical *ideal*, albeit impossible to achieve in this present reality. In other words, it is not demonstrated how conditional hospitality is able to interrogate the underlying premise of unconditional hospitality, other than being the inevitable conduit that the latter has to (begrudgingly?) use. It might be better said that it is the very im-possibility of unconditional hospitality that makes it an *ideal*.

Nonetheless, Derrida argues that there is an inevitable aporia between laws of hospitality and the Law of hospitality. The laws of hospitality are the concrete realities of legislating between guests, as either friend or foe, refugee or resident, temporary or permanent; and the Law of

---

7. Shepherd, *The Gift of the Other*, 80 (emphasis original); see also Caputo, *Deconstruction in a Nutshell*, 111.

8. Derrida, *Of Hospitality*, 27.

9. Derrida, *Of Hospitality*, 27.

10. La Caze, "Not Just Visitors," 319.

11. La Caze, "Not Just Visitors," 317.

12. La Caze, "Not Just Visitors," 317.

hospitality is as it were, the brains and more importantly, the heart. In this regard, both the Law and laws of hospitality are "contradictory, antinomic, *and* inseparable."[13]

In relation to nativism, it would seem the Law of hospitality is superior in terms of its ethical response. Yet I wish to interrogate this difficult relationship between Law, laws and nativism by reading Rahab through the above western locus of enunciation. So, I begin with those who side more easily with the Law of hospitality before looking at what I see as nativist responses.

Rahab as a Model of Hospitality

Much of western discourse up until the 2000s tend to see Rahab as a model of faith.[14] Space does not allow a more thorough interrogation of this idea but rather keeping to the question at hand, I re-direct some of their findings through the Derridean lens of hospitality.

If one accepts Derrida's reading of Lot as an exemplar of hospitality (which I discuss later), then by L. Daniel Hawk's estimate, Rahab would be by far a better Lot. According to him, there are remarkable parallels between both stories, particularly the house as the central point of both narratives (Gen 19:4–11; Josh 2:2–7); similar modes of crisis resolution by sending the aggressors away and the imminent destruction of both cities.[15] Tikva Frymer-Kensky adds how the men enter into a city that is about to be destroyed; both hosts disobey the command to "bring out the men" (Gen 19:5; Josh 2:3); and both guests are referred to as *mal'akim* (Gen 19:1; Josh 6:25).[16]

The similarities lay the ground to contrast the crucial differences. Lot's response is "feeble and fearful" (cf. Gen 19:18) while Rahab "offers a more confident response" (cf. Josh 2:4b–5a).[17] This is clear from how each handled the crisis at hand. Rahab negotiates the questioning better with deceit and succeeds, in contrast to Lot's futile attempt in offering his daughters that ultimately enrages the crowds. Rahab successfully redirects the pursuers, but Lot is stranded with men groping at his door (Josh 2:7; Gen 19:11). Furthermore, Lot is less successful in rallying his family to leave the city, but

13. Derrida, *Of Hospitality*, 81 (emphasis original).

14. One common theme revolves around the discussion of salvation in relation to the ban (*herem*). See Dozeman, *Joshua 1–12*, 54–59, 223–224.

15. Hawk, "Strange Houseguests," 89–90.

16. Frymer-Kensky, "Reading Rahab," 61.

17. Hawk, "Strange Houseguests," 91.

Rahab is able to seize the right opportunity to secure the salvation of her family (cf. Gen 19:14; Josh 2:9b–11).[18]

While appreciating the irony of handing one's daughters over to be raped in order to protect one's guests, Derrida's reading of Lot acknowledges "the moment when Lot seems to put the laws of hospitality above all, in particular the ethical obligations that link him to his relatives and family, first of all his daughters."[19] The textual witness seems to be positive about Lot's actions especially since he is willing to be hospitable "*at any price*" (Derrida's emphasis) as Derrida highlights that this echoes an earlier hospitality extended by Abraham to three messengers.[20]

It is possible to read Rahab in a similar light. By what Phyllis Bird describes as "her display of loyalty, courage and altruism," Rahab goes beyond what ancient audiences would have expected of her as a prostitute to be that "courtesan who sacrifices [her life] for her patron."[21] It is crucial to point out that she is a woman without a man's support and as Bird argues,[22] prostitution is one of the most despised and possibly vulnerable professions of her time.

If one were to reconsider Rahab's speech, it is possible to conclude that she is well aware that these spies in her home are the "undesirable foreigner . . . an enemy" who "encroaches on [her] 'at home', on [her] ipseity, on [her] power of hospitality, on [her] sovereignty as host."[23] Yet instead of resorting to "filtering, choosing . . . excluding and doing violence"[24] to these invaders, she chooses to defy the law of the land—which in this case is the king, who demands that these spies be found. In other words, she is willing to forego her ipseity and by Derrida's logic, her right to conditional hospitality. This is notwithstanding that she later negotiates for her own survival but to be fair, Rahab saves the spies *before* establishing any agreement with them.

It is worth mentioning that neither party gets the other's name. As I raised earlier, Derrida points out that unconditional hospitality does not ask of the guests "either reciprocity (entering into a pact) or even their names."[25] I explore the issue of reciprocity later but on the consideration of

18. Hawk, "Strange Houseguests," 92.

19. "The patriarch does not protect his women in the stories to which Derrida draws our attention—he abandons her to sexual predation to save himself or his male guest" (Still, *Derrida and Hospitality*, 72).

20. Derrida, *Of Hospitality*, 151.

21. Bird, "The Harlot as Heroine," 131.

22. Bird, "The Harlot as Heroine," 127–29.

23. Derrida, *Of Hospitality*, 54–55.

24. Derrida, *Of Hospitality*, 55.

25. Derrida, *Of Hospitality*, 25.

the name, I find that Rahab does indeed help without knowing their names, or at least the author(s) did not find it fit to include them. Therefore, all things considered, her act of hospitality is a moment of insanity for her to give such an excessive gift of protection over whom would be considered as wanted criminals in her own country.

In sum, Rahab fulfils some of the key criteria of unconditional hospitality as Derrida would have it—taking high risks to herself for her guests. This is while going the extra mile that despite indirectly knowing their identities, she is willing to submit even more to their power, rather than seeking to control or undermine it. While her act of hospitality is indeed laudable, there are some quarters of biblical scholarship that find her act of hospitality problematic.

Rahab as a Symbol for Conquering Guests

In this section, I call into question again the cost of Rahab's hospitality. At a banal level, the interlocuters in this section could come across as nativist reactions especially when the starting point is viewing the guests as not merely temporary tourists, but rather the "invader or colonist."

What is perhaps reprehensible is how Rahab does not seem to have *any* nativist reactions. Against the tendency of seeing Rahab as a heroine, commentators like Marcella Althaus-Reid would see her act as a "betrayal of her friends and compatriots, her culture and her traditional spirituality."[26] As to whether there is a nativist reaction, I take it up later from the Hong Kong locus of enunciation. Suffice to say here, Rahab does not appear to demonstrate the kinds of nativism that Betz has raised.

It seems to me that if there were any nativism present, it would be on the side of the guests. The narrative has chosen to use Rahab as the representation of Canaan. Like Rahab, Canaan would be quick to change its allegiance to the more powerful empire[27] which betrays how the land is easily available like a prostitute[28] and therefore, could be easily bought over.[29] To be fair, what appears to be symbolic nativism requires one additional enabler to become concrete. That would be the Israelites conquering the land in their name. In other words, if we were to think of natives as rightful inhabitants of the land, the Israelites are displacing Rahab through this narrative to be the (only?) legitimate owners (as ordained by YHWH).

26. Althaus-Reid, "Searching for a Queer Sophia-Wisdom," 137.
27. Crowell, "Good Girl, Bad Girl," 14.
28. Davidson, "Gazing (at) Native Women," 87.
29. McKinlay, "Rahab," 53.

An important note must be made here with respect to hospitality. Much as one would romanticize the host-guest relationship as *hesed* for *hesed*,[30] it is undeniable that reciprocity lies at the heart of her hospitality. Likely caught between the rock of Canaanite rule that has somehow relegated her to the boundaries as a prostitute and the hard place of an imminent invasion by marauding Israelites, Ira Mangillo (2015) argues through her experience as a multiply colonized woman in Indonesia that Rahab uses her postcolonial trickster imagination to secure for herself a better place. Nonetheless, even if indeed one were to view this as an ideal and even superior form of hospitality as compared to Lot as Hawk would have it, then the use of deceit in favor of the host seems to detract from Derrida's claim to unconditional hospitality.

As a possible way to rehabilitate this text, Erin Runions proposes that Joshua 2 comprises of two sources—an earlier, more indigenous folktale that is humorous in nature and a later Deuteronomistic redaction to include Rahab's conversion (Josh 2:9–11) and a more elaborate bargaining for her life (Josh 2:15–21).[31] In doing so, she separates the text what seems to me to be along Derridean lines of unconditional and conditional hospitality—the former as the earlier form of the text that devotes more narratival space to her selfless act of hospitality and the latter includes the Deuteronomistic insertion which incidentally focuses on aspects of the law. It is here that I deviate from Runions who argues that such a division places Rahab in the positive light but the spies in a negative light, "in anti-colonial fashion."[32] The seeming contradiction exemplifies more what Derrida often refers to as the aporia within hospitality where the folkloric part demonstrates the Law of hospitality and the Deuteronomistic redaction, the laws of hospitality.

So, we have within the western locus of enunciation at least three discernible positions. The first, by virtue of its emphasis on Rahab gaining salvation, would warm to the idea that hospitality needs to be unreserved and be likely more than willing to side with the Law of hospitality as ideal. The second problematizes this relationship of salvation and hospitality by highlighting the need for a nativist response especially in the light of the problematic portrayal of Canaan. The third is what I propose as a better rendering of the different divisions in the text as what Derrida sees as an aporia. Furthermore, I see that hospitality and nativism are often treated (subconsciously) as mostly mutually exclusive on the one hand. On the other hand, I would like to raise that it is not entirely clear what makes the

---

30. See for instance, Biddle and Jackson, "Rahab and Her Visitors."
31. Runions, "From Disgust to Humor," 58–59.
32. Runions, "From Disgust to Humor," 65.

Hundun and the Virtue of Hospitality

The second locus of enunciation is derived from the legend of *hundun* (混沌) at the conclusion of the seven inner chapters of an important Chinese philosophical work, Zhuangzi (莊子; 399—295 BCE) which is named after the author. It is a story that involves the protagonist playing host to two kings—King *Shu* of the South Sea and King *Hu* of the North Sea. Both kings are overwhelmed by the hospitality (*shan* 善) of *hundun* and decide to repay his kindness (*de* 德) by carving seven holes in him to make him look like the rest of humankind. *hundun* dies after the seventh hole is carved into him.

陈赟 points out that Zhuangzi writes this at the end of the era of kings (帝王时代). His main concern is the return to *de* (德) as an unconscious practice of virtue in opposition to *li* (礼) which is the way of the kings.[33] *hundun* then exemplifies a period where the person is governed by both inner virtues and external conventions (*neishengwaiwang* 内圣外王).[34] Meiyao Wu points out that Zhuangzi laments the passing of a time when people were internally motivated to virtue rather than requiring the external guidance of the king. The ultimate of virtue is practiced when the practitioner is completely unconscious of it.[35]

Therefore, being completely amorphous with no discernible human features, *hundun* exemplifies this important ethic by possessing "no subjectivity, no self, [and] thus no self/other difference and no bias regarding the goodness of others."[36] This is the true face of Dao embodied in *de* which has been rendered non-ideal or in Derridean terms, conditional, into different forms of *li*. What is perhaps even more coincidental as 陈 points out, reciprocity is a key foundation of relationships in Zhuangzi's time.[37] What his parable is pointing towards is the need to return to *de* from *li* which is founded on exchange, or moving beyond reciprocity to achieve the true virtue of hospitality.

---

33. 陈, ""浑沌之死"与"轴心时代"中国思想的基本问题," 136–37.
34. 陈, ""浑沌之死"与"轴心时代"中国思想的基本问题," 137.
35. Wu, "Hundun's Hospitality," 1437–38.
36. Wu, "Hundun's Hospitality," 1438; See also 杨 and 朱, "《庄子》 的"浑沌"解," 44.
37. 陈, ""浑沌之死"与"轴心时代"中国思想的基本问题," 137.

If we follow Runion's division of the tale, then it is possible to argue that up until verse 11, the risk that Rahab takes is almost analogous to *hundun* as she gives hospitality at the expense of her life—she could be killed either by the King of Jericho or by the invading Israelite army. Reading the lengths *hundun* is willing to go for his guests, this pushes me to see that Rahab is also willing to sacrifice her people and her land as her guests are after all, spies with a specific mission of scouting the land in preparation for conquest. However, when we move into the second half of the tale, it would seem that Rahab in entering into a trade with the spies for her life does not move beyond *li* because it still remains as reciprocity rather than an unconditional act. There is clearly no emptying of self even though her initial actions of protecting the spies might indicate as much.

Beyond the parallel between *de* and *li* with Law and laws of hospitality, what this legend shows is that turning one's host into one's image is not an act of any guest. Something that is relatively easy to overlook from the western lens is that not all guests are powerless, but some are like these kings with power. This enlivens the reality that Israel in the narrative is portrayed as a coming conqueror that has "utterly destroyed" the "two kings of the Amorites that were beyond the Jordan [and] Sihon and Og" (Josh 2:10). This is so much so that "[their] hearts melted, and there was no courage left in any of [them]" (Josh 2:11). The other important aspect that is elided, is that remaking another into one's image entails death. While the narrative in Joshua is leading us to believe that Rahab has lived because of her generous hospitality, reading with Zhuangzi leads me to wonder what had died.

So, how would this reversal of power dynamics trouble our attempts so far in reading Rahab for an ethic of hospitality? How has Rahab died in the process of her hospitality? Is there something more at stake here that is lost for fear of being called out as a nativist? It is here that I turn to the third section where I look at a film *Ten Years* to understand this ambivalent story of Rahab courting her conquerors.

Reading with the Future(s) of Hong Kong

Ten Years (2015) is a speculative fiction film that looks at possible dystopian futures of Hong Kong ten years from the year of its release. The film is heavily censored in mainland China where even the broadcast of its winning of the Best Film Award at the 35th Hong Kong Film Awards was prohibited to be aired. It is an anthology of five films but in the interest of space, I have chosen here to focus on what I consider to be more relevant to the story of Rahab: "Seasons of the End" and "Local Egg."

Being Remembered

The short film "Seasons of the End" touches on the theme of death through hospitality that was explored in the previous section. A couple attempts to seal up memories of Hong Kong through a process of taxidermy which is originally meant for animals. This segment opens with the couple sifting through the rubble of a recently demolished house which belonged to a close friend, Eddie and applying the principles of taxidermy to preserve what they view as important items. They struggle with the difficult task of cataloguing and ensuring that there are enough specimen boxes to contain what they have found. A sense of futility sets in as they wonder from the standpoint of taxidermy's original dilemma—species of animals are being wiped out faster than they could preserve them. Similarly, they wonder about the histories of Hong Kong. How much could they possibly preserve? Eventually, the male protagonist comes to ponder about his own life and makes the absurd request to his wife to turn him into a specimen while he is still living. The process is laborious as she takes samples of his sweat, hair and fingernails, prepares the chemicals he needs to consume presumably to preserve his inner organs, nurse and watch him go through the agonizing process. It is heart-wrenching, almost visceral to witness the struggle to preserve the memory of oneself. The story ends with the lament of the female protagonist whether despite their best efforts, no one will ever know.

Rahab's hospitality in this regard most certainly gives her a place in the recorded memory of her conquerors. While she preserves herself and her family, there is nothing more about her that is known other than her profession. The concerns about the future as reflected in this film also guides me to think about the afterlives of Rahab after Joshua 2 and 6 and what new insights it might shed on this passage. Within the Hebrew Bible, it is sad that Rahab melts away after Joshua 6.

That being said, as Frymer-Kensky points out, Rahab continues as a prominent figure in Jewish tradition as "one of the great religious proselytes" and in major Midrashic tradition, marries Joshua to be the "ancestress of priests and prophets."[38] She is also included in the genealogical list of Jesus in the gospel of Matthew as the mother of Boaz. While it would seem that Rahab received more honor than what the Hebrew Bible has given her, I still claim that the valorization of Rahab as heroine does not detract from what the "Seasons of the End" invokes—namely, her assimilation comes with almost complete erasure of her Canaanite identity and culture.

---

38. Frymer-Kensky, "Reading Rahab," 67; see also Charles, "Rahab," 208–9.

Another way of seeing this is through the trope of conversion. If we were to look at the afterlife of Rahab found in Hebrews 11 where she is numbered among the faithful Christians,[39] the writer of Hebrews lays claim that these Jewish (and Canaanite) heroes are part of the great cloud of witnesses that proclaim Christ as God. At the risk of oversimplification, one key theme of the letter is to establish Jesus as the rightful heir to God's throne, likely over and against what the Judaizers thought. Just as Rahab was once used as a polemic against her Canaanite people, what is seen as her faithfulness is now used against the Jews. In a similar fashion, Ronald Charles (2011) argues that James, despite his own leanings towards resisting oppression, sanitizes Rahab as a model of faith by violently caging her in Christian theology. So, her act of hospitality is now the faith of yet another—the Christians. If she had indeed cherished any hope of creating a taxidermy of her people, it is mostly lost.

Yet we must not forget that Rahab, however imperfectly it may be, is remembered as a Canaanite. Where records of their culture are few and far between, she has preserved her name. People remember that there was once a Rahab—a native woman of a very much disdained profession who lived in the wall. However hard the redactors and narrators of her story try to assimilate her story, it still continues to provoke, give leverage, afford slippage and grant ambivalence to her act of hospitality. It is so much so that no one can truly define the virtue of her act, much less lay claim to it as his or her own. Thus, following the taxidermic remnants of Rahab, I find that even the sparsest memories have unexpected effects.

Inevitable Erasure or Hospitality as Resistance?

The second story in the film anthology I explore is called "Local Egg." It features Sam who is struggling to keep his stall selling locally grown eggs afloat. He learns from his supplier that the farm is closing because it is deemed to be against the government. In reality, it is making way for other developments as Sam vocalizes that the farm has done nothing but try to obey government policies. His son is part of the Youth Guard who oversees policing local establishments for using "banned words." He finds his shop running afoul with the Youth Guard who accuses him of using the word 本地 which means "local." He tries to reason with the teenager who tells him that he can call his eggs "Hong Kong" but not "local." It is ultimately to no avail as the Youth Guard claims he is only enforcing the rules.

39. Butler, *Joshua*, 35.

The story ends with some hope that the next generation would not blindly accept mainlandisation of Hong Kong. Sam receives a call that the Youth Guard have gathered outside a bookshop to throw eggs and tries to intervene. He finds his son among the Youth Guard gathered outside and confronts him. His son points out to him that he has never thrown any eggs and he has no choice but stand with them. It is at this time the bookstore keeper opens the shutters and tells Sam that his son not only has warned him about the incoming attack, but also has been quietly sneaking the list of banned words to him. Sam and his son are brought to the underground bookshop where many banned books are kept.

Sam's son like Rahab is caught between the powers-that-be. What they appreciate is that survival could also be resistance. Here the battle is fought on the field of memory—keeping not only their own so-called high culture, but also the other cultural products within Hong Kong society, even Doraemon. It is here that Rahab seems to cohere yet deviate from this discourse. On the one hand, her presence, as mentioned earlier, in the text preserves some form of warped memory of Canaan while at the same time destabilizing the rhetoric of the text especially in the light of Deuteronomistic injunctions to cut off any connections to the land. All this could only be made possible if she survives. In some ways, if we consider her part of the wider world of biblical Israel, then recent modern efforts at archaeology could have the unintended consequence of recovering her memory. Without traces like her signaling presence, arguably we would not think of alternative discourses to the one preserved through the auspices of Judaism and Christianity.

The broader point I wish to make is that playing host can be resistance. Put differently, it is *ideal* that the unconditional becomes conditional because accommodating an imperial force comes with great cost to one's self. The very cost, in Levinasian terms, is murder. While we appreciate that Rahab's willingness to negotiate reminds us that survival is part of resistance, we can also say that it is possible she could have gone further. It is very likely that there are too many obstacles in the way especially since her story ends up in her oppressor's text. It is here that films like this in a troubled context like Hong Kong could fill in the gaps, destabilize the rhetoric of hospitality as unconditional and point to a different praxis.

Conclusion? The Conundrum of Hospitality and Nativism

In closing, reading Rahab through the western locus of Derrida, while it undoubtedly raises the aporia between unconditional and conditional hospitality, does not allow much room for sympathy for nativist voices, much less reconceiving nativism as viable resistance. This is reflective of much of biblical scholarship that is interested enough in the question of Rahab's hospitality in the way that they have taken sides with respect to her actions—either she is the better Lot, or she is an opportunistic betrayer typical of her own profession. Those who take the side of hospitality find themselves together with Derrida in condemning nativism, whereas those who find her hospitality questionable would raise nativist concerns of their right to live and perhaps as I have argued here, more sinisterly raise if the guests, that is the Israelites, are more capable of the excesses of nativism. Reading with *hundun* brings to light how not all guests are equally powerless before their hosts, where some even have the power to murder. More pertinently it raises the issue of death in the process of hospitality to which nativism arguably responds.

This leads us to read Rahab with *Ten Years* and highlight the need for survival. By foregrounding the power asymmetry between hosts and guests, it raises the question of why the Law of hospitality is the conscience of the laws of hospitality. The consequence of delinking unconditional from the Law makes room to think more broadly about nativism. Kuan Hsing Chen points out that one of the key gains of nativism is to bring back "people's focus from the imperial centers back to their own living environments."[40] While the tendency is to focus on the excesses of nativism (and there is a place for such critique), he also highlights the need to remember that the underlying motivation in many nativist movements is the desire for self-determination. As highlighted earlier, Rahab represents what the narrative caricatures as the weaker people before a strong invading army. Therefore, the power asymmetry as presumed between host and guests is inverted in favor of the guests. This seems more analogous to the Hong Kong situation which then casts doubt on the analysis of Lowe and Ortmann which utilizes populist responses of the West where it is clear that the white people are in a more superior position vis-à-vis the immigrants.

Enforced hospitality or welcoming the enemy becomes part of a bigger struggle. On the one hand, it problematizes the interruption to the self. The interruption to Rahab's self or more popularly known as "conversion"

---

40. Chen, *Asia as Method*, 81.

would be more than welcomed by New Testament writers and not surprisingly by Derrida himself. Yet in both "Seasons of the End" and "Local Egg," the loss in memory, language and even ways of life are experienced as visceral, as though it is attempting to invoke empathy for nativist struggles. Put differently, hospitality could be seen as resistance that veils different efforts to preserve self in the face of dominant guests. Where biblical scholars have to resort to wearing tinted glasses, the movie helps me to identify gaps in the text and fill it by facilitating the seeding of the imagination in these unspoken (and possibly hitherto unthought of) places. The silence of the text over Rahab's adaptation to a new culture, her own resistance to constant erasure and overwriting by dominant culture, is given as it were, some voice through the modern Rahabs of today.

Should we welcome as it were, the enemy into our homes, especially when we are the weaker Other compelled to accept our more powerful guests? This cannot be answered lightly, without dialogue. I am conscious on a reflexive note that my essay is playing host to a foreigner, an Algerian Jew brought up in France, who to my knowledge, had never travelled to East Asia. Even more conscious I am is the sacred text I read, though technically belonging to Asia despite the problematics of those boundaries, is mainly received on the sails of colonial ships, especially in the reading communities in Hong Kong. In thinking about hospitality, I am compelled to be hospitable to the thoughts and ideas of those foreign to this land. These complexities belie the many difficulties in striking the appropriate balance between hospitality and nativism.

What perhaps is the main difference in approaching this level of hospitality that deviates from Derrida, is that in this instance, the host is disadvantaged. Asian peoples receive western thought (and yes, I do still consider Derrida western) and foreign sacred texts not as equals, but as subordinates. I write as a minority, albeit still yellow-skinned, privileged yet not privileged in a foreign land. Perhaps like Hong Kong in relation to mainland China. And also, maybe Rahab in the face of an oncoming Israelite army. Therefore, in such a situation, I have argued that it is reprehensible to insist on the unconditional as ideal. Rather, the unconditional needs to be dissociated from the ideal and allowed to be in dialectical tension with the conditional on equal grounds that give room for context to speak into the ethics of hospitality. In so doing, hospitality can move from aporia to dialectics, unbridled hosting to praxis and hopefully, some resistance.

The converse might also ring true for nativism since not all such movements are the same. And those who approximate the power dynamics that Rahab faced such as the Palestinians or the Native Americans, I need to approach them with caution. While imperfectly preserved, Rahab insured that she, as the prostitute who resided in the wall, lives on in the narratives of her conquerors. As this essay hopes to show, this memory provokes, interrogates, and unsettles bourgeois conceptions of nativism and hospitality. More crucially, it reminds me that in the light of Hong Kong's inevitable full handover in 2047, we need to do better than what Rahab has achieved. We need to endeavor to leave behind for future generations something more than just a name, a profession and an address.

Works Cited

Althaus-Reid, Marcella. "Searching for a Queer Sophia-Wisdom: The Post-Colonial Rahab." In *Patriarchs, Prophets and Other Villains*, edited by Lisa Isherwood, 128–40. London: Equinox, 2007.

Betz, Hans-Georg. "Facets of Nativism: A Heuristic Exploration." *Patterns of Prejudice* 53.2 (2019) 111–35.

Biddle, Mark, and Melissa A. Jackson. "Rahab and Her Visitors: Reciprocal Deliverance." *Word & World* 37.3 (2017) 226–35.

Bird, Phyllis. "The Harlot as Heroine: Narrative Art and Social Presupposition in Three Old Testament Texts." *Semeia* 46 (1989) 119–39.

Butler, Trent. *Joshua*. Word Biblical Commentary 7. Waco, TX: Word, 1983.

Caputo, John D. *Deconstruction in a Nutshell: A Conversation with Jacques Derrida / edited with a commentary*. New York: Fordham University Press, 1997.

Charles, Ronald. "Rahab: A Righteous Whore in James." *Neotestamentica* 45.2 (2011) 206–20.

Chen, Kuan Hsing. *Asia as Method: Toward Deimperialization*. London: Duke University Press, 2010.

Crowell, Bradley L. "Good Girl, Bad Girl: Foreign Women of the Deuteronomistic History in Postcolonial Perspective." *Biblical Interpretation* 21.1 (2013) 1–18.

Davidson, Steed Vernyl. "Gazing (at) Native Women: Rahab and Jael in Imperializing and Postcolonial Discourses." In *Postcolonialism and the Hebrew Bible*, edited by Roland Boer, 69–101. Atlanta: Society of Biblical Literature, 2013.

Derrida, Jacques. *Of Hospitality: Anne Dufourmantelle Invites Jacques Derrida to Respond*. Translated by Rachel Bowlby. Stanford: Stanford University Press, 2000.

Dozeman, Thomas B. 2015. *Joshua 1–12: A New Translation with Introduction and Commentary*. Anchor Yale Bible 5. New Haven: Yale University Press.

Frymer-Kensky, Tikva. "Reading Rahab." In *Tehillah le-Moshe: Biblical and Judaic Studies in Honor of Moshe Greenberg*, edited by Mordechai Cogan et al., 57–67. Winona Lake, IN: Eisenbrauns, 1997.

Hawk, L. Daniel. "Strange Houseguests: Rahab, Lot and the Dynamics of Deliverance." In *Reading Between Texts: Intertextuality and the Hebrew Bible*, edited by Danna Nolan Fewell, 89–97. Louisville: Westminster John Knox, 1992.

Ip, Iam-chong. "Political De-institutionalization and the Rise of Right-wing Nativism." In *Routledge Handbook of Contemporary Hong Kong*, edited by Tai-lok Lui, Stephen W.K. Chui and Ray Yep, 462–73. London: Routledge, 2019.

Ten Years. Directed by Zune Kwok, Fei-pang Wong, Jevons Au, Chow Kwun-Wai and Ng Ka-leung. Golden Scene Co. Ltd.; Netflix, 2015.

La Caze, Marguerite. "Not Just Visitors: Cosmopolitanism, Hospitality and Refugees." *Philosophy Today* 48.3 (2004) 313–24.

Lim, Chin Ming Stephen. *Contextual Biblical Hermeneutics as Multicentric Dialogue: Towards a Singaporean Reading of Daniel*. Boston: Brill, 2019.

Lowe, John, and Stephan Ortmann. "Unmasking Nativism in Asia's World City: Graffiti and Identity Boundary Un/making in Hong Kong." *Continuum* 34.3 (2020) 398–416.

McKinlay, Judith E. "Rahab: A Hero/ine?" *Biblical Interpretation* 7.1 (1999) 44–57.

Mangillo, Ira D. "When Rahab and Indonesian Christian Woman Meet in the Third Space." *Journal of Feminist Studies and Religion* 31.1 (2015) 45–64.

Mignolo, Walter D. *Local Histories/Global Designs: Coloniality, Subaltern Knowledges, and Border Thinking*. Princeton: Princeton University Press, 2000.

Runions, Erin. "From Disgust to Humor: Rahab's Queer Affect." In *Bible Trouble: Queer Reading at the Boundaries of Biblical Scholarship*, edited by Teresa J. Hornsby and Ken Stone, 45–74. Atlanta: Society of Biblical Literature, 2011.

Shepherd, David. *The Gift of the Other: Levinas, Derrida, and a Theology of Hospitality*. Cambridge, UK: James Clarke, 2014.

Still, Judith. *Derrida and Hospitality: Theory and Practice*. Edinburgh: Edinburgh University Press, 2010.

Wu, Meiyao. "Hundun's Hospitality: Daoist, Derridean and Levinasian Readings of Zhuangzi's Parable." *Educational Philosophy and Theory* 46.13 (2014) 1435–49.

杨, 宝春, and 占青 朱. "《庄子》 的"浑沌"解." 天中学刊 18.6 (2003) 44–45.

陈, 赞. ""浑沌之死"与"轴心时代"中国思想的基本问题." 中山大学学报(社会科学版) 50.6 (2010) 125–37.

8

Deleted and Reclaimed Borders

Embracing My Native Self

CRISTINA LLEDO GOMEZ

DELETED. DISREGARDED. DISMISSED. LOST. I found myself expressing these words after day-long conversations with fellow migrant and native theologians. The chapter I proposed for this book was to focus solely on the necessity of establishing borders within churches for survivors of abuse. I however think that it is important to show that borders can also be a good thing, given that borders in relation to nations and migration can often have negative associations and thus they are to be crossed and re-crossed, dismantled, disempowered, and redefined.

The desire for dismantled borders in migration is not unreasonable, given that there are many examples all over the world of borders being used to exclude and dehumanize people desperately seeking help and safety, as exemplified by the way asylum seekers have been treated here in Australia.[1] And yet borders serve a purpose for the common good, such as containing and keeping inhabitants safe, and creating an identity for persons and communities within those borders which in turn enable them to relate with others.

---

1. See for example, Australian Human Rights Commission, *Lives on Hold*.

In faith communities, borders determine identity and unity (in diversity) and are vital for love and covenantal relationships. These are evidenced in various early church controversies such as with the Arians, Donatists and Gnostics who mimicked Christian beliefs. Without the borders that distinguished the church from these so-called heresies, church communities became vulnerable to confusion and disunity. In the end, ecumenical councils set the borders of belief, through the Nicene-Constantinople Creed, distinguishing between what was true to the Good News delivered by Jesus Christ and what was not, even though initially they presented as innocuous or seemingly life-giving as a contemporary expression of the Gospel.[2]

In Scripture, borders have importance too. When Abraham and Sarah made a covenant with God, God promised them ancestors but also land for themselves and their ancestors (Gen 15:18–21). The description of the boundaries of those lands are quite detailed (see Ezek 47:13–21), evidencing the significance of borders in relation to the divine covenant. God grants peace to the borders of Jerusalem (Ps 147:14), reinforcing the significant role of borders in regard to divine covenants. Borders also establish divine peace.

With set ideas for this chapter, I had not expected to rewrite it after meeting a second time with fellow collaborators on this book, engaging in what the Pacific Islanders among us described as the *talanoa* process. Whilst *talanoa* has been used by Pacific islander cultures for centuries, in the western world it is a fairly new concept, only recently taken up as the methodology for the United Nations Conference of the Parties at their Paris convention in 2015 (COP21).[3] According to the United Nations Framework Convention on Climate Change (UNFCCC):

> Talanoa is a traditional word used in Fiji and across the Pacific to reflect a process of inclusive, participatory, and transparent dialogue. The purpose of Talanoa is to share stories, build empathy and to make wise decisions for the collective good. The process of Talanoa involves the sharing of ideas, skills, and experience through storytelling. During the process, participants build trust and advance knowledge through empathy and understanding. Blaming others and making critical observations are inconsistent with building mutual trust and respect, and therefore inconsistent with the Talanoa concept. Talanoa fosters stability and inclusiveness in dialogue, by creating a safe space

---

2. See Lledo Gomez, *The Church as Woman and Mother*.

3. United Nations Climate Change, COP 21 (https://unfccc.int/process-and-meetings/conferences/past-conferences/paris-climate-change-conference-november-2015/cop-21).

that embraces mutual respect for a platform for decision making for a greater good.[4]

Fellow collaborators and I followed a similar process as we sought to encourage the final shaping of this book. After hearing the stories of my colleagues, their own grappling with borders, their various issues as migrants and natives of their countries, and as Christians from various denominations, I found myself blurting out the words "deleted, lost, dismissed" and "disregarded" in terms of my own experience of being a theologian and a native of my country, the Philippines. In the safe space of *talanoa* I shared how I had felt for some time that only the white male European Western voice, the classical way of theologizing, the form in which I was taught, seemed to have the voice that was most respected and accepted in many of the theological circles I had been engaging. Yet, those same circles showed a desire to be supportive of what they called "global theologies," such as Latinx, Womanist and Asian-American theologies. I see this same dissonance between a desire to provide a space for the non-white voice and the actual practice of providing this space in the way Australian Aboriginal people are treated. Wiradjuri man, Glen Loughrey, writes that in terms of the 2019–20 bushfires in Australia, people are showing interest in giving the Indigenous a voice, to share their fire practices,[5] but are then unwilling to give them a real voice by embedding them into the Australian constitution, as having rights. As Loughrey notes: "I am always amused when people want to appropriate our practices to resolve their problems but won't allow us a Voice, recognise our sovereignty or the freedom of self-determination. Colonialism is still alive and well. We are good little black fellas only when what we have is useful to those in power."[6] Listening to Loughrey speak on postcolonialism in Australia, my experience of feeling out of place in a country still operating predominantly in the "white way" is somehow affirmed:

> Post-colonialism is the state after colonisation where those who colonised and those who were colonised come together and reimagine the space, in this case Australia, and rewrite a narrative inclusive of all. That is yet to happen here. We are living in a neo-colonial state where little has changed. The story

---

4. Tunufa'i shows the complexities of adopting 'talanoa' as a methodology; its misuse can be a reinforcement of colonisation (see Tunufa'i, "Pacific research").

5. See Higgins, "Indigenous fire practices"; Fisher and Altman, "The world's best fire management system is in northern Australia and it's led by Indigenous land managers"; Nikolakis *et al.*, "Goal Setting and Indigenous fire management."

6. Loughrey, Facebook Post, January 9, 2020 (https://www.facebook.com/glenn.loughrey/posts/1417574135087187).

is still white and still told through the European imagination. Aboriginal people are the exotic other, the 'Ooga Booga' people useful for didge playing, footy and welcomes to country, but little more. They have no voice about what happens to them or about what they intrinsically know, except when the dominant society thinks it might be of assistance to fix up the mess they have made—cultural or firestick burning is an example.[7]

To be clear, my white male lecturers did not prevent me from speaking in my native voice. Rather, it was the opposite: they believed they were equipping me, a minority, to have a voice, to be heard in the white male hegemonic theological space. The problem was the lack of colored female migrant mentors. There was no one to encourage the development of my native voice in a sustained way—neither teacher (no colored lecturers), nor elder (no mother or aunts to guide me).

This chapter is thus an exploration and a reclamation of the lost borders of my native self as a woman from the Philippines and as a theologian—beginning with the experience of feeling deleted as a migrant and a woman of color, discovering the colonial mentality I carried as part of the Philippine diaspora, then "being seen" by an Australian Aboriginal woman and ending with being empowered to "see" others through the reclamation of a babaylan value called *kapwa*.

The methodology used in this chapter is ethnoautobiography which is an "indigenously grounded form of personal storytelling as a means of restoring wholeness and reconnection to the alienated modern self . . . an approach to decolonization and reclamation of the indigenous self that reconnects the atomized individual to place, history (including stories and myths), nature, spirit, ancestry (indigenous origins), and community."[8] It presents the layers of intersectionality experienced by a woman of color, a theologian, and a migrant from the Philippines to Australia.

Colonial Mentality, Internalized Oppression, and the Filipina Migrant

Since migrating to Australia, I have felt rootless and without a community that could pass on the ways of being a native of my country, the Philippines. Apart from my parents, one of whom died when I was 18 years old and the other became incapacitated from a stroke when I was 24 years old, there was

7. Loughrey, "Lament and Hope on Australia Day."
8. Mendoza, "Back from the Crocodile's Belly."

no one to teach me about being Filipino, about being part of the "Lledo" (my father's family side) or "Nava" (my mother's family side) families/clans. As migrants we were keen to learn about the ways of our new country and become like one of its citizens. So, we spent less of our energies recovering the culture and ways of the country we had left behind and more on integrating ourselves into the new land we had settled into.

As part of a colonized people, we carried with us a sense of inferiority because of our non-white skin. The inferiority is reinforced in advertisements for skin whitening and hair straightening products. It is reinforced by family themselves as exemplified by experiences with aunts and uncles who in the first instance would ask whether or not I had spent too much time in the sun because my skin had become darker—the very skin color which we shared through our common ancestry and for which I had already received numerous compliments from white-skinned strangers in Australia. Growing up too, I had memories of my mother massaging my nose every night in the hope that it would become less broad and more pointed and slimmer like white-Europeans or *mestizas* (those of mixed Filipina and white parentage), reminding me of my own inferiority as a native Filipina, dark skinned and flat-nosed. E.J.R. David, Dinghy Kristine B. Sharma, and Jessica Petalio state similar colonizing experiences in contemporary society by other Filipinos:

> The abundance of skin bleaching products and skin-whitening clinics in the Philippines is evidence that the masses [of modern-day Filipinos] may have accepted the notion that Filipino physical characteristics are not as desirable as European physical traits. The discrimination against, and low regard of, non-Christians, non-Urban, and non-Westernized Filipinos send the message that the more Western you look, think, and behave, the better off and more accepted you will be. These ubiquitous inferiorizing messages in modern day Philippines, have their roots in colonialism.[9]

Colonial mentality (CM) is one of the effects of colonialism. CM is "a broad multidimensional construct that refers to personal feelings or beliefs of ethnic or cultural inferiority."[10] Its characteristics are:

1. denigration of the self;
2. denigration of the culture or body;

---

9. David, Sharma and Petalio, "Losing Kapwa," 44.
10. David and Okazaki "Assessing the Psychological Consequences of Internalized Colonialism," 198.

3. discriminating against less Americanized in-group members; and
4. tolerating historical and contemporary oppression.[11]

In regard to Filipinos, CM is viewed as a form of internalized oppression (IO), resulting from a history of colonization by the Spaniards and Americans.[12] It is defined as "an automatic and uncritical rejection of anything Filipino and an automatic and uncritical preference for anything American."[13] Based on the named CM characteristics shown above, Tuazon et al. specify the particular CM characteristics of Filipinos:

a. denigration of the Filipino self (i.e., feelings of inferiority, shame, embarrassment, resentment, or self-hate about being Filipino);

b. denigration of the Filipino culture or body (i.e., the perception that anything Filipino is inferior to anything White, European, or American, including culture, language, physical characteristics, material products, and government);

c. discriminating against less-Americanized Filipinos (i.e., distancing oneself from characteristics related to being Filipino and becoming as American as possible); and

d. tolerating historical and contemporary oppression of Filipinos and Filipino Americans (i.e., the acceptance of oppression as an appropriate cost of civilization, believing maltreatment is well intentioned).[14]

The power of CM is as such that even when the colonization by Spaniards and Americans had occurred in a by-gone past, numerous Filipinos continue to carry CM as part of their diaspora experience.[15] David and Okazaki argue that colonial mentality negatively affects the mental health of Filipino Americans.[16] Meanwhile, in Australia, a 2010–11 joint study between scholars from the University of Technology Sydney and

---

11. David and Okazaki "Assessing the Psychological Consequences of Internalized Colonialism," 198.

12. See Tuazon et al., "Colonial Mentality," 354.

13. See Tuazon et al., "Colonial Mentality," 354.

14. See Tuazon et al., "Colonial Mentality," 355. See also David and Sharma, "Losing Kapwa"; Marcelino, "Towards Understanding the psychology of the Filipino."

15. David and Okazaki, "Colonial mentality"; David, "A colonial mentality model of depression for Filipino Americans"; David, "Testing the validity of the colonial mentality."

16. David and Okazaki, "Colonial mentality"; David and Okazaki, "The colonial mentality scale (CMS)."

the University of Western Sydney show similar acculturative stress and depressive results among Filipino Australians.[17]

But there are scholars who are reluctant to use the phrase "colonial mentality." For Elaine Marie Carbonell Laforteza, while the idea of "colonial mentality" might seek to bring awareness to the superstructure that supports and perpetuates this form of oppression, it is limited as a descriptive because it "fails to invade the realm of the 'superstructure.'"[18] That is, if superstructure "refers to the norms that underpin society, its governmentalities and individual ways of being/becoming," then it fails to critique the "assymetrical relations of power engendered by colonizing power."[19] Thus, we have the visceral experience as described by Delia D. Aguilar in Laforteza in which power is engendered by colonizing power and remains largely uncritiqued:

> Every day we are bombarded by advertisements where the light-skinned girl gets the admiring stares, the fair mestiza lands the job, the fairer girl gets the man. Notice the billboards that literally gobble up the highway [in Manila]. Plastered on them is either some blond foreigner or the pale, smiling face of a local mestiza movie star. To be a model or an actor in this country, you have to be *tisoyin* or *tisayin* meaning, on the fair side (never mind that you can't act!).[20]

Laforteza thus prefers to use the descriptive "the somatechnics of whiteness and race" as explained in her similarly named publication from 2015 (kindle edition published in 2016):

> somatechnics is revealed as the means through which everyday belonging to the world becomes constituted. It reveals the ways in which technologies of power/knowledge become consolidated through embodied practice. Consequently, the concept of somatechnics considers the ways in which *soma* [body] and *techne* [technologies] intersect to inform interpersonal/intercorporeal relations. This focus on embodied practice and its enmeshment with technologies of power is relatively absent from the concept of colonial mentality which depends on a Cartesian logic and a subject/object split. As the concept of somatechnics pays

---

17. https://opus.lib.uts.edu.au/bitstream/10453/35919/1/SEM_accepted%20version29052015MD.pdf.

18. Laforteza, *The Somatechnics of Whiteness and Race*, 4.

19. Laforteza, *The Somatechnics of Whiteness and Race*, 4.

20. Laforteza, *The Somatechnics of Whiteness and Race*, 4.

particular attention to the bodily technologies of power that the concept of colonial mentality elides.[21]

This idea of the somatechnics of whiteness and race thus leads me to question the role of Christian churches, and particularly in regard to the theological academy—how they either resist or reinforce whiteness as the norm and thus also resist or reinforce oppression of the non-white and non-native person in their spaces.

A Somatechnic Experience of Western Theological Academic Space

At our second gathering to bring to realization the ideas for our book on *Bordered Bodies*, I explained to my colleagues through tears that: "This is the first academic space where I feel I am allowed to speak in the first-person, as an I, my, me, or myself. In other spaces theological or Christian, I feel overwhelmed by the dominance of white people, white culture, and the white way of doing anything. I've spent a lot of my life trying to fit in despite being a woman and a person of colour." Konai Helu Thaman's 1987 poem "Our Way" expresses well the feelings and thoughts that were brewing in me in regard to myself and white academic spaces. The white academic space ("your way") is objective, individualistic, and driven by evidence. On the contrary, I feel more at home with what Thaman calls "our way"—it is subjective, and driven by gut-feelings.[22]

In my experience, the purpose of speaking in a white Western theological academic space is to teach, rather than to share one's own theological journey. To share one's own intellectual, spiritual and emotional developments—which would resonate with fellow academics who themselves believe, laugh, love, and struggle in their own theological journeys—is not considered academic-theological in the white Western theological academic space. Rather it is considered narrative and personal, and not objective and academic enough.

To practice theology differently from the classical white European-Western way I had been taught was beyond my imagination. But in my view, this is the effect of white colonization onto native peoples and their descendants—it holds up whiteness as the norm and ideal, and deletes native identity and native ways by marginalizing practices fundamental to claiming the personal, the self—such as the use of first person pronouns (in an attempt to

---

21. Laforteza, *The Somatechnics of Whiteness and Race*, 6.
22. In Konai Helu Thaman, *Hingano*.

uphold non-bias), or the use of personal story (again to justify validity of the research piece), or the use of song, poetry and myth as theology themselves rather than as contributors to a theology of something.

I recognize too that because of IO resulting from CM, I myself have participated in the upholding of white culture and the erasure of my native voice. As a result of colonization, the colonized internalize and reinforce their own oppression, their own silencing. For Filipinos, this is even more pointed as they were colonized three times over: trying to fit in, rejecting their own ways in preference for the white or *mestiza-mestizo* (mixed race) ways and normalizing this.[23] It is without surprise I sought to fit within the new borders of Australia by rejecting my native borders and holding up Western-European ways and considering them as more superior. Engaging in the *talanoa* process, researching for, and writing this chapter, unintendedly resulted in the process of beginning to recover and reclaim the lost, rejected, and deleted borders of my native self.

In her article exploring colonial mentality and Filipina-American experiences of racism and sexism, Lou Collette S. Felipe explains the process of internalized oppression for Filipinas (also known as *Pinays*), what Laforteza would view as the dynamics of the somatechnics of whiteness, race, and/or gender:

> Though directionality or causality cannot be assumed, it is possible that repeated exposure to oppression, whether based on gender, race, or in combination, contributes to the development of negative internalizations about cultural identity. As recipients of dehumanizing treatment, *Pinays* may embody the stereotypes imposed on them and move about the world accepting false notions of insignificance. With large numbers of Pinays in service positions, including nursing, the mail-order bride industry, domestic work, and prostitution, it is worthwhile to consider whether internalized inferiority plays a role in this worldwide phenomenon.[24]

I acknowledge that thanks to my doctorate I felt an increase in my self-esteem and yet remained in a cloud of self-inferiority until only recently. For deeply ingrained in my body was the feeling of inferiority over the darkness of my skin color.

---

23. David, "Filipinos, Colonial Mentality."

24. Felipe, "The Relationship of Colonial Mentality with Filipina American Experiences," 29.

From a Vision of Whiteness to Babayi Theology

In 2015, the first year of my PhD, I was diagnosed with a form of reading dyslexia in which the whiteness of the page dominated over the black text. The effect of this reading dyslexia is that I would fall asleep after fifteen minutes of reading, for I would spend most of my energies distinguishing the black writing from the glaring white background. Words appeared to simply converge whilst I sought to make the letters distinct and separated from one another. The dyslexia is called "Irlen Syndrome" after Helen Irlen who discovered it in children and found a solution by introducing color corrective glasses.[25] I was a sceptic until I wore my own color corrective glasses and the muscles of my face instantly relaxed. This made a great impression upon me, pointing out that I had been straining to read and distinguish letters and words all of my life. This condition presented as a poignant metaphor for how I have also engaged with the academic world—my training in white theology was what dominated, and I strained, if at all, to see a trace of theology from a *babayi* perspective.

Here I have begun to use the word *babayi* and not Filipina because it derives from the word *babae* which means woman in Tagalog, my native language, whilst Filipina is the word imposed by colonizers to describe the women of the Philippines. To date, there is no such thing formally called *Babayi* theology, theological research by the *Babae*. Whilst women theologians from the Philippines have written articles on colonialism in addition to a number of other topics (for example Mary John Mananzan, Agnes Brazal, and Christina Astorga), none have acknowledged their work as *babayi* theology. Only one article refers to the beginnings of a *babae* theology and interestingly it is by a Filipino male priest, Alfonso P. Suico:

> This paper on methodology is an attempt to find a distinct Filipino theology and ethics by retrieving the sense of the *babayi* (woman). The *babayi* comes from the ancient Asiatic script called the *baybayin*. Inspired by the Filipina women's courage and resiliency, the goal is to map out a theo-ethics that is uniquely reflective of the Filipino woman within the broader feminist and liberation ethics. As a method, it critiques the prevailing framing of Western feminism common among Filipino women writers. Inspired by intersectionality, a paradigm that analyzes oppression as the crossroad of racism and poverty, this

---

25. For research on this syndrome, see Crabtree, "Educational implications of Meares-Irlen syndrome"; Chouinard et al., "A Functional Neuroimaging Case Study of Meares." This diagnosis is viewed controversially—see Uccula et al., "Colors, colored overlays, and reading skills."

method locates the Filipina in the multiaxial framing of history, the struggle of poverty and discrimination, displacement, religion and dialogue, and ecology. This multidimensional approach considers the long history of oppression experienced by our people, reflects inherent Filipino values and provides a method for understanding the Filipina and her allies today.[26]

The renowned Filipina Catholic theologians, Brazal and Astorga, have indeed been writing using Western frameworks or structures. For example, Astorga's books are entitled: *The Beast, the Harlot and the Lamb: Faith Confronts Systemic Evil*,[27] and *Catholic Moral Theology and Social Ethics: A New Method*.[28] Meanwhile, Brazal's work is exemplified in the following publications: *Feminist Cyberethics in Asia: Religious Discourses in Human Connectivity*,[29] and "Church as Sacrament of Yin-yang Harmony: Toward a More Incisive Participation of Laity and Women in the Church."[30] In contrast, Mananzan shows attempts at a reclamation of the *babaylan* tradition in her co-authored work, *Babaylan: Filipinos and the Call to the Indigenous* (2010), and more recently, *Shadows of Light: Philippine Church History Under Spain A People's Perspective* (2016).[31]

My own research evidences not only the use of Western frameworks but also Western-focused content as seen in my first book, *The Church as Woman and Mother: Historical and Theological Foundations*.[32] My other publications also evidence the use of Western frameworks alongside Western-focused content as seen in the following titles: "From Infants to Mothers: Recovering the Call to the People of God to Become Mother Church in *Lumen Gentium*" in *Ecclesiology Journal*,[33] and "Early Motherhood and the Paschal Mystery: A Rahnerian Reflection on the Death and Rebirth Experiences of New Mothers" in the *Australasian Catholic Record*.[34] *Babae* theology is needed more than ever to encourage Filipina women theologians to integrate and express their native selves, presenting *babae* theology as an equally valid framework as a Western-European framework, and thus contributing to the decolonization of theological

---

26. Suico Jr., "In Search of the *Babayi*," 199.
27. Astorga, *The Beast, the Harlot and the Lamb*.
28. Astorga, *Catholic Moral Theology and Social Ethics*.
29. Brazal and Abraham, *Feminist Cyberethics in Asia*.
30. Brazal, "Church as Sacrament of Yin-yang Harmony."
31. Strobel et al., *Babaylan: Filipinos and the Call to the Indigenous*.
32. Lledo Gomez, *The Church as Woman and Mother*.
33. Lledo Gomez, "From Infants to Mothers."
34. Lledo Gomez, "Early Motherhood and the Paschal Mystery."

academia and churches as much as *Womanist, Mujerista,* and Asian-American feminist theologies have attempted to do.

What can *babayi* theology look like? Suico explains that *Babayi* refers to woman in *Babayin*, "the early script or writing system used by pre-colonial Filipinos [. . .] closely related with the Proto-Austronesian word *bahi* or *babahi* for female."[35] Before the Christian Spanish colonizers arrived in 1564 (and stayed for over 300 years until 1898), a priestly caste consisting mainly of elderly *babayi* called the *babaylan* or *catalonan* existed within the *barangay* (community) which was the basic unit of social structure in pre-colonial Philippines. The *babaylan* presided over religious rituals and ceremonies and were seen as the healers of spiritual, mental, and physical illnesses of community members.[36] Exercising such roles gave the *babaylan* a vital and powerful position within the *barangay*. But women in pre-colonial Philippines were highly regarded in general. Sociologist Marie Lou Frias Bautista claims that "women in this period held a special position. They were not only involved in the decision-making process and economics of the family but they participated and held power on all levels of the barangay's economic, political, social, and religious activities."[37] Of greater note is the equal partnership between men and women in pre-colonial Philippines. There was no such thing as sexism or abuse or subjugation of women by men because cooperation and interdependence between them was the norm. Both women and men could rise to political leadership. Equality even extended to the language used in pre-colonial Philippines: "For instance, the natives never used *tu* (thou) or spoke in the second person, plural or singular. It was considered most respectful to speak in the third person. In the Tagalog dialect, there is no word for he or she, instead the word *siya* stood for he or she. Likewise, Tagalog terms such as *anak* (child) and *apo* (grandchild) and the Kalinga term *olitog* (child) were used for both males or females."[38]

In addition, if insults were directed at women, chiefs and elders, perpetrators were subject to the severest types of punishment. When the Spanish Catholic colonizers invaded the Philippines, they introduced the concept of dominance of the man over the woman, and man as being in the public realm whilst the woman was to remain in the private realm. Men accordingly received education in occupations that belong to the public realm such as law and medicine whilst women's education were limited to matters of the private realm such as clothing and social etiquette. Eventually, it was difficult for

---

35. Lledo Gomez, "Early Motherhood and the Paschal Mystery," 201.
36. Bautista, "Historical Influences on Gender Preference in the Philippines," 144.
37. Bautista, "Historical Influences on Gender Preference in the Philippines," 144.
38. Bautista, "Historical Influences on Gender Preference in the Philippines," 145.

women to acquire jobs outside the home, and they became dependent and inferior to men. In contrast to this, authors and activists who utilize the word and concept "babaylan" seek to reclaim a tradition of empowered women, equal partnership between men and women, and an emphasis on interconnectedness and kinship between peoples, their land, their spirit ancestors, and their God. As the Center for Babaylan Studies state, *babaylan* is a tradition carried inside both Filipino women and men:

> Babaylan Tradition concerns the Filipino Wisdom and Power within us. Filipinos everywhere can be empowered by traditions preserved, upheld, passed on by Babaylan women and men. Filipino leaders can individually and collectively strengthen, evolve and uphold this intensifying, re-emerging respect for indigenous traditions and identity, and can in turn empower communities they serve.
>
> You may carry the traditions of the Babaylan within you because you have answered a calling of leadership in one or more of the following: advocacy, activism, teaching, increasing awareness, healing, spirituality and vision, struggling and working for justice—actions and motivation deeply connected to the context of being Filipino.[39]

The Centre for Babaylan Studies quotes their founder and former executive director, Leny Strobel, to allude to the embrace of *babaylan* tradition as a way of engaging in decolonization, enabling them to heal and become empowered for activism against colonization which remains in the psyche of many Filipinos: "Decolonization transforms the consciousness of the colonized through the reclamation of the Filipino cultural self and makes space for the recovery and healing of traumatic memory, and healing leading to different forms of activism. It is an open-ended process. It is a new way of seeing. As a way of healing, it is also a promise and a hope."[40]

Babayi theology then can be a reclamation of the *babaylan* tradition for theologizing, by women of the Philippines, for women of the Philippines, and their descendants, inside and outside of the Philippines. It is a reclamation in which the women begin to see in their heritage and consequently in themselves as having the ability to be leaders, decision-makers, changemakers and healers (spiritual, physical and mental) in equal partnership with men, of their communities. Reclaiming the *babaylan* tradition for the Filipina

---

39. Centre for Babaylan Studies, *What Is Babaylan?* (https://www.centerforbabaylanstudies.org/history).

40. Centre for Babaylan Studies, *What Is Babaylan?* (https://www.centerforbabaylanstudies.org/history).

theologian affects her God-speaking and God-writing wherein interconnectedness with God, community, and land of origin and current living, with ancestors, and descendants and/or relatives, become evident.

Over the last decade I have come to realize how much I have been longing to recover the richness of my roots as a Filipina, as a Lledo woman (my father's side) and as a Nava woman (my mother's side). To learn about the *babaylan* tradition was a bonus for me. I had a glimpse of the lost part of my native self after spending just a week with my aunties from the Lledo family and a day with my Nava family. There were traits that I saw about myself which I thought only belonged to me personally but in fact were traits which I shared with family members such as preferring to eat with my hands rather than utensils (even when I began a meal with utensils), preferring to walk barefoot rather than with shoes or slippers, having an affinity with the spirit world and being comfortable in speaking with spirit ancestors as if they were physically present, here, today. It is through *babayi* theology that I have found a way to reclaim my lost and deleted native borders and roots.

From Being Seen to Seeing Others

"You are a native of your country" was the first thing that Australian Aboriginal elder, Miriam Rose, said to me at our first meeting.[41] It was shocking to hear these words because I had never thought of myself as a native person. I associated "native" with being indigenous but according to *Fowler's Concise Dictionary of Modern English*, "native" has various meanings and does not necessarily equate with "indigenous": "In many of its meanings, *native* is uncontroversial: *native speaker, native of Liverpool, native oak* are typical examples of innocuous usage. The danger comes when the word is used as a noun to mean "an original inhabitant of a country," because of the notions of cultural inferiority it conveys."

Whilst the danger of associating *native* with cultural inferiority remains, I have come to embrace the description as part of my reclamation of my home country and the best of its culture. When Miriam Rose called me a native, I was called from within myself to reclaim the very origins I had erased or placed little energies into in order to fit into the melting pot of multicultural and yet white hegemonic Australian society. It took a woman of color (Miriam, and her full acceptance of her indigeneity) to recognize and truly see another woman of color (myself). There and then I wanted to be mentored by Miriam, so that she could show me how to

---

41. For more on Miriam Rose, go to www.miriamrosefoundation.org.au/.

embrace that neglected/lost part of myself, the non-white, olive-brown-skinned self that dealt with racism, discrimination, and social profiling more often in some places than others. I felt I could learn from Miriam how to deal with being lost and displaced from my own home country and how to resist the effects of being colonized, one of which is to internalize my oppression. It seemed to me that Miriam had grappled with these issues and moreover, she did not change according to whoever was in front of her. Rather' she remained consistently herself and if people misunderstood her or were offended through cultural misunderstanding, she was unapologetic about being her consistent self.

From my encounter with Miriam, I came to believe that Australian Filipino/Filipina first generation (Gen-1) migrants in general could learn a lot from Australian Aboriginal and Torres Strait Islanders. For there are affinities in ways of thinking such as connection to the land and ancestors and the effects of being colonized and displaced as a people; Filipino-Australian Gen-1 migrants can also learn quite a lot too from Australian Aboriginal and Torres Strait Islanders such as Glen Loughrey and Miriam Rose about recovering or rebuilding borders of lost native selves and fighting for recognition, rights, and platforms for their people. I imagined Miriam's mentoring would be different from aunts and older female cousins who had internalized white oppression. For Miriam would not ask at every first meeting after years of not seeing each other: "Have you been out in the sun again? Look how dark you have become!"

Nearly 35 years after migrating to Australia, with my brown skin, my distinctly Filipino face, my attraction to song, paintings, stories, and dance, my feeling of coming home to myself after seeing palm trees, rice fields, and straw homes and feeling the wind on my face as I rode a jeepney from point A to point B in my mother's hometown in the Philippines—these were the things that reawakened the desire to explore the undeveloped parts of my native self. Even though the native parts of myself were what made my spirit soar, they were not part of my theologizing and communicating theology. I learnt that the most superior way of "doing theology" and therefore the only way of being guaranteed of being listened and heard is to speak in the language and manner of white theologizing—a structured essay on a page, with a clear introduction, body and conclusion, black writing on a stark white page, involving the theological lexicon which included words and phrases that impressed from the Western world such as *magisterium, apostolicum, semper reformanda, aggiornamento, mater ecclesia,* and *ressourcement.* They are texts that have been used for centuries by bishops in church council debates, theologians in journal articles, and monks and seminarians in their places of living and learning.

My new challenge is to incorporate Filipino words, song, story, phrases and values as part of my theological lexicon. Words and values such as *kapwa* (others as self or shared inner self), *utang na loob* (debt of gratitude), or *pakikisama* (getting along with others) must have equal place as words that have traditionally held *gravitas* in the Western classical theological tradition. For example, the word *kapwa* has deep significance for the men and women in the Philippines, even as far back as the *babaylan* era because it is associated with the concept of *kinship* which was the way of organizing of the *barangay* (the community) by pre-colonial Philippines, politically and socially.

David et.al. quote Enriquez explain *Kapwa*: it means "the unity of the 'self' and 'others'. A recognition of a shared identity, an inner self that makes one connected with and equal to others."[42] Quoting the same author, Enriquez, Levy Lara Lanaria explains *kapwa*: "Enriquez refers to kapwa as 'shared inner self,' which presupposes the sharing of 'collective values with the rest of humanity and deep respect for the dignity and inherent worth of a fellow human being.' It is marked by 'a reflexive quality, such that what is good for one is shared and is good for the other, what would be to the detriment of one is accepted in fact as detrimental to the other.'"[43] Lanaria further explains the deeply humanizing implications and better ways of relating and behaving because of a "shared inner self" with one's own neighbor:

> A person starts having *kapwa* not so much because of a recognition of status given him by others but more because of his awareness of shared identity. The *ako* (ego) and the *iba-sa-akin* (others) are one and the same in *kapwa* psychology: *Hindi ako iba sa aking kapwa* (I am no different from others). Once *ako* starts thinking of himself as separate from *kapwa*, the Filipino "self" gets to be individuated in the Western sense and, in effect, denies the status of *kapwa* to the other. By the same token, the status of *kapwa* is also denied to the self. To be denied of the selfhood or personhood (*pagkatao*), that last remaining 'line of defense' of the individual, is a terrible misfortune for a Filipino ... *Kapwa*, then, has an innate ethical dimension which a priori recognizes and respects and advances the cause of human dignity.[44]

As theological text, *Kapwa* communicates not only the deep dignity of human beings but also the interconnectedness of all creation. It is about

---

42. Enriquez in David et al., "Losing Kapwa", 44.
43. Lanaria, "*Kapwa* in *Pamilya*," 36.
44. Lanaria, "*Kapwa* in *Pamilya*," 37.

"seeing" the other as oneself. The concept of *Kapwa* supports Pope Francis' push for greater ecological integrity in the world where humanity begin to see their interconnectedness with all of creation and therefore their need to work towards the common good even with and sometimes because of their differences. These are seen in Pope Francis' 2015 *Laudato Si* encyclical letter, and more recently in his 2020 *Querida Amazonia* post-synodal apostolic exhortation.[45] *Kapwa* is also non-gendered language. Thus, it communicates that the focus is on a relationship of equals rather than the traditional Roman hierarchy of domination-subjugation between male and female, between master and slave, or between parent and child (cf. Gal 3:28—"There is neither Jew nor Gentile, neither slave nor free, nor is there male and female, for you are all one in Christ Jesus").

At this point I have reached full circle in my attempts to reclaim deleted borders. I began with the feelings of being deleted, dismissed, disregarded, and lost. I then came to terms with colonial oppression and my participation in its perpetuation. I moved from being deleted and unseen to being seen and eventually being empowered to see others as myself. The hope is that I continue to discover and incorporate more Tagalog words, concepts, images, story, and song which can be used as part of my theological reflecting and writing rather than simply as part of a reflection. My eventual hope is to engage in a more developed *babayi* theology which engages in an integral ecology viewed from the lens of *kapwa* and the *babaylan* tradition, in conversation with my Western theological training and contemporary issues.

A Final Note—Beginning Practices to Resist Colonialism in Academia

After attending a feminist theological conference in which my Pacific Islander colleague and I lamented and explained to our other colleagues in the room how academic practices can reinforce colonialism, I was inspired to list some beginning practices to resist colonialism in academia. The list includes:

- Build relationships—listen first, in order to learn—this is primary above everything else.
- Be aware whose voice is not being heard. Ensure all voices have a chance to speak, repeatedly.

---

45. Pope Francis, *Laudato Si* (2015); Pope Francis, *Querida Amazonia* (2020).

- Acknowledge that the hermeneutics of theology is still white even if it opens up other non-white voices.
- Provide the space to express theology beyond the written word in "white" terminology.
- Provide spaces for non-white theologians to gather, make sense and articulate their theologies.
- Affirm non-white Western ways of theologizing as equally valid and very much welcomed, appreciated and necessary.
- Ask permission to cite, to research.
- Give recognition where it is due.
- Wherever you are in a place of power, provide opportunities for those not in power to step up.
- Acknowledge that an Anglo-European Westerner is an 'outsider' to *Babayi*, Pasifika and other global theologies.
- Acknowledge that to express *Babayi*, Pasifika and other theologies in academic speak is a translation into white language and culture, not a movement from something inferior to something superior.

Works Cited

Astorga, Christina. *The Beast, the Harlot and the Lamb: Faith Confronts Systemic Evil*. Quezon City, Philippines: New Day, 1999.

———. *Catholic Moral Theology and Social Ethics: A New Method*. Maryknoll, NY: Orbis, 2014.

Australian Human Rights Commission. *Lives on Hold: Refugees and Asylum Seekers in the Legacy Caseload*. 2019. www.humanrights.gov.au./our-work/publications.

Bautista, Marie Lou Frias. "Historical Influences on Gender Preference in the Philippines." *Journal of Comparative Family Studies* 9.1 (1988) 143–53.

Brazal, Agnes M. "Church as Sacrament of Yin-yang Harmony: Toward a More Incisive Participation of Laity and Women in the Church." *Theological Studies* 80.2 (2019) 414–35.

Brazal, Agnes M. and Kochurani Abraham. *Feminist Cyberethics in Asia: Religious Discourses in Human Connectivity*. New York: Palgrave, 2014.

Centre for Babaylan Studies, *What Is Babaylan?* https://www.centerforbabaylanstudies.org/history.

Chouinard, Brea, Crystal Zhou, Stanislau Hrybouski, Esther Kim, Jacqueline Cummine. "A Functional Neuroimaging Case Study of Meares–Irlen Syndrome/Visual Stress (MISViS)." *Brain Topography* 25.3 (2012) 293–307.

Crabtree, Elaine. "Educational Implications of Meares-Irlen Syndrome." *British Journal of School Nursing* 6 (2011) 182–87.

David, E. J. R., and S. Okazaki. "Colonial Mentality: A Review and Recommendation for Filipino American Psychology." *Cultural Diversity and Ethnic Minority Psychology* 12.1 (2006) 1–16.

———. "The Colonial Mentality Scale (CMS) for Filipino Americans: Scale Construction and Psychological Implications." *Journal of Counseling Psychology* 53.2 (2006) 241–52.

David, E. J. R., and Dinghy Kristine B. Sharma. "Losing Kapwa: Colonial Legacies and the Filipino American Family." *Asian American Journal of Psychology* 8 (2017) 43–55.

David, E. J. R., Dinghy Kristine B. Sharma, and Jessica Petalio. "Losing Kapwa: Colonial Legacies and the Filipino American Family." *Asian American Journal of Psychology* 8.1(2017) 43–55.

———. "A Colonial Mentality Model of Depression for Filipino Americans." *Cultural Diversity and Ethnic Minority Psychology* 14.2 (2008) 118–127.

———. "Filipinos, Colonial Mentality, and Mental Health: A psychological exploration of the effects of colonialism among Filipinos." *Psychology Today* (Nov 2, 2017). https://www.psychologytoday.com/au/blog/unseen-and-unheard/201711/filipinos-colonial-mentality-and-mental-health.

———. "Testing the validity of the colonial mentality implicit association test and the interactive effects of covert and overt colonial mentality on filipino american mental health." *Asian American Journal of Psychology* 1.1 (2010) 31–45.

Felipe, Lou Collette S. "The Relationship of Colonial Mentality with Filipina American Experiences with Racism and Sexism." *Asian American Journal of Psychology* 7.1 (2015) 25–30.

Fisher, Rohan, and Jon Altman. "The World's Best Fire Management System Is in Northern Australia and It's Led by Indigenous Land Managers." *The Conversation*, 10 March 2020. https://theconversation.com/the-worlds-best-fire-management-system-is-in-northern-australia-and-its-led-by-indigenous-land-managers-133071.

Helu Thaman, Konai. *Hingano*. Suva, Fiji: Mana Publications, 1987.

Higgins, Isabella. "Indigenous Fire Practices Have Been Used to Quell Bushfires for Thousands of Years, Experts Say." *ABC News*, 9 Jan 2020. https://www.abc.net.au/news/2020-01-09/indigenous-cultural-fire-burning-method-has-benefits-experts-say/11853096.

Francis I, Pope. *Laudato Si* (2015), Encyclical Letter On Care for Our Common Home. http://www.vatican.va/content/francesco/en/encyclicals/documents/papa-francesco_20150524_enciclica-laudato-si.html.

———. *Querida Amazonia* (2020), Post-Synodal Papal Exhortation to the People of God and All Persons of Good Will. http://www.vatican.va/content/francesco/en/apost_exhortations/documents/papa-francesco_esortazione-ap_20200202_querida-amazonia.html.

Laforteza, Elaine Marie Carbonell. *The Somatechnics of Whiteness and Race*. Studies in Migration and Diaspora. London: Taylor & Francis. Kindle Edition, 2016.

Lanaria, Levy Lara. "*Kapwa* in *Pamilya* Rooted in *Loob* of Divine Image: Thoughts from a Filipino Catholic Theologian." *Religions* 6 (2014) 34–43, 63.

Lledo Gomez, Cristina. "Early Motherhood and the Paschal Mystery: A Rahnerian Reflection on the Death and Rebirth Experiences of New Mothers." *The Australasian Catholic Record* 88.2 (2011) 131–50.

———. "From Infants to Mothers: Recovering the Call to the People of God to Become Mother Church in *Lumen Gentium*." *Ecclesiology* 11.1 (2015) 32–62.

Lledo Gomez, Cristina. *The Church as Woman and Mother: Historical and Theological Foundations*. New Jersey: Paulist, 2018.

Loughrey, Glen. "Lament and Hope on Australia Day." *Red Shoes Walking*. https://www.redshoeswalking.net/lament-and-hope-on-australia-day/.

Mendoza, S. Lily. "Back from the Crocodile's Belly: Christian Formation Meets Indigenous Resurrection." *HTS Teologiese / Theological Studies* 73.3 (2017) 1–8. a4660.https://doi.org/10.4102/hts.v73i3.4660.

Marcelino, Elizabeth Protacio. "Towards Understanding the Psychology of the Filipino." *Women & Therapy* 9 (Oct 2008) 105–28.

Nikolakis, William, Emma Roberts, Ngaio Hotte, and Russell Myers Ross. "Goal Setting and Indigenous Fire Management: A Holistic Perspective." *International Journal of Wildland Fire* 29.11 (2020) 974–82.

Strobel, Leny Mendoza et al. *Babaylan: Filipinos and the Call to the Indigenous*. Santa Rosa, CA: Center for Babaylan Studies, 2010.

Suico, Alfonso P., Jr. "In Search of the *Babayi*: A Quest for a Distinct Filipina Theoethics." *Journal of Asian Orientations in Theology* 1.2 (2019) 199–218.

Thaman, Konai Helu. "Our Way." In *Hingano: Selected Poems 1966–1986*, 40. Suva, Fiji: Mana, 1987.

Tuazon, Victor E., Edith Gonzalez, Daniel Gutierrez, and Lotes Nelson. "Colonial Mentality and Mental Health Help-Seeking of Filipino Americans." *Journal of Counselling and Development* 97 (October 2019): 352–363.

Tunufa'i, Laumua. "Pacific research: Rethinking the Talanoa 'methodology'." *New Zealand Sociology* 31.7 (2016) 227–39.

Uccula, Arcangelo, Mauro Enna and Claudio Mulatti. "Colors, Colored Overlays, and Reading Skills." *Frontiers in Psychology* 5.833 (2014) 1–4.

Utsey, Shawn O., Jasmine A. Abrams, Annabella Opare-Henaku, Mark A. Bolden, Otis Williams. "Assessing the Psychological Consequences of Internalized Colonialism on the Psychological Well-Being of Young Adults in Ghana." *Journal of Black Psychology* 41 (2015) 195–220.

9

Second-generation Migrant Bodies

Site of Ideological Reproduction and Implications for the Body of Christ

Joy J. Han

THE USE OF "SECOND-GENERATION" (second-gen) to denote the children of those who migrate from the homeland as adults is common across migrant communities but is especially popular in the contemporary Korean diaspora. This acceptance of the term is most documented in the United States for the Korean diaspora's long history and large size there, and it is also found in my context, Australia, including in the Uniting Church in Australia (UCA).

Whereas a few of the UCA's *national conferences* (national meetings among UCA members who identify with a particular cultural group) have developed vibrant second-gen chapters organized across regional councils, the Korean national conference (despite the significant numbers it represents across the UCA) has no formal second-generation organization on any inter-regional scale. The purported failure of second-generation Korean migrants to be consolidated in a worshipping community is named as a persistent point of anxiety in the Korean migrant church. This state of affairs dovetails with the trope of the "silent exodus" of second-generation Koreans, about which I say more later.

This essay problematizes the very categorization of second-generation Christians as the source of such anxieties. Before causing anyone any anxiety, they are real people in real bodies who narrate their identities. This essay argues that, especially for diasporic identities born outside the homeland who find themselves perpetually reterritorialized, adequate agency ought to be afforded to individuals and communities as they develop narratives for the sake of "meaningful personal identity."[1] As a result, the entrenchment of terminology and their meanings within a community may serve people an oppressive context for their identity formation.

Although, as mentioned above, there is no visible organization of specifically Korean second-generation identities beyond a local scale in the UCA, an increasingly prominent banner that is intended to include Korean and other second-generation migrant identities in the UCA is that of "NextGen." But how different is this term from "second-gen," and even if it is different, might its function as an identifier still be subject to some of the concerns and criticisms that this essay raises regarding the term "second-gen"?

This essay examines the history and the contemporary state of affairs for the usage of the term "second-generation Korean American" as an example of how "second-generation" is as ideologically value laden as it can also present opportunities to resist and reform both ideologies and communities. In particular, this essay considers the ideological function of settler colonialism and heteropatriarchy in the evolution of the meaning of "second-generation," and recommends that this term be reimagined particularly in the context of Christian community.

Three-generations Analysis

The work of three twentieth-century US researchers constitutes the most oft-credited foundation for contemporary three-generations analyses of migrant cohorts and the associated terminology.[2] Marcus Lee Hansen, Oscar Handlin, and Will Herberg studied the nineteenth- and early twentieth-century migration of European nationals to the US. A couple of general observations about their work will enable comparison later with more recent analyses that use the same terminology in relation to Korean Americans. First, their work sought to analyze migrant cohorts' acculturation in relatively broad terms. Their inquiry was not limited to any one "generation" (howsoever defined) of a given migrant cohort, but instead it was their exploratory analysis of social

1. Pak, *Korean American Women*, 42.
2. Warner, "Ethnicity, Race, and Religion," 433.

cohorts distinguished broadly by ethnicity that produced their observations about intergenerational differences and interdependencies in acculturation. Second, as much as they themselves and their research shared similarities in context, it is possible to situate their findings within that context and thence critically analyze those findings. In particular, it is possible to identify a number of ideological assumptions that contribute to the context within which their conclusions can make sense.

Positivist Methodology

In an essay published in 1938, Hansen wrote that "what the son wishes to forget the grandson wishes to remember."[3] Time has since honored this statement with the title "Hansen's Law": a shorthand statement of the differing postures embodied by an immigrant's children and grandchildren towards the culture of the immigrant's sending country. But the promotion of this statement to axiomatic status detracts from the fact that Hansen was seeking to apply a general principle of historical study to his survey of European migration to the US around his own time. True to the positivism that was foundational to modern social science and particularly influential for how American sociology developed in the 1930s,[4] Hansen took as dogma the "possib[ility] for the present to know something about the future,"[5] thanks to the operation of certain discoverable "laws of history." One such law was what he called "the principle of third generation interest."[6] When Hansen illustrated this principle with what is now called Hansen's Law, he was not limiting the application of the principle to migrant generations. Instead, he was appealing to a general observation about how the historical legacy of events can outlive those events' primary historiography and so eventually prompt secondary historiography. For Hansen, this continuing historiography and collective memory are mutually sustaining, making possible the historical study not only of immigration events but of any historical event.

When read in methodological context, Hansen's Law, even when applied narrowly to the historical study of immigration, is primarily an assertion about the predictability and observability of the intergenerational shape of cultural resilience. The statement's provision of a typology of first-, second- and third-generation migrants' acculturation is to be taken stock of

3. Hansen, *The Problem of the Third Generation Immigrant*, 9.
4. Abercrombie, Hill, and Turner, "Positivism," 299.
5. Hansen, *The Problem of the Third Generation Immigrant*, 9.
6. Hansen, *The Problem of the Third Generation Immigrant*, 9.

secondarily. That was the approach taken by Will Herberg and Oscar Handlin, who were both born in Hansen's lifetime and also researched European migration to the US. For example, Handlin's characterization of the second-generation migrant's acculturation differs marginally from Hansen's,[7] while his observations about the fact and overall shape of intergenerational cultural resilience among migrant cohorts are consistent with Hansen's. Meanwhile Herberg, too, focused not on the acculturation profiles of the generations but examined the intersection between ethnic identity and religion in the acculturation process.[8] Even for Hansen, a motivating concern was to expand the scope of the study of immigrant acculturation beyond what he believed had been too narrow a focus on the role of religion alone.[9]

Ideological Context

The originating context of modern three-generations analyses consists, however, in more than just the methodology and historical locale in which Hansen, Herberg and Handlin worked. That context also entails various ideological assumptions that in turn imbue three-generations analyses and associated terminology. For example, and most obviously, Hansen's formulation "what the son wishes to forget the grandson wishes to remember" linguistically reflects patriarchal norms. The following paragraphs critically appraise just a few of the ideological assumptions of not just Hansen's Law but three-generations analyses in general. These assumptions will later be revisited as part of the ideological inheritance of contemporary three-generations analyses of Korean Americans.

Settler Colonialism

As already pointed out, modern three-generations analysis was developed in the US. The characterization of that time and place as opposed to one of First Nations signifies the ongoing operation of settler colonization as the fundamental context for modern three-generations analyses. The basic

---

7. Handlin, *The Uprooted*, 226.

8. Herberg, *Protestant, Catholic, Jew*, 27–28; Herberg, "The Integration of the Jew into America's Three-Religion Society," 28.

9. Hansen, *The Problem of the Third Generation Immigrant*, 15.

function of settler colonization, as Patrick Wolfe reminds us, is violent[10] dispossession: invasion in perpetuity.[11]

In turn, the very characterization of European nationals who arrived in the US with the permission of the originating settler community specifically as "migrants" (rather than as additional invaders) signifies its own complicity with the dispossession of First Nations. Conversely, the refusal to describe the originating settler community as "migrants" reflects the ideological impetus to legitimate the violently enforced dominance and normative status of that community's invading institutions and culture.

As a result, the only kind of acculturation that is of any interest to researchers in the given context is that into the dominant culture of the earliest settler colonizers. Alternatively, the very conceptualization of so-called migrants' acculturation as a specific phenomenon may be critiqued as a ruse for what is just another ordinary process in settler colonization's fundamental project of self-expansion and self-legitimation. Either which way, this process has as both its condition and outcome the continued dispossession of First Nations.

This ideological glossing of so-called migrants' complicity in the violence of dispossession is girded by a willful ignorance of any settler colonial structures that may be found in sending countries. As Gayatri Chakravorty Spivak reflects personally in an interview, one's well-meaning or relatively marginal status in one locale does not discount one's membership of or complicity with a dominant or otherwise violent structure in another.[12] This means that the substitution of inquiry into settler colonialism in sending countries with a focus on incoming minority groups' "acculturation" in the US serves to legitimate settler colonization not just in the US but in other parts of the world as well.

Finally, as Wolfe argues, the basic currency of settler colonialism is race.[13] Nation-based ethnicity and its reconstruction (at least in part) as a function of race in the categorization of migrant groups first by race and then by ethnicity signifies that the most elementary identification of migrant groups is indeed a function of settler colonialism.

10. Ecocide, increasingly visible in the face of anthropogenic climate change, is part and parcel of settler colonialism's attempted elimination of first nations and their relationship to (and scientific knowledge of) their lands and waters; and is just one among many of the violences that invasion entails.

11. "Settler colonies were (are) premised on the elimination of native societies"; Wolfe, *Settler Colonialism and the Transformation of Anthropology*, 2.

12. Gayatri Chakravorty Spivak, interview by Steve Paulson, 26 July 2016, 2016.

13. Wolfe, *Traces of History*, 5.

Heteropatriarchy

The structure of settler colonialism corresponds to that of rape in the context of heteropatriarchy. A couple of observations are offered here as additional evidence of how Hansen's Law and associated research engages heteropatriarchy uncritically and so perpetuates it. Handlin's treatment of how intergenerational acculturation played out in attitudes to marriage is formulated under the legal as well as cultural assumptions that marriage was available only to cis-gendered and heterosexual male–female couples. Furthermore, marriage was normally expected to be endogenous and produce biological children.[14] Similarly in Herberg's examination of acculturation the diversity of gender and how major religious institutions and traditions have usually sought to delimit and control sex/gender through heteropatriarchy is not of interest, even as he argues that America is a "three-religion country" comprising Protestants, Catholics, and Jews.[15]

Korean American Diaspora

The typology of the three generations as suggested by Hansen's Law has gained such currency among ethnic Koreans in America and beyond that in the 1980s Korean Americans developed the term "1.5 generation" to describe people born in Korea who migrate as child dependents of their parents.[16] This, being just one example of the popularization of three-generations terminology in the Korean diaspora, suggests people's successful appropriation of that terminology for themselves. It seems as though the language of "three generations" has proved useful for Korean migrant communities in their pursuit of meaningfully articulated personal identity. Since, however, this essay is concerned with the adequacy of the agency of certain bodies and their identity formation, the task at hand is to critically examine specific examples of how Hansen's Law has been appropriated in relation to Korean American second-generation Christians. Of particular interest is to identify how the ideological assumptions that shaped the development of modern three-generations analyses may have been appropriated together with the terms, even while the terms undergo recontextualization.

---

14. Handlin, *The Uprooted*, 228.
15. Herberg, "The Integration of the Jew into America's Three-Religion Society," 28.
16. Hurh, "The 1.5 Generation."

Emergence of three-generations typology

The methodological influence of positivist empiricism, "the justifying foundation of advanced capitalist neocolonialism,"[17] is evident in the contemporary usage of three-generations terminology. The term "1.5 generation" highlights the methodological shift that characterizes contemporary scholarly research into Korean Americans. Instead of the earlier more macroscopic approach that examined the acculturation of multiple generations over time, the first, second and third generations of Korean Americans signify sociological types. The characteristics of each generation have been so narrowly canonized that "1.5 generation" was coined, and generational identifications to two decimal points are commonly heard in the community.[18]

The differing acculturating traits that Hansen and his contemporaries observed from generation to generation have been pinned to particular types of bodies that are categorized according to various biological criteria. In an extreme turn of positivist empiricism, the terminology that was intended to illustrate the acculturation of an ethnic group has become shorthand for certain bodies that are predicted and in fact empirically and culturally expected to exhibit various traits. Sociologists routinely operationalize popular definitions of "the second generation" into criteria for identifying human subjects the study of whom will reveal more and more facts about second-generation Korean Americans. But this research approach can essentialize its subjects, as the following examples demonstrate.

"Silent Exodus": Second-generation Koreans Who Quietly Leave the Immigrant Church

The notion of the "silent exodus"[19] of second-generation Korean Americans from ethnic Korean migrant church communities is an example of how three-generations terminology now serves the purposes of reductionist typology: "Korean religious leaders, including second-generation Korean Americans, have used the term "silent exodus" to predict or indicate the drastic drop in second-generation Korean American adults' participation in ethnic churches."[20]

---

17. Spivak, "Can the Subaltern Speak?," 275.

18. Anecdotally speaking, an individual with biological parents who identify as 1.5- and second-generation respectively may classify herself as "1.75 generation."

19. A related characterisation is that of second-generation Korean Americans as "the lost generation." Kang and Hackman, "Toward a Broader Role in Mission," 73.

20. Min and Kim, "Intergenerational Transmission of Religion and Culture," 267.

The identification of withdrawal from cultural tradition with "the second generation" is consistent with Hansen's observation of a relatively early decline in a given social cohort's interest in its own origins. But in fact, the prevailing method hypothesizes that this behavior is to be exhibited by certain biologically defined bodies that are classified from the outset as "second-generation Korean Americans." The conclusion comes not from a longitudinal study of a multi-generation cohort but is sought among a subcohort and expected to present as a persistent characteristic. The silent exodus is anecdotally a meaningful observation, but the attempt to validate it by examining a somehow delimited group called "the second generation" in isolation amounts to little more than a self-fulfilling prophecy, and an as-yet dubious one at that: "to date, no concrete evidence has been provided that shows drastic declines in ethnic church participation among 1.5- and second-generation Korean Americans."[21]

Second-generation Korean Americans' Missionary Capacity?

More spurious than the characterization of the silent exodus as a collective second-generation Korean American trait is the aggrandizement of second-generation Korean Americans and how they organize themselves and others in Christian community. A colorful example follows: "The potential for the future of the Korean American church lies with the [second generation], which is exploring its symbolic ethnicity under the influence of the Korean American church while relating as an ethnic "block" to both the American and the Korean cultures."[22]

Kang and Hackman's insistence on an untapped mission to Asia among second-generation Korean Americans is premised on an essentialization of some second-generation Korean identity. Even more measured and multipart claims remain problematic. For example, the observation that second-generation Korean American Christians, both individually and collectively, responsively moderate their racial and ethnic identity depending on social context[23] is premised on an operational definition of "second-generation Korean American Christian" that is developed without reference to the diversity of people's exercise of their agency in identity formation.

21. Min and Kim, "Intergenerational Transmission of Religion and Culture," 267.
22. Kang and Hackman, "Toward a Broader Role in Mission," 73.
23. Kim, "Shifting Boundaries within Second-Generation Korean American Churches," 115–16.

"Second-generation Korean American" as Catachresis

What the above tropes have in common and what they share with the very usage of the term "second-generation Korean American" both colloquially and in scholarship today is a catachresis or an "abuse of a figurative move."[24] The figurative move in question is Hansen's Law. The abuse thereof is that the term "second-generation" no longer serves to demarcate an overall phase or movement of a community that may be found to exhibit various distinctive characteristics, but instead it denotes particular types of behavior in a subset of bodies. In the context of the Korean American community, the second generation is not a figurative generation as in Hansen's Law but an actual son who wishes *a priori* to forget.

Theological Implications

This catachresis facilitates the essentialization of "the second generation" into predefined types of bodies and their behaviors. The following paragraphs critically examine how the ideologies and the history of both settler colonialism and heteropatriarchy that shaped Hansen's Law have been recontextualized in the Korean American diaspora. Given the violence of those structures, this serves as a problematization of the phrase "second-generation Korean American." Furthermore, this discussion points theologically to how the joining of that phrase with Christian identity may entrench and even attempt to gloss certain violence in the Body of Christ.

Settler Colonialisms Again

In the same way that the term and the entire concept of "the United States" can be read for its history of settler colonialism, the term "Korean"—not least as found within the phrase "second-generation Korean American"—can also be read for its colonially and neocolonially imbued meaning. Certainly, history provides witness to enduring Korean self-determination through a distinctive linguistic and cultural tradition tied to the Korean peninsula. But history also bears witness to numerous foreign imperial attempts on Koreans' distinct identity. The Japanese annexation of Joseon, the last Korean dynasty, from 1910 until Japan's defeat in World War II involved the violent reconfiguration of Korean cultural identity. The Japanese colonial agenda

---

24. Spivak, *A Critique of Postcolonial Reason*, 14.

continues to express itself in contemporary negotiation of Koreanness, even three-quarters of a century after Hiroshima and Nagasaki.

The modern meaning of "Korean," influenced by Japanese colonial government propaganda and European colonial understandings of race, is heavily ethnicized and in turn racialized in that it features familism, an overtly heteronormative biological understanding of ethnicity that appeals to blood-relatedness.[25] The contemporary nationalism that conflates national identity with a biological conceptualization of ethnicity is traced to the Japanese colonial policy of *naisen ittai* that sought to assimilate Koreans into Japanese culture by constructing a biohistory in which Koreans and Japanese shared a common ancestry.[26]

Sharon Kim observes that the nature of the persistent racialization experienced by non-white bodies in the US means that in some cases, "ethnic boundaries at second-generation Korean American churches have been stretched to include other Asian American groups."[27] On the one hand, this is accompanied by the *prima facie* positive report that "[s]econd-generation churches provide the institutional spaces where Asian Americans, bound by shared values, life orientations, and experiences, can congregate together under a common religious identity,"[28] but Kim also notes that the diversification of otherwise Korean American leadership that followed and facilitated the emergence of pan-Asian congregations has come at the cost of some suppression of Koreanness. This indicates that what presents itself as a certain ecumenism spearheaded by second-generation Korean American Christians is complicit with settler colonialism. In the structure of settler colonialism, expressions of cultural diversity are not granted self-determination but are ultimately subjected to the rule of political and cultural institutions established in the image of the ruling invaders.

What is under scrutiny here is not so much second-generation Korean American churches' complicity with the American instance of settler colonialism. After all, the pervasive nature of settler colonialism means complicity is never far away. Rather, the call is to a greater awareness and confession of that complicity. Without our ongoing sociologically reflexive negotiation of a term such as "second-generation Korean American," the trace of the violent dispossession of certain people groups that is found

25. Han, "The Archaeology of the Ethnically Homogeneous Nation-State and Multiculturalism in Korea," 23.

26. Shin, *Ethnic Nationalism in Korea*, 54.

27. Kim, "Shifting Boundaries within Second-Generation Korean American Churches," 15.

28. Kim, "Shifting Boundaries within Second-Generation Korean American Churches," 15.

across "Korean" and "American" histories remains unchecked. It will not be enough to give unqualified thanks for the vibrancy or resilience of a second-generation Korean American Christian community or for its leadership of a pan-Asian congregation as an end in itself, because it must be recognized that either such type of church exists in relation to violently dispossessed First Nations and others. Indeed, no Christian community can be content to predefine or consolidate a single ethnic or racial identity for itself because the very nature of Christian community is its "sent-ness" to those beyond itself as it is called to participate in *missio Dei*.

Ethnobiological Essentialism

The popularization of "second-generation Korean American" as a category of bodies that gets populated among immigrants entails a number of normative values. These values include reproductive heteronormativity; construction of Korean identity that services ethnic nationalism and racism; marginalization of exogenous marriage; and marginalization of adoptive identities, even despite Korea's vast postwar adoptee population. Those are some of the structures through which second-generation Korean American identity implicates sex/gender and gender relations.

As many churches (not least in the settler colonized West) continue to search for and formulate their responses to sexual violence, gender fluidity and the diversity of sexualities, the "second-generation Korean American" identity—at least as it is typically defined in ethnobiological terms—quickly becomes exclusive and privileged by largely heteropatriarchal norms. Scripture witnesses to communities that were able to renegotiate attitudes towards exogenous marriage as they came to terms with their historical circumstances. We too, then, receive and are invited into a tradition in which ethnic identity can be dynamic, ranging from narrow exclusivity to postures of radical welcome. Once again, the complicity might be unavoidable: in this case, the complicity of one's identification as second-generation Korean American with heteropatriarchal norms and structures. The call therefore is to recognize the relevant norms and be prepared to interrogate them and seek justice for those of us who may experience marginalization or other violence as a result of such norms.

Concluding Remarks

The two broad areas of concern raised about the notion of the "second-generation Korean American" are about methodological form and ideological content. Both areas of concern ultimately relate to ideology. Both the positivist empiricist methodology enabling the essentialization of "second-generation" identities and the ideological traces of settler colonialism and heteropatriarchy have been traced to Hansen's Law. The methodological shift from Hansen's use of "second-generation" as sub-cohort to the contemporary use of "second-generation" as a social type, I have described as catachresis or category mistake. But it ought to be noted here that that methodological shift represents an intensification rather than an insertion of ideology—namely the ideology of positivist empiricism, which indeed was foundational for Hansen and other scholars of his time. Similarly, in the contemporary concept of "second-generation Korean American" we see the intersection of Japanese and American settler colonialisms and associated heteropatriarchy, all functioning to inscribe traces of historical violence in the term "second-generation Korean American."

As much as this critique examines the function of ideology, the resulting caution is not limited to the territory of America but is applicable to any locale in which real people and real bodies are engaged in identity formation within the structural contexts of settler colonialism and heteropatriarchy. In the UCA, with its codified commitment to radical reconciliation between First Peoples and second peoples in Australia and its proactive tradition of seeking for a diversity of identities, the growing use of the term "NextGen" alongside but also as an alternative to "second-generation" presents an opportunity to articulate anew a vision of the Body of Christ for the UCA's local context. Inasmuch as the biblical vision emphasizes the interdependency of different members, the imagining of any given "generation" need not demarcate certain bodies without due regard for their self-determination, much less prescribe any of their behaviors. Instead, language can be harnessed to critically interrogate and resist the ideologies that entrench generational, ethnic, racial, sex/gendered and other borders between different members of the Body of Christ. Immanuel's own movement that loosens and crosses borders calls us to encounter and join with one another not for the sake of uniformity but fully expressing our created diversity and seeking unity through, among other things, reflexive ecumenical dialogue and witness to our common experience of the mission of God.

Works Cited

Abercrombie, Nicholas, ed. *The Penguin Dictionary of Sociology*. 5th ed. New York: Penguin, 2006.

Han, Kyung-Koo. "The Archaeology of the Ethnically Homogeneous Nation-State and Multiculturalism in Korea." [In English] *Korea Journal* 47.4 (2007) 8–31.

Handlin, Oscar. *The Uprooted: The Epic Story of the Great Migrations That Made the American People*. 2nd ed. Philadelphia: University of Pennsylvania Press, 2001.
Hansen, Marcus Lee. *The Problem of the Third Generation Immigrant*. Rock Island, IL: Augustana Historical Society, 1938. Microform.
Herberg, Will. "The Integration of the Jew into America's Three-Religion Society." *Journal of Church and State* 5.1 (1963) 27–40.
———. *Protestant, Catholic, Jew: An Essay in American Religious Sociology*. Doubleday Anchor Book A195. New ed. Garden City, NY: Anchor, 1960.
Hurh, Won Moo. "The 1.5 Generation: A Cornerstone of the Korean American Ethnic Community." In *The Emerging Generation of Korean-Americans*, edited by Ho-Youn Kwon and Shin Kim, 47–49. North Park College: Kyung Hee University Press, 1993.
Kang, S. Steve, and Megan A. Hackman. "Toward a Broader Role in Mission: How Korean Americans' Struggle for Identity Can Lead to a Renewed Vision for Mission." *International Bulletin of Missionary Research* 36.2 (2012) 72–76.
Kim, Sharon. "Shifting Boundaries within Second-Generation Korean American Churches." *Sociology of Religion* 71.1 (2010) 98–122.
Min, Pyong Gap, and Dae Young Kim. "Intergenerational Transmission of Religion and Culture: Korean Protestants in the U.S." *Sociology of Religion* 66.3 (2005) 263–82.
Pak, Jenny Hyun Chung. *Korean American Women: Stories of Acculturation and Changing Selves*. Studies in Asian Americans. New York: Routledge, 2006.
Shin, Gi-Wook. *Ethnic Nationalism in Korea: Genealogy, Politics, and Legacy*. Studies of the Walter H Shorenstein Asia-Pacific Research Center. Stanford: Stanford University Press, 2006.
Spivak, Gayatri Chakravorty. "Can the Subaltern Speak?" In *Marxism and the Interpretation of Culture*, edited by Cary Nelson and Lawrence Grossberg, 271–313. Urbana: University of Illinois Press, 1988.
———. "Critical Intimacy: An Interview with Gayatri Chakravorty Spivak." By Steve Paulson. *To the Best of Our Knowledge* (26 July 2016).
———. *A Critique of Postcolonial Reason: Toward a History of the Vanishing Present*. Cambridge: Harvard University Press, 1999.
Warner, R. Stephen. "Ethnicity, Race, and Religion Beyond Protestant, Catholic, and Jewish Whites." In *The Oxford Handbook of American Immigration and Ethnicity*, edited by Ronald H. Bayor, 430–51. New York: Oxford University Press, 2016.
Wolfe, Patrick. *Settler Colonialism and the Transformation of Anthropology: The Politics and Poetics of an Ethnographic Event*. Writing Past Colonialism. London: Bloomsbury, 1998.
———. *Traces of History: Elementary Structures of Race*. London: Verso, 2016.

Part Three

Troubling Voices

10

This Body

Valentina Satvedi

THIS VERSE SPEAKS OF that which binds me: I was born as an Asian woman into the borders of gender, religion, family, culture, and tradition. I have walked and crossed borders in search of freedom from that which binds, and find the constant need to unbind and permeate, in order to find release, to "chrysalis" into being (see Figure 10.3). Restrictive in nature, borders can be dismantled and rendered permeable, yet there is an ongoing building of borders that are fixed, permanent and non-permeable (see Figure 10.1).

As a migrant, immigrant and settler with a body that was birthed in and through borders, I give voice to the internalizations and socializations that continue to affect the ongoing dismantling of my borders (see Figure 10.2). I bring to this the lens of an individual influenced by colonialism, raised in a patriarchal society, racialized on an ongoing basis. I continue to experience the borders of this world and am in an ongoing process of unlearning, dismantling and uncaging the self.

Figure 10.1: these bodies . . . these temples
Photo courtesy of Ian Ferguson

This body
a temple
in my mother's body,
a body in God
the Divine within my body
    for me
the Divine without this body
    for some.

This body
    bound in the confines of the sacred
        the permeable sacred
        the nourishing sacred
this body
    ready to push
    and being pushed out
    arrives into another world

    unbound
        tether severed
release . . .
oh freedom!

This body
a temple
perceived freedom
    un-lasting freedom
this body
    bothered
    by culture
this body
    bound
    by tradition
        sit like this
        stand like that
        wear this
        eat this
        walk this way
        speak when permitted
        do not resist when I lust
the Divine within my body
    for me
the Divine without this body
    for many.

Figure 10.2: time to be bound
Photo courtesy of Ian Ferguson

This body
a temple
bound
   within the confines of the unsacred
bound
   within impermeable traditions
bound
   within life denying norms.

This body
a temple
perceived freedom short lived
   assimilation
   stipulation
   classification
   the secular
   the religious.

This body
a temple
bound
    by the cage of oppression[1]
bound
    by the intersections of the world
    into which it took birth.

This body
a temple
always in God
the Divine always in this body
yet this body considered as 'the other'
    an unwelcome color
    an unwelcome gender
    an unwelcome age
    an unwelcome other
        at the intersections
        constructed of this world
        into which it escaped for freedom
bound now ...
oh, captivity!

---

1. In her 1983 collection of feminist essays *The Politics of Reality: Essays in Feminist Theory* (Crossing Press), Marilyn Frye speaks of oppression being an interconnected system of forces and perimeters which collectively is perceived as a cage.

Figure 10.3: presenting the bound sacred
Photo courtesy: Ian Ferguson

This body
a temple
    conversing with the Divine within
    sacred acknowledgement
    to push once again
begin the push
    the pushing begins
    resistance
    resistance
    resistance
push . . .
time to push in a new way
    unlearn the old
    relearn anew
    unleash the self
        the sacred
sever the tethers
unravel the cage.

This body
a temple
   the cage is strong
   still holding
this sacred body
   still learning
   new ways of being
   unraveling the self
   unraveling the tethers
   suddenly
   the air turns red and grey
   breathing labored
   the body seeking shelter
   the air then clear and potent
   the body sheltering again
   this is a self binding
   a masking
   a preservation . . .
   awaiting once again
   for the unmasking
   for the unraveling
awaiting freedom!

This body
   ready to push again
      to push out the self
         to arrive into a new world
            another world
               perhaps a different world.
This body
   ready to push again
      to be unshackled
      to severe the tether
release . . .
oh freedom!

11

Kalanga

(sh)Outing Bodily Abuse in the Bible, Society, and Churches

Nāsili Vakaʻuta

THIS ESSAY SPOTLIGHTS ONE of the key global realities of our time: *bodily abuse*.[1] The term "bodily abuse" is herein used in a broad sense to include any treatment of a person's body (sexual or otherwise) with harmful intention *and* without that person's consent. It includes, but not limited to, sexual abuse; I however hover over sexual abuse in this essay because this is a reality that we often overlook.[2] Open conversations about critical issues like this is avoided in many venues (cultural and religious in particular) because silence is a safe and comfortable option. But in many cases, silence is perilous and life-denying.

This essay is a *kalanga*[3]: it *speaks up, speaks out* and *(sh)outs loudly in public* against the cultures that perpetuate and justify bodily abuse and the silence on, and silencing of, response to bodily abuse. It sets forth a challenge

---

1. I use the term "bodily abuse" hereinafter instead of "sexual abuse" or "sexual violence" in order to align this essay with the volume title, *Bordered Bodies, Bothered Voices*.

2. See also Havea and Havea, "Sex: Suicide, Shame, Signals."

3. A Tongan word for "shouting," "crying out" aloud in public. It carries a sense of urgency with the intention to protest, resist, expose, attract attention, and to interrupt.

to break the silence on bodily abuse and invites in-depth *kōrero* (*talanoa*, conversation), because it is inexcusable to hide behind culture, church, and scriptures.[4] By the same token, it is irresponsible to ignore cases of bodily violence that *occurred, covered up, validated* and *supported* within the so-called sacred spaces of religion (in this case, church).[5]

Surfing the #MeToo Waves

This essay rides upon the waves of the global #MeToo movement.[6] Born out of resistance against sexual violence with a vision of justice and healing, #MeToo began in 2006 as a grassroot movement founded by Tarana Burke, a black woman and victim of sexual violence. She sets the movement in motion to help survivors of sexual violence (particularly young women of color from low-income communities) find *pathways to healing*. Using the idea of *empowerment through empathy* the movement was created to ensure survivors know they are not alone in their journey.[7] Since October 2017, the #MeToo movement managed to build a community of survivors from all walks of life, and they have brought the conversations about, and resistance against, bodily abuse/sexual violence into the mainstream.

Those at the forefront of the movement (most of them victims of sexual violence) decided to *kalanga* (speak out) against their abusers, most of whom have been powerful men (and a few women) from different sectors of society including the church. For that reason, *Time Magazine* called these courageous individuals—"The Silence Breakers," and honored them collectively as *Time Magazine*'s 2017 Person of the Year.[8] Since then, this movement rippled far and wide through social media and became a global phenomenon.

---

4. This is a revised version of a paper delivered at the 2018 Annual Conference of the Methodist Church of New Zealand with the title: "#MeToo: Troubling Sexual Abuse in Scriptures." I am indebted to the editor, Jione Havea, for his comments on the penultimate manuscript.

5. Those who have watched the movie *Spotlight*, and the Netflix docuseries *The Keepers*, would know what I am talking about here. Both documented the extent to which religion and its agencies go to cover up their corrupt practices.

6. A lot have been written on the movement and its impact. The following are examples: Fileborn and Loney-Howes, *#MeToo and the Politics of Social Change*; Boyle, *#MeToo, Weinstein and Feminism*; Palmer et al., "#MeToo for Whom?"; Bartlett, Clark, and Cover, *Flirting in the Era of #MeToo: Negotiating Intimacy*. See also Philipose and Kesavan, "The #MeToo Movement."

7. Suk et al., "#MeToo, Networked Acknowledgment, and Connective Action."

8. Available online: https://time.com/time-person-of-the-year-2017-silence-breakers/.

The #MeToo movement helps to de-stigmatize survivors by highlighting the breadth and impact bodily abuse has had on thousands of women and men alike. It assisted those who need to find entry points to healing, and thus aid the fight to end bodily abuse worldwide. The #MeToo movement uplifts radical community healing as a social justice struggle, and it is committed to disrupting all systems that allow sexual violence to flourish.[9]

The key phrase here is "disrupting systems," because any act of bodily abuse is not an isolated incident; it is symptomatic of a violent-supportive system that denies victims their humanity. Any attempt to end such violence requires a collective effort to dismantle/disrupt (in words and actions) the system that allows it. There is a name for one of the systems that supports bodily abuse/sexual violence: patriarchy.[10]

(sh)Outing Patriarchy

To end bodily violence and create a life-affirming pathway for victims, patriarchy has to be confronted and dismantled.[11]

Patriarchy literally means "the rule of the father." In a Weberian sense, patriarchy can be defined as "a system of government in which men ruled societies through their position as heads of households."[12] From a feminist standpoint, patriarchy is "a system of social structures and practices in which men dominate, oppress, and exploit women."[13] The use of the term "social structure," according to bell hooks, implies a rejection of biological determinism, and the notion that every individual man is in a dominant position and every woman in a subordinate one.

Another interesting take on patriarchy comes again from bell hooks. She defines patriarchy as "[a] political-social system that insists that males are inherently dominating, superior to everything and everyone deemed weak, especially females, and endowed with the right to dominate and rule over the weak and to maintain that dominance through various forms of psychological terrorism and violence."[14]

---

9. For more information, visit https://metoomvmt.org/.

10. See hooks, "Understanding Patriarchy"; Hunnicutt, "Varieties of Patriarchy and Violence Against Women"; Walby, *Theorizing Patriarchy*.

11. The need to dismantle patriarchy is not new, but it requires a renewed effort to bring it to pass. See Ademiluka, "Patriarchy and Women Abuse"; Brown, "The End of the Story: Patriarchy"; Hill and Allen, "'Smash the Patriarchy.'"

12. Walby, *Theorizing Patriarchy*, 19.

13. Walby, *Theorizing Patriarchy*, 20.

14. hooks, "Understanding Patriarchy," 1.

She also coins the phrase "imperialist white-supremacist capitalist patriarchy"[15] to describe the interlocking political systems that are the foundation of American politics and society. Here, patriarchy is theorized alongside colonialism, racism, and capitalism. As such, patriarchy becomes not only the oldest system of domination/oppression known to, and practiced by, humanity, but also "the single most life-threatening social disease assaulting the male body and spirit."[16] That is, in the process of trying to dominate/oppress others, we are violently assaulting ourselves as well. Patriarchy in this sense is *a self-destructive system*—it is not good for anybody. Such a system needs dismantling.

Patriarchy has several manifestations.[17] One is what some radical feminists call *rape culture*.[18] Rape culture refers to a setting in which rape is pervasive and normalized due to societal attitudes about gender and sexuality. Behaviors commonly associated with rape culture include victim blaming, slut-shaming, sexual objectification, trivializing rape, denial of widespread rape, refusing to acknowledge the harm caused by some forms of bodily abuse or some combination of these.

Another equally disturbing manifestation of patriarchy is *toxic masculinity*. This refers to society's expectations of how a traditional male should behave. Ideas related to toxic masculinity have been normalized in society, which include comments like, "be a man," "that's girly," and "man up."[19] It is important to underline that toxic masculinity relates to the cultural perspective given to masculinity, not the biological traits of (the male) gender.[20] It is founded upon societal norms that frame cisgender men as the domineering gender, creating harmful stereotypes that incite violence and sexism across cultures. In addition, toxic masculinity disregards non-conforming genders, and imposes gender binarism (that is, the belief that only two genders exist), which allows the ongoing problem of homo-/bi-/trans-phobia in many societies, including Aotearoa New Zealand and many island nations in Oceania.

Toxic masculinity enforces the societal ideology that males must attain control in relationships, the household, and in public places (such as the church, business, and education sectors). This attitude promotes aversion

15. hooks, "Understanding Patriarchy," 1.

16. hooks, "Understanding Patriarchy," 1.

17. See Hunnicutt, "Varieties of Patriarchy and Violence Against Women," 553-573.

18. For further reading on the subject vis-a-vis the Bible, the volume from the Shiloh Project is highly recommended: Blyth, Colgan, and Edwards. *Rape Culture, Gender Violence & Religion.*

19. "Feminism 101: What Is Toxic Masculinity?"

20. "Feminism 101: What Is Toxic Masculinity?"

towards expressing emotions that would be deemed as feminine for fear of emasculation.[21] This is directly linked to the misogynistic mentality that male qualities are superior to feminine qualities.

Toxic masculinity seeps through everyday life, yet it is often excused as normal behavior, or "locker-room talk," as we have seen in the Trump (USA), Modi (India) and Bolsonaro (Brazil) administrations (among other patriarchs of the modern age). Society uses the popular belief that "boys will be boys" to disregard, or deny, the existence of toxic masculinity. However, comments that reinforce the social hierarchy by placing traditional masculinity above femininity cannot be ignored. The normalization of this rhetoric underpins the continuing existence of toxic masculinity.

Ryan Douglas, in a column published in *The Huffington Post*, explains that *toxic masculinity* is built on two fundamental pillars: *sexual conquest* and *violence*. He further remarks: "If sex and aggression are the measuring sticks of manhood, it's no wonder rape education remains a conversation of what women should be doing to not get raped rather than what men should be doing, which is not raping. *How can we hope to stop violent sexual behavior if violence and sexuality are still considered primary virtues of manhood?*"[22]

To end bodily abuse and gender violence, patriarchy has to be demolished. Patriarchy is not just a male problem; it is everyone's problem. The promotion and maintenance of patriarchy is not just a male business. A lot of women across cultures and religions are also complicit because they either benefit from patriarchy or yet to comprehend the violence involved.

(sh)Outing the Bible

Patriarchy shapes the narratives on, and attitudes to, bodily abuse or sexual violence in scriptures. The Bible, despite the sacred status and authority attributed to it by ecclesial tradition, is a foreign place where norms are determined by imperial ethos, by slavery systems, and patriarchal values. These combined create an environment of aggression, domination, and control.

Katie Edwards of the Shiloh Project points out that "rape is endemic in the Bible (both literally and metaphorically) and, more often than not, functions as a conduit for male competition and a tool to uphold patriarchy."[23] She also notes that "a common thread in the biblical text is

21. "Feminism 101: What Is Toxic Masculinity?"
22. Douglass, "Men Should Learn the Difference."
23. Edwards, "How the Bible Shapes the Contemporary Attitudes to Rape and Sexual Assault."

that women are responsible for maintaining their sexual 'purity', which is to ensure that as male properties, women remain 'undamaged' and thereby maintain their 'full market value' when 'ownership' is handed over from father to husband at the time of marriage. Their interests and consent are never considered."[24] Examples of #MeToo moments in the Hebrew Bible include Hagar and the unnamed daughters of Lot; in fact, there are #MeToo moments in the New Testament and the Bible as a whole.

#HagarToo (Genesis 16)

In Gen 16, we read that Abram went into Hagar obediently because of Sarai's command. Throughout the narrative, Abram hardly spoke. The following points are worth noting: Abram, being the chosen one of God and recipient of God's promise is portrayed positively as a passive, innocent male who took Sarai's slave girl (without her consent) to serve Sarai's interest. Sarai, the female figure, is painted as an impatient, barren wife who took matters into her own hand to bring to pass the promise of offspring (which is a patriarchal concern). Abram is also positioned favorably as if he reluctantly "went into" Hagar (or abuse Hagar, the slave-girl) in obedience to Sarai's advice.

The text is narrated in a way to persuade readers to believe that whatever went wrong was Sarai's fault, and what Hagar experienced was the norm because she had no control over her enslaved body. Consent therefore is out of the question, so this case is closed, and most churches and Christians are comfortable with that.

When churches normalize and internalize such narratives, they allow the problem within the text to spill over into the contemporary context. Such narratives must be problematized and resisted.

#Lot'sDaughtersToo (Genesis 19)

In Gen 19, we encounter another patriarch who offered his "virgin" daughters to people of Sodom/Gomorrah *to save his male visitors*. Like Gen 16, this narrative also deals with producing male heirs and preserving the family line. But there is something fishy about this story: the narrator got rid of those who were best candidates for the heir-producing task—namely, the sons in law who were left behind (because they were too busy partying),

---

24. Edwards, "How the Bible Shapes the Contemporary Attitudes to Rape and Sexual Assault."

and Lot's wife who was turned into a pillar (because she looked back). That leaves Lot and his two daughters.

Instead of settling in Zoar, Lot moved with his daughters to a cave. In that cave, the narrative explained, the two daughters *whom no men knew* ("virgin") were so concerned with preserving their father's offspring. What follows is a classic feature of patriarchy, namely, shifting the blame to female characters and depicting the male figure as an innocent victim. The daughters, according to the narrative, made their father drunk with wine, and they slept with him. Here, like the Hagar narrative, the female characters are portrayed negatively as if they were the perpetrators. Here again, Lot, the patriarchal figure is situated as an innocent father *who knew nothing* about what happened because *he was so drunk*.

In both cases, Abram and Lot are narrated to cover up the sexual abuse committed in both narratives. Covering up of bodily abuse/sexual violence is a popular tool of patriarchy; a tool to manage male anxiety, fear and insecurity.

#NewTestamentToo

The New Testament is also marked with bodily abuse/sexual violence. Meredith Warren (also of the Shiloh Project) discusses this with reference to the Apocalypse/Book of Revelation.[25] Written in the first or second century CE, Revelation is widely read as early Christianity's rejection of the sinful, violent Roman Empire and the hopeful expectation of justice for true believers. This understanding of the Apocalypse, Warren argues, overlooks the rampant violence omnipresent in the text, which depicts sexual violence as a punishment ordained by God. This reflects the strange world of the Bible where sexual violence and rape were frequently depicted as just punishments for conquered peoples. The defeat of an army represented a power dynamic between enemies, where the victors upheld the masculine role of empowered penetrator and the conquered were made effeminate in their weakness, their penetrability. It is perhaps not so surprising, then, that Revelation not only portrays its enemies in feminized terms, but also punishes them with sexual assault.

---

25. Warren, "Sexual Violence and Rape Culture in the New Testament."

#BibleToo

The Bible has an abusive orientation. In the volume *Rape Culture, Gender Violence, and Religion: Biblical Perspectives*, the editors made this opening statement: "The Bible is a violent book. Its pages are inscribed with an abundance of traditions that bear witness to the pervasiveness of gendered aggression and abuse within biblical Israel. Its narratives attest to the commonality of wartime rape, forced marriage, and sex slavery; we can read stories of stranger rape, acquaintance rape, and gang rape (both threatened and actualized)."[26]

Attributing to the Bible sacred status made it more dangerous in the sense that its instructions are seen as given from the divine and therefore has to be followed. When stories it contains are violent and abusive, those who live by them are most likely to become violent and abusive.

Communities (like churches) whose lives and works revolved around the Bible, the so-called "people of the book," are perilously exposed to texts of abuse and affected by them in unimaginable ways. This is particularly harmful to vulnerable members of the community, such as women and children. These violence and abuse are internalized and normalized when members of the community are encouraged to learn texts taken out of context by heart. Churches and Bible-obsessed communities need to be careful not to allow narratives of abuse spill over to social and public spaces.

#usToo

These biblical #MeToo moments present us with a challenge to do something about sexual violence and violent-supportive systems among and around us.

#AotearoaToo

This abusive system of patriarchy exists in our own societies in Oceania and Aotearoa. We only need to look at research findings to realize the severity of its impact.[27]

The crime figures from the 2018 State of the Nation Report (by the Salvation Army)[28] show that from 2015 to 2017, there were 16,783 *reported*

---

26. Blyth, Colgan, and Edwards, *Rape Culture, Gender Violence & Religion*, 1.
27. "Feminism 101: What Is Toxic Masculinity?"
28. Johnson, "Kei a Tātou."

cases of sexual assault and related offences (5620 for 2015, 5430 for 2016, and 5733 for 2017). Statistics from the Rape Prevention Education website (http://rpe.co.nz/) identifies that 1 in 3 girls is likely to experience unwanted sexual experience by the age of 16 years. Amongst adults, 1 in 5 women experience sexual assault. Both Māori and Pasifika women are at statistically greater risk of sexual violence. There are incidences of sexual violence offences against males at a rate of 1 in 7 amongst boys.

Despite these figures, sexual violence, according to RPE, has a very low conviction rate in Aotearoa New Zealand, with only 13% of cases recorded by the Police resulting in conviction.

Media reporting of sexual violence is often under-informed and defends public myths and misconceptions about the dynamics of sexual violence. This misinformation affects society's shared understanding of and attitudes to sexual violence, promoting false narratives and rape-supportive attitudes in society.

#churchesToo

Those of us who belong to churches need to ask: How might we as members of the Christ-body respond to this issue? How safe is our Church spaces for our children, women and those who are vulnerable to such acts of violence? How might we conduct ourselves in a way that respects and promotes the dignity and humanity of those subjugated by patriarchy? I extend an invitation to consider the following:

- pay attention to the facts about sexual abuse because facts do matter (many churches are not very good in appreciating facts);
- listen closely to the stories of sexual abuse victims, because their stories are our stories too, and they must be heard (churches do not have a good record in this matter);
- radically smash the roots of sexual abuse, because it is vital to the healing process (and churches cannot play safe and be comfortable, because such a church is a danger to society);
- shift the way we read narratives of abuse in the Bible, because traditional (or the so-called objective, neutral, heaven-bound, divinely-inspired) readings of such texts have become irrelevant and abusive.

Kalanga

We need to *kalanga* at the complicity of faith communities, particularly those who have turned a blind eye to the violence in/of the Bible; those who validated the sins of the chosen and the illusion of patriarchal innocence (Abraham, Lot) through their violent-friendly theologies and militant readings of scriptures; those who closed their ears to the *cries of the forgotten/ abused* (Hagar, Lot's daughters); those who subscribe to, live by, the toxic values and violent norms of *patriarchy*.

Finally, let us *acknowledge* (and tweet!) that bodily violence/sexual violence in the bible is *troubling* (disturbing, alarming). That requires, on the one hand, a serious reconsideration of the sacred and authoritative status given to the bible, and a critical analysis of norms and values inscribed onto its pages, on the other hand.

Let us also learn to become *troubling/disruptive* readers; readers who have the radical edge demonstrated by Jesus in his ministry, and the courage to engage, confront, interrogate, resist, and shatter all systems (like patriarchy) that support any form of violence. In so doing, there is hope to experience life, bodily healing, and a life-flourishing society.

Works Cited

Ademiluka, Solomon Olusola. "Patriarchy and Women Abuse: Perspectives from Ancient Israel and Africa." *Old Testament Essays* 31.2 (2018) 339–62.

Bartlett, Alison, Kyra Clark, and Rob Cover. *Flirting in the Era of #MeToo: Negotiating Intimacy.* Cham, Switzerland: Palgrave Macmillan, 2019.

Blyth, Caroline, Emily Colgan, and Katie Edwards. *Rape Culture, Gender Violence & Religion: Biblical Perspectives.* Cham, Switzerland: Palgrave Macmillan, 2018.

Boyle, Karen. *#MeToo, Weinstein and Feminism.* Cham, Switzerland: Palgrave Macmillan, 2019.

Brown, Kimberley Juanita. "The End of the Story: Patriarchy." *Differences: A Journal of Feminist Cultural Studies* 30.3 (2019) 152–65.

Douglass, Ryan. "Men Should Learn the Difference Between Masculinity and Toxic Masculinity." *Huffington Post*, August 2017. https://www.huffpost.com/entry/the-difference-between-masculinity-and-toxic-masculinity_b_59842e3ce4b0f2c7d93 f54ce.

Edwards, Katie. "How the Bible Shapes the Contemporary Attitudes to Rape and Sexual Assault." *Conversation*, May 2, 2017. https://theconversation.com/how-the-bible-shapes-contemporary-attitudes-to-rape-and-sexual-assault-76900.

FEM. "Feminism 101: What Is Toxic Masculinity?," n.d. https://femmagazine.com/feminim-101-what-is-toxic-masculinity/.

Fileborn, Bianca, and Rachel Loney-Howes. *#MeToo and the Politics of Social Change.* Cham, Switzerland: Palgrave Macmillan, 2019.

Havea, Jione, and Diya Lākai Havea. "Sex: Suicide, Shame, Signals." In *Theologies from the Pacific*, edited by Jione Havea, 323–36. New York: Palgrave, 2021.

Hill, Rosemary Lucy, and Kim Allen. "'Smash the Patriarchy': The Changing Meanings and Work of 'Patriarchy' Online." *Feminist Theory* 22.2 (2021) 165–89.

hooks, bell. "Understanding Patriarchy." Louisville Anarchist Federation, n.d. http://laff-experiment.org/.

Hunnicutt, Gwen. "Varieties of Patriarchy and Violence against Women: Resurrecting 'Patriarchy' as a Theoretical Tool." *Violence Against Women* 15.5 (2009) 553–73.

Johnson, Alan. "Kei a Tātou—It Is Us. State of the Nation Report." Salvation Army, February 2018. https://www.salvationarmy.org.nz/research-media/social-policy-and-parliamentary-unit/latest-report/State-of-Nation-2018.

Palmer, Jane E., Erica R. Fissel, Jill Hoxmeier, and Erin Williams. "#MeToo for Whom? Sexual Assault Disclosures before and after #MeToo." *American Journal of Criminal Justice* 46.1 (2021) 68–106.

Philipose, Pamela, and Mukul Kesavan. "The #MeToo Movement." *Indian Journal of Gender Studies* 26.1 & 2 (2019) 207–14.

Suk, Jiyoun, Aman Abhishek, Yini Zhang, So Yun Ahn, Teresa Correa, Christine Garlough, and Dhavan V. Shah. "#MeToo, Networked Acknowledgment, and Connective Action: How 'Empowerment Through Empathy' Launched a Social Movement." *Social Science Computer Review* 39.2 (2019) 276–94.

Tolliday, Dale. "'Until We Talk about Everything, Everything We Talk about Is Just Whistling into the Wind': An Interview with Pam Greer and Sigrid ('Sig') Herring." *Sexual Abuse in Australia and New Zealand* 7.1 (June 2016) 70–80.

Walby, Sylvia. *Theorizing Patriarchy*. Oxford: Blackwell, 1990.

Warren, Meredith. "Sexual Violence and Rape Culture in the New Testament." The Shiloh Project: Rape Culture, Religion and the Bible, May 31, 2017. https://www.shilohproject.blog/sexual-violence-and-rape-culture-in-the-new-testament/.

12

Tautua Lē Pa'ō and Toxic Masculinity
Voicing a Pisa *Theology*

Brian Fiu Kolia

The Samoan proverb *O le ala i le pule o le tautua* (The path to authority/chiefhood is service/toil) has been baptized for the Samoan way of living. Samoans are taught to serve and respect their elders, their *matai* (chiefs), their *faifeau* (church ministers), their *aiga* (family), their *nuu* (village), and their *ekalesia* (church). The reward for such hard service, is *pule* (authority) through a *matai* title. The desire for a *matai* title is high, as it carries prestige and grants the *matai* the power to make important family and village decisions. The authority extends to the national level seeing that one cannot sit on Samoan parliament without a *matai* title. The proverb therefore has proved to be an effective way of maintaining the status quo for Samoans in the village (local) and national context.

But often, the *pule* and *tautua* are stressed and not so much the *ala* (path/way). It is in the *ala* that *tautua* (toiling) and hard work occur. *Tautua*, which I explain further below, exhibits the livelihood of the village. But who can perform *tautua*? In the Samoan setting, every member performs *tautua* in some way or form. Men and women perform *tautua*, and so do *fa'afafine* who have long been referred to in Samoa as the third gender. Johanna Schmidt explains that "The Samoan word 'fa'afafine' literally translates as 'in the manner of' or 'like'—'fa'a'—a woman or women—'fafine'. Fa'afafine are biological Samoan 'males' whose gendered behaviours are feminine."[1]

In a typical Samoan setting, men do all the heavy labor: building churches and *maota* (Samoan housing), clearing the land, tending the lawns, agrarian work, fishing, pig hunting, outdoor cooking (*umu*), putting up fences, bird shooting, and anything that requires a *sapelu* (machete/bush knife). The women perform lighter domestic duties, and indoor cooking. *Fa'afāfine* can perform the same duties as the men, but also "domestic chores along with the women, albeit with the physical strength of men."[2]

The brunt of *tautua* is performed by the *taule'ale'a* (young untitled man). Ultimately, much of the *pule* (authority)—primarily through *matai* titles—is afforded to these young men in recognition of their *tautua*. This is extremely discriminatory to women, for whom I cannot speak. Here, I want to speak for my *uso* (my brother)[3], who struggles to come to terms with this androcentric agenda. An agenda that discriminates against women and *fa'afāfine* yet plays on the masculinity of the Samoan male, propagated by expectations to perform *tautua* regardless of physical and mental health. Which beg the questions: Does *tautua* promote a cultural propaganda? Does *tautua* incite toxic masculinity?

In this essay I argue that *tautua* is a border that can be a quandary for a number of bodies, such as the Samoan male body, and also the psychological body, i.e., mental well-being. I offer a biblical response to this dilemma, specifically how Qoheleth breaks the border of *tautua*, through the common theme of *hebel* (ambiguity) in the book of Ecclesiastes.

Tautua as Border: Hegemonic Masculinity

Bordering the Physical Body

The starting point for perceiving *tautua* as border is in the term itself, given that most Samoan terms are compound words created from what is observed in everyday life. The term *tautua* is a compound of the words *tau* and *tua*. *Tau* can mean "to strive," "to fight," "to pluck" or "to reach/reach the end." *Tua* can mean "back," "behind," or "depend upon/lean on." The compound term *tau-tua* purport to say, "strive from behind," "strive from the back," or "to strive with your back into it." *Tautua* talks of service that

---

1. Schmidt, *Migrating Genders*, 2.
2. Prower, *Queer Magic*. See also Schimdt, *Migrating Genders*, 1.
3. *Uso* is a male's brother, or a female's sister. Hence, a male cannot call his sister *uso*, and vice versa.

is performed from the back. *Tautua* is hard and laborious service, as *tua* implies service that is strenuous on the back.

On the islands, Samoans live agrarian and subsistent lifestyles. Many tasks are performed manually and *tautua* exemplifies hard work and determination contrary to quick and effective methods of labor offered through machinery and technology. For instance, in spite of the availability of lawn mowers and weed eaters, many village councils prefer the *taule'ale'a* to use machetes so that the young men feel the strain and pain of the work performed. It also stands to justify the status of *matai* who uphold and idealize the old ways of doing things as tradition, and necessary to attain *pule*. Samoan society is also very traditional and anything that is stamped as tradition will be revered and adulated.

The problem here is that while the status quo is successfully maintained, the impact of its preservation are felt by those in the margins: the untitled, *tautua* performers. In this essay, I focus on the *taule'ale'a*, collectively known as *aumaga*. It is apparent already that to get to *pule*, one must first become *taule'ale'a* and thus a member of the *aumaga* in order to perform *tautua*. But who are the *aumaga*? Aiono states:

> The *aumaga* have earned the honorific *o le malosi o le nuu* [strength of the village] because they are the physical strength *api*[4] support upon which the *matai* group (*nuu*) depend. They are the tillers of the soil; the planters; the *tautai* (fishermen or literally those who are involved in the sea and marine activities); the catchers–snarers of birds; the builders; the makers of weapons and tools; the preparers; the cooks and servers of food and drink; the poets, the singers, the dancers, the entertainers; the sportsmen and the fighters in times of war. They are the heirs of matai titles who give the uniquely Samoan service called *tautua*, to honour the chosen *matai*.[5]

Aiono's definition heightens masculinity, particularly through the honorific *malosi* (strength). The expectation upon the *taule'ale'a* is to be *malosi* else they fail the village and their *matai*. Ultimately, the dangling of the carrot (qua the *matai* title) becomes elusive for the *taule'ale'a*. As the honorific shows, the expectation of *malosi* increases masculinity, and I argue that such masculinity becomes toxic because there is no room for weakness, particularly as the *taule'ale'a* works together with other members of the *aumaga*. To fail leads to embarrassment and ridicule by fellow

---

4. The Samoan word *api* often means "rest" but can also mean "rely upon."
5. Aiono and Crocombe, *Culture and Democracy in the South Pacific*, 118–19.

aumaga members and disgrace to the family name. It is better to just put the head down, be quiet and keep working.

Psychological Bordering: *Tautua Lē Pa'ō*

Vaitusi Nofoaiga speaks of a type of *tautua* that is often praised in Samoan culture known as *tautua lē pa'ō* or *tautua lē pisa* which is "to serve with silence."[6] *Pisa* or *pa'ō* means "sound" or "voice" and in this instance, it has a negative connotation associated with unwanted sounds or voices. Therefore, *tautua lē pa'ō* is *tautua* performed without disturbing voices. This type of *tautua* is praised openly in the Samoan context, because it is aligned with the principles of hard work and determination. Nofoaiga argues that working in silence "does not mean submission to oppression but respect to a commitment to carry out a service role to the best of his ability, thus ensuring the survival of the family."[7]

Nofoaiga favors *tautua* in light of family survival and the needs of the village, but the definition neglects the *tautua* himself. What is going through the mind of the persons performing *tautua*? Do they mind waking up in the early hours? Do they mind the heavy and mundane labour? Do they mind adopting traditional methods of doing things when there are quicker and more effective methods available? Is there room for the *tautua* to voice their concern? In a traditional and conservative setting, can the *tautua* be skeptical?

I argue that *lē pa'ō* (in silence) is a psychological border to the *tautua*. The *tautua* does not want to complain because silence is praised and glorified, and as Nofoaiga claims, it shows commitment. Those who break the silence by complaining are depicted as weak, and in the village context, such males are labelled—some derogatory—*kaea* and *kipi*.[8] At times, those who break silence are viewed mockingly as *fafa* (short for *fa'afāfine*, equivalent of "poofter") or *mala* (literally means "curse") thus marginalizing homosexuals and transgenders.[9] Avoiding such name-calling, and dishonoring one's *aiga*, serve as impetus for one to remain silent. This is toxic or hegemonic masculinity.

---

6. Nofoaiga, *A Samoan Reading of Discipleship*, 38.

7. Nofoaiga, *A Samoan Reading of Discipleship*, 38.

8. *Kaea* (formal: *taea*), from the word *tae* (shit) is a derogatory term that means "shitty"—someone who is incompetent or useless. *Kipi* (formal: *tipi*) literally means "cut" which refers to someone who takes shortcuts or avoids hard work, a bludger.

9. See Kupers, "Toxic Masculinity as a Barrier to Mental Health Treatment in Prison," 716.

Being a part of the *aumaga* entails a masculinity analogous to "hegemonic masculinity" which R. W. Connell defines as "the configuration of gender practice which embodies the currently accepted answer to the problem of the legitimacy of patriarchy, which guarantees (or is taken to guarantee) the dominant position of men and the subordination of women."[10] The life of the *taule'ale'a* in the *aumaga* collective manifests the legitimacy of such masculinity. And given that they are all male, the *aumaga* largely guarantees the dominant position of men in the Samoan context.

In recent times, there has been a turn in the tide with increased female and *fa'afāfine* representation in *matai* positions. This is because *tautua* in other forms, such as education and academic success, professional roles, sporting achievements, and monetary contributions, have been accepted and acknowledged by the *aiga* and village. Appropriately, they have also been granted *pule* through *matai* titles. However, the village setting is still very traditional, and the *aumaga* is a prominent part of village life. The patriarchal systems remain in place, while the desire for *pule* driving the *aumaga* and feeding the hegemonic masculinity.

Such hegemonic apparitions still speak of patriarchy. *Tautua lē pa'ō* continues to border the male from voicing their concerns. Because, in reality, the *tautua* may not *pa'ō* but within the realms of the *aumaga*, there is plenty to *pa'ō* and *pisa* about. *Tautua* is somewhat romanticized but, in reality, *tautua* confines different kinds of masculinity under the one umbrella. Connell maintains that this is a problem: "We must also recognize the relations between the different kinds of masculinity: relations of alliance, dominance, and subordination. These relationships are constructed through practices that exclude and include, that intimidate, exploit, and so on. There is a gender politics within masculinity."[11]

There is certainly gender politics at play in *aumaga*, as *matai* seek to exploit such physicality and strength expected from the *malosi o le nuu*. Here, the body of the *fono* (village council) acts as a border to the masculine body of the *taule'ale'a*. The *fono* dictates the work they are to carry out, however strenuous it may be, and for no monetary compensation. Those in the *fono* propagate the *matai* title to the *aumaga* in order to gain their *tautua*. Intimidation is also glaring through a culture of hegemonic masculinity within the *aumaga*, which seeks to devalue the *taule'ale'a* as unmanly if they were to veer away from the masculine norm.[12]

---

10. Connell, *Masculinities*, 77.
11. Connell, *Masculinities*, 37.
12. Kupers, "Toxic Masculinity as a Barrier," 716.

There are many forms of masculinity, as not all males are the same. Ironically, while *faʻafafine* are not restricted from *matai* title, they are commonly excluded from the *aumaga*, despite being biologically male.[13] The masculine agenda promoted through the *aumaga* is therefore oppressive, especially towards weaker males, transgenders and homosexuals who may not exhibit the masculine qualities expected from the *malosi o le nuu*. Yet their voices remain suppressed, as they *tautua* in silence, and in a physical form not consistent with their own unique masculinity. So, what happens if the *tauleʻaleʻa* cannot perform *tautua*? How valuable is *tautua* if they do not have the required strength to do so? How can women perform *tautua*? How can their voices be heard?

There are theological implications of these questions. The issue of masculinity carries over to the ecclesiastical setting. *Tautua* is used in the church setting where it is associated with androcentric tendencies. Church offerings, and work done for the church are labelled as *tautua*. The physical underpinnings of *tautua* carry over the masculine overtones of the *aumaga*. For instance, those who cannot give as much as others may be called *kaea* or *kipi*.

This toxic masculinity contextualizes theological interpretation of *tautua* by praising those who *tautua* in silence in the church. This can only be toxic for the church as it promotes determination and a reluctance to *pisa*. I propose an alternative theology that seeks to un-silence the silent voices being suppressed through toxic hegemonic style theology. As a basis, I am drawn to Qoheleth's[14] musings, particularly the theme of *hebel* (vanity)[15] that is reflective of his own skepticism towards wisdom, toil, wealth, and life itself. I bring this in conversation with *tautua lē paʻō* and the toxic effect it has on Samoan masculinity. The aim of this theology is to remove the oppressive borders through a *pisa* (vocalize) theology. Qoheleth helps to vocalize the silent *tautua*, and to vocalize women.

---

13. Schoeffel, "Representing *Faʻafafine*, 79.

14. Qoheleth refers to the author of Ecclesiastes.

15. *Hebel* (הבל) is translated in the NRSV as "vanity" and this is the most common translation amongst commentators on the book of Ecclesiastes. However, the word's definition as "vanity" is a topic of debate among scholars. For the purposes of this paper, I will not argue the meaning of *hebel* but rather utilise its various interpretations in order to gauge a fuller understanding of the theme.

Pisa across Borders

Pisa is noise, but not all noise is unwelcome. In fact, *pisa* may cause a necessary disruption because *pisa* causes reaction and creates an opportunity for things to be corrected. *Pisa* crosses borders. It crosses gender borders as well as cultural borders, church borders, and theological borders. In crossing these borders, *pisa* allows for reconciliation. This is the purpose of a *pisa* theology. It is not just to vocalize, but to lead to reconciliation.[16]

Pisa theology is contextual and, as Stephen Bevans puts it, it takes into account our experiences of the past—i.e., Christian tradition and Scripture—and our experiences of the present (in my case, culture) which come together in dialogue.[17] Here I bring into conversation the Samoan concept of *aitaumalele* which represents my present experience, in dialogue with the skeptical wisdom of Qoheleth in the book of Ecclesiastes.

Aitaumalele

The traditional Samoan village setting does not allow for much *pisa*, however migration beyond the village and into diasporic communities overseas have changed the landscape of Samoan families and villages. It has brought about a type of *tautua* known as *aitaumalele*.

As an Australian Samoan, I am located outside my home villages, and it is from afar that I perform *tautua*. Those who *tautua* in the village perform *tautua tuāvae* and are considered to be *taumalae*. *Tuāvae* can mean "behind the legs/feet" or "depending on the legs/feet." Both notions help explain *tautua tuāvae*: The second meaning is best explained through the phrase *vae ma lima* (feet and hands). *Vae ma lima* is a common Samoan idiom that points to service with *vae* (feet) resonating with the haste of the *tautua* while *lima* (hands) points to the strength and skill of the *tautua*.[18] The second meaning of *tuāvae* fits this understanding, in that the *tautua*'s *vae* is depended upon to provide service to the *aiga*. The first meaning of *tuāvae* points to the proximity of the *tautua*, i.e., right behind one's feet. This meaning alludes to the *tautua* who lives on the land.[19]

---

16. I must point out that Samoan culture is founded, guarded and nurtured by *fa'aaloalo*—a cultural term that speaks of the respect shown between two or more parties. The ultimate goal of *fa'aaloalo* is the harmony in relationships, and if the relationship had been violated, *fa'aaloalo* advocates for and guides the path to reconciliation. See Vaai, "Faaaloalo," 161–200.

17. Bevans, *Essays in Contextual Theology*, 2.

18. Cf. Mulitalo-Lauta, "Pacific Peoples' Identities," 255.

19. One who grew up and lives on the land is known as *taumalae*, hence the term

The weight of *aitaumalele* lies in the word *lele*. *Lele* refers to migration, like a bird that flies away from its nest or home.[20] This idea of a bird flying away from its nest is consistent with the Samoan proverb: *E lele le toloa ae maau i le vai* (the wild duck flies but always comes back to the water). The proverb means that no matter to where Samoans travel, they know where home is. *Aitaumalele* carries the spirit of this proverb if we liken *tautua* to the wild duck (*toloa*). To imagine this, I break the word up as *ai-tau-ma-lele*: *ai* means "to eat," *tau* means "to snatch," *ma* means "and" and *lele* means "to fly." In this connection, *ai-tau-ma-lele* means "to snatch their food and fly" which is consistent with the dabbling form of feeding for which the *toloa* is known.[21] The *toloa* is a "great wanderer" and is "found across a huge geographic area, extending from Indonesia to French Polynesia, and south to New Zealand and Australia."[22] The connotations of the *toloa* flying away help to understand the premise behind *aitaumalele* as a *tautua* who has taken what they have learnt from their homeland into new and foreign territories. Like the *toloa*, the *aitaumalele* crosses borders, and no longer lives on the land. Mema Motusaga summarizes *aitaumalele* as those family members who do not live on the land but live afar.[23] Tui Atua Tupua Tamasese Efi further explains that despite their distance, they still *tautua* (serve) for the village.[24] Despite their *aitaumalele* status, they still have *monotaga* (village membership).[25]

Efi's statement regarding *monotaga* is important because it implies that connection to land, family and village is not only physical but also spiritual and hence permanent. *Monotaga* ensures that even if the *aitaumalele* lives afar, it still has a voice in village and family matters.[26] The *aitaumalele* views from afar and consequently *pisa*-s as well as crosses borders from afar.

---

aitaumalele stands on the opposite spectrum to *taumalae* and *tuāvae*. Motusaga, "Women in Decision Making in Samoa," 99. See also Pratt's discussion of *tāumalae* as the same as *anomalae* which defines "those living nearest the *malae*" with the *malae* being the family land (*A Grammar and Dictionary of the Samoan Language*, s.v. "Anomalae").

20. Mulitalo-Cheung, "*E lele le toloa 'ae ma'au i le vai*," 2.
21. The *toloa* is the dabbling duck because it doesn't dive under the water, but dips its head in and snatches its food and flies away. Cf. International Business Publications, *Samoa (American)*, 187.
22. International Business Publications, *Samoa (American)*, 187.
23. Motusaga, "Women in Decision Making in Samoa," 99.
24. Efi, "Samoa o le Atunuu Tofi," 5.
25. Efi, "Samoa o le Atunuu Tofi," 5.
26. Efi, "Samoa o le Atunuu Tofi," 5.

Aitaumalele are also in the diaspora, a precarious position to *pisa* from. They live and survive in difficult spaces, but they also enjoy certain liberties. For instance, in the current climate of racism and discrimination, the *aitaumalele* are marginalized. At the same time, compared to what is available in the homeland, the *aitaumalele* access better education, employment, welfare and other services. The position of *aitaumalele* in this regard may be deemed privileged. As an Australian Samoan, the *aitaumalele* must be aware of the privileged state so as not to draw unfair comparisons with those who are *taumalae* (see n.19). The marginalisation of the *aitaumalele* in foreign lands could highlight the injustices in the borders that continue to oppress and decapitate the spiritual, cultural, psychological, and physical body of the *tautua*.

Aitaumalele is a significant way of breaking down borders. They first break down the border of how *tautua* is performed. Traditionally, *tautua* could only be performed in the village. The *aitaumalele* has changed the stage for *tautua* by taking it beyond the village border, and into outside (foreign) territory. A crossing of borders occurs as the *aitaumalele* leaves their village and enters the urban contexts of Samoa, and further into foreign lands such as New Zealand, Australia, USA, UK, Europe, Hawaii, and Fiji.

The *aitaumalele* also crosses cultural borders. Specifically, the procession for the *tautua* is to work as part of the *aumaga* or the *aualuma* before becoming a *matai*. Aitaumalele does not work as part of the *aumaga* nor *aualuma* but can *tautua* by sending remittances or commodities back to the family in the village. They also honor the village through achievements in education, professional careers, sports, music, and other entertainment. The recognition the *tautua* receives in these contexts, in turn gives honor to the family name and to the village. The *aumaga* and *aualuma* no longer provide the direct path to chiefhood.

The other significant border that *aitaumalele* break is the gender border. The distinction between the *aumaga* and *aualuma* forms of *tautua* is glaring in that the *aumaga* do most of the heavy work. In the Samoan context, this is highly admirable. As such, the honor and prestige of being a *matai* tend to favor the *aumaga* form of *tautua*. In the context of the *aitaumalele*—men, women and *fa'afāfine* are on equal footing. The endorsed achievements do not favor a particular gender; men, women and *fa'afāfine* have equal access to become *matai*. Anybody can be *aitaumalele*, and they can *pisa* from afar![27]

27. While there are positive aspects to *aitaumalele*, there are also negative aspects that could propel *pisa* into chaos. The obvious difficulty is the tension between *aitaumalele* and those in the homeland. My proposal anticipates this tension and welcomes it. Not to cause division, but as mentioned earlier, to provide a point for reconciliation.

Qoheleth as *Aitaumalele*

I bring Qoheleth into conversation with *aitaumalele*. Qoheleth is extremely vocal.[28] The first-person perspective is proof of this, and he proclaims those famous words: "vanity of vanities! All is vanity" (Eccl 1:2).[29] He is a *tautua* as he has "made great works;" he has "built houses and planted vineyards" (2:4), and he also made "gardens and parks, and planted in them all kinds of fruit trees" (2:5). He also made "pools" for irrigation (2:6). But then in 2:11, Qoheleth's vocality makes a turn, declaring: "Then I considered all that my hands had done and the toil I had spent in doing it, and again, all was vanity and a chasing after wind, and there was nothing to be gained under the sun" (2:11).

Qoheleth's frustrations are vocalized, alerting his audience to the absurdity of toiling—the effort is in vain. Ancient Jewish Wisdom promotes a deeds-consequence (retribution) theology that is prominent in the book of Deuteronomy: if one performs good deeds, one accrues reward or blessing. Conversely, if one performs evil deeds, one becomes cursed. This theology is also promoted in the book of Proverbs. On the other hand, Ecclesiastes and Job question this theology.

The voices of dissonance in Ecclesiastes and Job counter the orthodoxy in Proverbs. I read Qoheleth's voice of dissonance as *aitaumalele* from diaspora. Stuart Weeks states that we should not discount a diasporic setting for Ecclesiastes,[30] and Daniel Smith-Christopher navigates our thinking to that possibility: "Ecclesiastes reads far more subversively if the famous "cynicism" is directed not towards a Jewish state, or even toward traditional Jewish values of social existence, but rather toward the gentile state—the *goyim naches*—absurd preoccupations of the non-Jews under whom Jews are forced to live."[31]

I argue then that Qoheleth is vocal from afar, possibly from a diasporic context. Qoheleth can therefore be read as *aitaumalele*. Qoheleth vocalizes the discrepancies and contradictions of the deed-consequence theology. In the process, he gives those who are silent a voice. A voice to those who are *lē pa'ō* or *lē pisa*. Qoheleth's reckoning thus invites a new theology, a theology that seeks to dispel the myths that fuel hegemonic masculinity by allowing men to speak up about the fallacy of masculine dominance; dominance over

---

28. Qoheleth's voice could be perceived as either liberating or oppressive. For Qoheleth's liberating voice, see Deik, "Justice in Ecclesiastes," 72. For an oppressive sense of Qoheleth's voice, see Vijayan, "Qoheleth Silences Women," 44, 50.

29. All Biblical quotes are from the NRSV unless otherwise stated.

30. Weeks, *Ecclesiastes and Scepticism*, 7.

31. Smith-Christopher, *A Biblical Theology of Exile*, 173.

women, homosexuals and transgender, and also over other males who do not fit in the mold of the "ideal man."

The reality is that hegemonic masculinity is alarming and more so given the restraint of cultural borders over the voiceless *tautua*. A theological response is needed to provide the voiceless *tautua* with the confidence to *tautua* and *pisa*, to create a platform for reconciliation. Reconciliation between masculinities, between genders, between *tautua* and *pule*, between *tautua* and the church.

After Qoheleth's *pisa*, reconciliation comes in Eccl 12:13–14, namely, that in spite of the contradictions, the audience must fear the Lord. Most commentators see these verses as a redaction. For instance, Roland Murphy argues that "a third epilogist gave a direction to the book for its practical use by means of the edifying ending."[32] The postcolonial reader could see these verses as colonizing the voices of the oppressed, leading the audience back to a position of orthodoxy, despite Qoheleth questioning the status quo.[33] But the ambiguity of Ecclesiastes allows for different perspectives, and I argue that *pisa* leads to reconciliation.

Although *tautua lē pisa* is preferred, the Samoan culture of *fa'aaloalo* (respect) and *va tapuia* (sacred space) always prevail. While some might consider *pisa* to be disrespectful, advocating for reconciliation could never be deemed *lē fa'aaloalo* (disrespectful). In this connection, *pisa* upholds *fa'aaloalo* by giving voice to those who are wronged. Relationships are mended under *fa'aaloalo* through the cultural process of *teu le va* (mending the space) whereby the *va* (space) is rectified and reconciled (*teu*).[34] Indeed, in *tautua*, relationships that are tainted through hegemonic agendas are reconciled after *pisa*. Rather than promoting *lē pisa* which conforms to the status quo, *pisa* can challenge the notions of masculinity that threaten to harm one's masculinity, while subjugating women and other genders. *Pisa* unsettles borders, and if *pisa* is loud enough, it can destroy borders.

Conclusion: *Pisa* from Afar

In Samoa, there is not enough *pisa*, but in the diaspora, *pisa* is emphatic. Qoheleth's *pisa* may have also come from afar, causing a stir in the traditions of conventional Israelite wisdom. This may be the way of doing *pisa* theology, to *pisa* from afar. Those who *pisa* from afar are known as

---

32. Murphy, *Ecclesiastes*, 127.
33. See Tamez, *When the Horizons Close*, 10–13.
34. Cf. Anae, "Teu le Va," 225.

aitaumalele. They are the voice of critique in order to inform the establishment of areas worthy of reforming and reconciling.

From afar, *tautua lē paō* is a form of toxic masculinity. Against that border, we need to *pisa*! From afar, we must *pisa* to vocalize the voiceless *tautua* so that strained relationships may be reconciled. So that different masculinities and different bodies may be acknowledged. So that women and *faʻafāfine* may not be subjugated. So that the marginalized may not be bordered away in their traditional roles, but to *tautua* in their unique ways.

Works Cited

Aiono, Fanaafi Le Tagaloa, and R. G. Crocombe. *Culture and Democracy in the South Pacific*. Suva, Fiji: Institute of Pacific Studies, University of the South Pacific, 1992.

Anae, Melani. "Teu le Va: Toward a *Native* Anthropology." *Pacific Studies* 33.2 & 3 (2010) 222–40.

Bevans, Stephen B. *Essays in Contextual Theology*. Theology and Mission in World Christianity 12. Leiden: Brill, 2018.

Connell, R.W. *Masculinities*. 2nd ed. Berkeley: University of California Press, 2005.

Deik, Anton. "Justice in Ecclesiastes (3:16—4:3 and 8:10–17): A Missional Reading from and for Palestine." In *Reading Ecclesiastes in Asia and Pasifika*, edited by Jione Havea and Peter H. W. Lau, 69–84. International Voices in Biblical Studies 10. Atlanta: Society of Biblical Literature, 2020.

Efi, Tui Atua Tupua Tamasese Taʻisi. "O Samoa o le Atunuu Tofi, e lē se Atunuu Taliola." Paper presented at the NUS Measina Conference, Samoa, 2012.

International Business Publications. *Samoa (American): Doing Businsss, Investing in Samoa (American) Guide—Strategic Information, Regulations, Contacts*. Washington, DC: International Business Publications, 2007.

Kupers, Terry A. "Toxic Masculinity as a Barrier to Mental Health Treatment in Prison." *Journal of Clinical Psychology* 61.6 (2005) 713–24.

Motusaga, Mema. "Women in Decision Making in Samoa." PhD diss., Victoria University, 2016.

Mulitalo-Cheung, Tamari. *"E lele le toloa ʻae maʻau i le vai": Toe taliu mai i fanua le ʻau Saʻili Matagi*. National University of Samoa, 2008.

Mulitalo-Lauta, Paʻu Tafaogalupe. "Pacific Peoples' Identities and Social Services in New Zealand: Creating New Options." In *Tangata o te Moana Nui: Evolving Identities of Pacific Peoples in Aotearoa/New Zealand*. Edited by Cluny Macpherson, Paul Spoonley, and Melani Anae. Palmerston North, NZ: Dunmore, 2001.

Murphy, Roland E. *Ecclesiastes*. Word Biblical Commentary 23A. Dallas: Word, 1998.

Nofoaiga, Vaitusi. *A Samoan Reading of Discipleship in Matthew*. International Voices in Biblical Studies 8. Atlanta: Society of Biblical Literature Press, 2017.

Pratt, George. *A Grammar and Dictionary of the Samoan Language*. London: Trubner 1878.

Prower, Tomás. *Queer Magic: LGBT+ Spirituality and Culture from Around the World*. Woodbury MN: Llewellyn, 2018.

Schmidt, Johanna. *Migrating Genders: Westernisation, Migration, and Samoan Faʻafafine*. Anthropology and Cultural History in Asia and the Indo-Pacific. London: Routledge, 2010.

Schoeffel, Penelope. "Representing *Faʻafafine*: Sex, Socialization, and Gender Identity in Samoa." In *Gender on the Edge: Transgender, Gay, and Other Pacific Islanders*, edited by Niko Besnier and Kalissa Alexeyeff, 73–90. Hong Kong: Hong Kong University Press, 2014.

Smith-Christopher, Daniel L. *A Biblical Theology of Exile*. Overtures to Biblical Theology. Minneapolis: Fortress, 2002.

Tamez, Elsa. *When the Horizons Close: Rereading Ecclesiastes*. Translated by Margaret Wilde. Maryknoll, NY: Orbis, 2000.

Vaai, Upolu Lumā. "Faaaloalo: A Theological Reinterpretation of the Doctrine of the Trinity from a Samoan Perspective." PhD diss., Brisbane: Griffith University, 2006.

Vijayan, Laila. "Qoheleth Silences Women: Rereading Ecclesiastes 2:25–26, 4:1, 7:26, and 28 from India." In *Reading Ecclesiastes from Asia and Pasifika*, edited by Jione Havea and Peter H.W. Lau, 43–52. International Voices in Biblical Studies 10. Atlanta: Society of Biblical Literature, 2020.

Weeks, Stuart. *Ecclesiastes and Scepticism*. Library of Hebrew Bible/Old Testament Studies 541. New York: T. & T. Clark, 2012.

13

Silence

STEPHEN BURNS

MY TALANOA (STORY, TELLING, conversation)—the Pasifika practice described by Jione Havea and others[1]—is, at the suggestion of Monica Melanchthon,[2] about silence. I reflect here on silence/near silence, gaps, and absences. I am conscious that I am, in a way, out of place[3]: I am not, to use another phrase of Jione Havea, "another brown face in the crowd."[4] My face is not brown. In the context of the initiative out of which this collection emerged, mine was the only *white* face, my voice was the only white person's in the conversation. I am mindful of the privilege. Amidst migrant and native perspectives (I am a migrant, and everyone is native somewhere), I realize that I was initially invited to have voice *at all* because of my efforts sometimes to respond to and contend with the challenge I recognize in Rasiah Sugirtharajah's work: that European theologians (add: churches)

---

1. See Havea, "Welcome to Talanoa"; Havea, "Negotiating with Scripture and Resistance"; Vaka'uta, *Talanoa Rhythms*. It is important to me to note with gratitude that I was both invited and encouraged by colleagues in this project to engage this Pasifika way of learning.

2. In the talanoa towards this publication on August 3, 2019, Pilgrim Theological College.

3. I recall Havea and Pearson, *Out of Place*.

4. In the talanoa towards this publication on December 7, 2019, Pilgrim Theological College.

need to deal with the influence of European colonialism upon their discipline and upon their own thinking (add: practice).[5]

I am well-aware that my efforts are partial, piecemeal, fragmentary, broken; and in what follows I reflect on that and relate it to silence. I have kept in mind Franz Wright's sage comment in his poem "Alder Street,"

> Someone new may speak
> if I, today, keep silent.[6]

Yet, whatever I manage to say herein, my hope is that the inclusion of my white voice highlights in reverse as it were a dynamic that sometimes goes on, but that at other times does not go on at all: for as a remarkable amount of what passes for theology happens without including "brown faces," and is silent in terms of voices beyond those—such as myself—we might call the "usual suspects," that is, those from colder climes around the North Atlantic and its nearby seas. And even if we recognize—as we must—a shift in Christianity to the global south, as Jione Havea asserts, "It does not really matter that the Bible is in the hands of Africans, and of Asians and Islanders, if they are to interpret it according to the teachings of white men"[7]—a point that can be elaborated from Bible to the tradition at large and to many ways of theologizing.

Voice and Body

Voices, of course, come from bodies, bodies with hands perhaps holding the Bible, amongst other things (I recall a US president, Trump, with Bible aloft at a church near the White House, while much of "his" country was protesting in Black Lives Matter marches—who was on the side of right?). Bodies *at borders* can provide us with glimpses of some of the most joyous and heroic moments of human life: a border might assure people that they have arrived in safety, and maybe at the border they fall into others' arms, embraced and held by friends or lovers—or merciful strangers. But borders can also be fraught and dangerous, the place of some people's deepest fears, and worst nightmares. Bodies at borders may be searched and frisked at others' hands; or stripped. At borders, bodies can be tracked by deadly

---

5. See Sugirtharajah, *Postcolonial Reconfigurations*, 143, discussed in Jagessar and Burns, *Christian Worship: Postcolonial Perspectives*, 126 and Burns, "Introduction: Postcolonial Practice of Ministry," 2.

6. Wright, *God's Silence*, 24.

7. Havea, "The Cons of Contextuality," 44, discussed in Burns, "A Fragile Future for the Ordo?," 160.

hand-held weapons; targeted, put under fire. And borders can and do keep people apart, out of touch, lost from one another for years, for decades, for ever. Think among a plethora of awful real-life possibilities:[8] tense soldiers standing guard at the DMZ that divides Korea; watchtowers along the Berlin Wall, gunners stationed there turning bodies limp with bullets; military showmen, kicking their heels, on the India/Pakistan borderline; IDF personnel training their weapons on Palestinian kids; parents and children being pulled apart by immigration officials in New Mexico; lines of armored police and their vehicles on Hong Kong or Ferguson (Missouri, USA) or London streets; exhausted bodies collapsing out of dinghies onto Mediterranean beaches, while others wash up dead.

Over time, I have come to think that all theology should be humanized, with, as John Vincent insists, every possible theme having an "anatomy": not poverty, but poor *people*, not malnourishment, but malnourished *children*, not dereliction but the derelict *human* environment, and so on.[9] Having "bodies" as a keyword might make us more readily humanize, able to *see* suffering?

Art and Stories

To help that humanizing process, it is also important to hear stories, including ones in bothered voice, so that, in Charlotte Delbo's terms, those who don't know but don't know that they don't know are better informed by those who do know—or so she insists with unequivocal authority in her memoir *Auschwitz and After*. A vivid, at first trivial example of the difference she identifies is that: "when most people say 'I am thirsty,' they 'just go to the bar and order a beer.'" Trivial, that is, until "she insists that anyone able to exercise this kind of freedom can *only think they know* what survivors of [Holocaust] experience like her *do* know."[10]

Alongside stories, or when it is difficult (as it often is) to hear them, I find art can sometimes help—and usefully remind us too that theology is not just about voice. For a happy example, think of Frank Mesaric's "She Went in Haste to the Hill Country" (2006), a powerful image of the pregnant young woman of Luke 1, striding off to see Elizabeth, looking with

---

8. I acknowledge my debt here to Ann Loades' sermon on the face of Christ: "Imagine the ways in which we look for one another at railway stations or at bus depots . . . ," which I go on to invert with miserable encounters. Loades, *Grace and Glory in One Another's Faces*, 81.

9. Vincent, *Hope from the City*, 15.

10. Burns, "Forgiveness in Challenging Circumstances," 146.

resolve right at the viewer.[11] Yet Mary is much more depleted as depicted by Kelly Latimore in his transposition of Matthew 2's narrative of the flight into Egypt. Latimore's contemporary icon "Refugees la Sagrada Familia" (2016) is a scene of moonlit mountain and river being crossed by vulnerable Latinx, their inadequate footwear (flip-flops/thongs) just one indicator of the precariousness of the journey by which they put their lives at risk. Latimore's "Mother of God: Protectress of the Oppressed" (2019) is even more alarming: she stands, haloed babe in arms, behind a wire barrier, sad eyes staring down those who look at her[12]—somewhat of a contrast with Mesaric's strong girl in her stride.

But borders are not just physical, walls and fences, hills and rapids, however dangerous; they can consist in the insulating power of privilege and the oftentimes unseen privilege of power. Vanessa Beecroft's "Madonna with Twins" (2006)—a white woman in a pretty dress (Beecroft herself) breastfeeding two black babies—starkly suggests that privilege, even when the intimacy of the scene collapses other boundaries,[13] while her "Black Christ" (2007)—a young Sudanese man sprawled out in the shape of a cross, dressed only in his underpants—is another visual comment on the ambiguities of colonial "charity" in Dafur where she once lived.[14] Discomforting, Beecroft's images contrast with the like of Margo Humphrey's "Fear Not. I Got You" (2013): a black mother and black child, mother weeping, son dead in her arms, Skittles tumbling from his hand (even as the boy's other hand is curled in a fist and lifted up in a gesture of black power)—with the sweets/lollies/candies a direct allusion to the killing of Trayvon Martin;[15] or Kehinde Wiley's various images of nativity and passion, such as "Mary Comforter of the Afflicted" (2016), glass art in which a young black male, crowned like Mary in images of her Assumption, carries in his arms the limp body of a child—another modern day *pieta* consciously crafted to reflect the realities of the Black Lives Matter movement.[16]

Like these Marian scenes, Ron Mueck's "Youth" also references "classic" (read: western) images of Jesus, in Mueck's case, the resurrected body

---

11. http://frankmesaric.com/gallery-8/ (accessed November 22, 2019).

12. https://kellylatimoreicons.com/ (accessed November 22, 2019).

13. https://en.wikipedia.org/wiki/Vanessa_Beecroft (accessed November 22, 2019).

14. https://oneroom.eu/products/vanessa-beecroft-vbss-006-mp-2006 (accessed November 22, 2019).

15. See Douglas, *Stand Your Ground*, with Margo Humphrey's image on the cover.

16. See versions I and II here: https://www.pri.org/stories/2016-11-02/kehinde-wiley-reimagines-old-portraits-because-if-black-lives-matter-they-deserve and https://ocula.com/art-galleries/daniel-templon/artworks/kehinde-wiley/mary-comforter-of-the-afflicted-ii/ .

of Jesus (especially in encounter with Thomas, as John 21), but the youth is dressed as a urban teenager, sagging pants, flank and shorts on show—and with a knife wound in his side, so resonant not just with the like of Carravagio's "The Incredulity of St. Thomas" but with the realities, and statistics, about victims of knife-crime in many modern cities.[17] And another "classical" reference might be found in the work of another plastic artist, Reza Aramesh—significantly for this piece of art, an Iranian. His "Action 105: An Israeli soldier points his gun at a Palestinian youth asked to strip down as he stands at a military checkpoint along the 'separation barrier' at the entrance of Bethlehem, March 2006" (2011) shows, as the long title suggests, a fraught, undressed Arab man—and it seems to me to have echoes of the "Ecco Homo" (1999) by Mark Wallinger displayed in London where Aramesh now lives, and so via Wallinger's theme also older invitations to behold Christ, by Carravagio as well as Botticelli, Mantegna and many others. Where words fail, or are hard to hear, images like these ones might play their part in humanization, just as the pained savior ("man of sorrows") of the medieval artists just mentioned supposedly did in their day. Art and stories can evoke visceral knowledge for theology.

And: of course, all of the contemporary art I have just cited are racialized. To link this back to my earlier point about my out-of-place-ness, my inclusion in this collection reminds of the kind of tokenism which often goes on with the balance more typically tipped to perspectives shaped by experience more like my own:[18] We all know that some borders are more possible for white bodies to cross than they are for others, and maybe especially white hands holding certain visas or cash; and maybe I am a rare white voice in this collection because we know that some borders are easier for me to cross than many others. I might not even be conscious of the borders, given that I am not "constantly asked to explain myself," pulled over when driving, stopped at airports, or looked at with suspicion when I walk the street or travel on public transport.[19] In Charlotte Delbo's terms, I don't know what others do know with acutely personal awareness.

---

17. Mueck and Beecroft's art is included in Rosen, *Art and Religion in the Twenty-first Century*.

18. I use the word tokenism here consciously, recalling Seforosa Carroll's comments in the talanoa towards this publication on August 3, 2019, which for me brought two particular cautions in mind: Thistlethwaite, "Beyond Theological Tourism"; and Althaus-Reid, "Gustavo Gutierrez Goes to Disneyland."

19. To cite some examples from recent conversation about racism in which I have been a part. I noted in *Pastoral Theology for Public Ministry*, viii, however, that I have become aware that, in Australia, I am avoided when wearing a clerical collar in public (a practice I have abandoned), such, I think, is the mistrust of clergy in the public of Christian institutions—but that is another matter.

After gathering various thoughts to frame my reflections, in the next couple of sections I move my talanoa to narrative about my own experience of becoming aware of gaps, before then turning specifically to some fragments on silence.

Gaps and Absences

This past couple of years I have been working on a project, *Twentieth-century Anglican Theologians*,[20] awareness of the need for which came to me when I co-taught a class with that title with Kwok Pui-lan. A generation ago—and less—it was commonplace to find Anglicanism being discussed only and wholly in terms of the Angles/Atlantic Isles/British Isles, a context to which, of course, the very name of the tradition still ties it, one way or another. But in *what way* it does so needs to be up for grabs. Even worse, sometimes the theology of this tradition has been discussed—seemingly without sense of the limits of such a view—in terms of the work only of male clerics in professorships in British universities.[21] That is, it has left out a lot of voices because it has included only bodies that have white skin; bodies that (rather than say, with shovels or fishing nets in hand) work at writing desks and library carols and speaking lecterns; bodies (rather than being "blue collared" or clothed in overalls) tog up in the haberdashery of—academic (and often also ecclesial)—office; bodies in some very small—and privileged—spaces even in the wider societies of which they are a part. It is, then, not so surprising to find that the chapter in which the British-based male professors are valorized is edited by an Anglican male professor in one of those institutions, or that he constructs the book in which the chapter is found by starting with "classics," all European—of course white and male too—with "perspectival theologies" from anywhere else, and the women, consigned to part 5, well towards the back.

Twentieth-Century Anglican Theologians is not conceived as an *ancillary* list of Anglican theologians (that is, all made up with folks from the blue-yonder instead of the North Atlantic and its nearby seas—and all playing second fiddle to the usual suspects). But, for sure, it has still not made perfect, even good-enough, work of recalibrating a decent/honest list of twentieth-century thinkers in this tradition; it is a book with plenty of gaps remaining. I hope, though, that maybe at least it does something rather

---

20. Burns, Cones, and Tengatenga, *Twentieth-century Anglican Theologians*. I write on Dorothy L. Sayers, Ann Loades, Ken Leech, and Carter Heyward, as well as the introduction, "Un/usual Suspects," the latter two with Bryan Cones.

21. Sedgwick, "Anglican Theology."

than nothing to put the usual suspects in wider perspective: as it is, 12 subjects are from Britain, 17 from the west—including 1 from Australia (and of the westerners, 4 are women, and 2 openly gay or lesbian); of the rest, 2 are Chinese, 1 Ghanaian, 1 Indian, 1 Kenyan, 1 South African. In noting what has been absent from other all too common telling(s), the full story is still far from being told (not least as six chapters fell through, and had they emerged there would have been another five tri-continentals included),[22] but this book may fill *some* gaps, perhaps puts some overlooked bodies in the frame, raises up some usually ignored voices, and starts to transgress some if not all questionable conventions about "who counts." There's a reaching towards the idea that "someone new may speak if I, today, keep silent," though for reasons that will become obvious below, I hesitate to say that, such as it is, it is done with "good intentions."

Similar problems with gaps and absence afflict the discipline in which I mainly work, liturgical theology, wrapped up in and warped as it is by western "norms." A particular northern climate—nothing like Australia's—influences liturgical seasons that are observed worldwide at least in many traditions, and in turn these shape lectionary sequences at least in much of the mainline (old-line).[23] In liturgical theology, there is a near total blank on Southern Hemisphere experience of these seasons.[24] Further, images grounded in northern climes also determine key metaphors in the tradition which wends its way—in compassion and conquest—around the world. I learned about some of the problems with the characteristic pairing of light and goodness/divinity and darkness and evil, in Advent especially, but far too much at large, when myself a minority in a congregation with a Caribbean-heritage majority in Birmingham, Britain—a parish where when Caribbean people turned up after stepping off the Windrush ships, were told by the then vicar that "this will never be your church." To which, as one Caribbean elder told me, "we sat right down and waited for the bastard to die."[25] Which he did. In that company, the like of "God is light and in him there is no darkness at all," and "the darkness of sin" *ad infinitim*, grated in ways I had never experienced because I had never *seen* the gross correlation

---

22. A further volume is now in progress, comprised of all tri-continental contributions: Tengatenga and Burns, eds, *Anglican Theology: A Postcolonial Pastiche*.

23. See Jagessar and Burns, *Christian Worship*, Chapter 3. For counter-voice to the mainline reading schema, see Havea, "Local Lectionary Sites."

24. Burns and Monro, *Christian Worship in Australia*, brings forward some alternatives.

25. For more on racism in Birmingham and British churches, see Barton, *Rejection, Resistance and Resurrection*. which strongly informs Jagessar and Burns, *Christian Worship*.

of these words mouthed out of black bodies, and about which a number of people in that company were aware and disturbed. Initially horrified, I become intrigued to discover that biblical narratives—from which the liturgical traditions are drawn (or twisted)—also depict both skin disease and the Anti-Christ as white (though these don't turn up in liturgical texts), as well as that churches in black-majority settings have at least sometimes reworked the too often unexamined correlation of light and goodness/divinity, darkness and sin. Light may be contrasted not with darkness but with heaviness, after Paul's talk of the weight of glory (2 Cor. 4). "Lighten our hearts with the glory of Christ" is the lovely appeal of confession in some Kenyan rites, for example.[26] In this current collection, U-Wen Low's exploration of charismata in India is of great interest to me (chap. 2), an important recalibration of Pentecostal tradition given that narratives of its contemporary origins tend to focus in on William Seymour's remarkable assembly in Azusa Street, Los Angeles, and (albeit much less so) on similar manifestations in the mainstream (old-line) churches like St. Gabriel's (Church of England), Sunderland, in the north-east of England.[27] I welcome this work because we need much more attention to the many gaps and absences that persist in my discipline, just as in so much other theology.

Apologies and Good Intentions

One of the things I have learned about tokenism, and specifically about tokenism among and by the majority, is that it is important to move beyond "good intentions." Anthony Reddie writes (and I quote from him at length to make space for his story), "'theology of good intentions' is a phenomenon that I (along with many other Black people) have lived with for many years [. . .] when, as a Black person, I have been on the end of some thoughtless or insulting words, expressions, actions or behaviours." A "catalyst" arose one year at the British Methodist Conference, of which he is a member: "What I remember most clearly about that incident is the number of people who, following the incident and the resulting apology, demanded that I 'rise above' the whole thing and empathize with the other person. While I was being advised to be a good forgiving Christian, I

---

26. See Jagessar and Burns, *Christian Worship*, chap. 2.

27. On the latter, see Wakefield, *William Boddy: Pentecostal Anglican*. Somewhat strangely to my mind, Pentecostal scholarship is not always so interested in the charismatic movement, despite, for example, Amos Yong's recognition in *Renewing Christian Theology* that nearly 30% of the Roman Catholic Church is charismatic. For work on Roman Catholic experience, and published in India, see Alva, *The Spirituality of the Catholic Charismatic Renewal Movement*.

wondered what injunctions were being placed upon the other person?" He continues, "I thought about every occasion, when despite repeated pleas and assurances, the same offences, oversights and injustices were perpetuated against Black and minority ethnic people. I thought about the many occasions when complaints were made by Black people in response to these constant mistakes or unfortunate incidents."

What Anthony Reddie found in reflection was that "in response to our pleas, the inevitable reply was a simple apology. The comments or incidents were never intended. It was always a mistake, and 'sorry' was the appropriate, if indeed the only response to yet another unfortunate event." So "a 'theology of good intentions' is a way of responding to situations of injustice, in which the perpetrator fails to take full responsibility for their actions." Moreover, "It is a way of responding to the oppressed and powerless, by refusing to take the experiences or perspectives of these people seriously." Because "I am sorry" was like "a mantra for those who constantly use it," Reddie sarcastically remarks, "I began to think that it might be infused with magic properties." While offence may never have been meant by this much-used phrase's speakers, as Reddie observes, "the accidental nature of the events would be less offensive [. . .] if they were not repeated on a regular basis."[28]

I find this story compelling, and I am trying to learn from it,[29] even if *Twentieth-century Anglican Theologians* is an instance—one among many: partial, piecemeal, fragmentary, broken, as I said in my introductory comments—where I haven't been able to better enact what I hoped for. Yet what I know is that better books might be possible and feckless apologies less needed where more time is taken to listen, from the beginning and along the way. Here, silence comes in:[30] "someone new may speak if I, today, keep silent." Silence allows for listening, yet it is also important to be clear that like apologies, it *can* also collude. Silence *can* be used to close down to people as well as open up to others, so I am not sure that it is better than apology in some situations. As Catherine of Siena is purported to have said: "Be silent

---

28. Reddie, *Nobodies to Somebodies*, 152–53.

29. It is striking to me how many references in this essay are from immediate faculty colleagues at one time or another: Mukti Barton, Jione Havea, Michael Jagessar, Kwok Pui-lan, Anita Monro, Clive Pearson, Anthony Reddie, Katalina Tahaafe-Williams, and Gavin Wakefield, to whom I should add Bryan Cones (my "supervisee," a term that hardly does him justice), Ann Loades (my supervisor, a term that hardly does her justice) and James Tengatenga (a visiting professor who made a deep impression on me)—all of whom are mentioned in my footnotes in this essay.

30. Two relatively recent and enjoyable studies in theology are Macculloch, *Silence: A Christian History* and Maitland, *A Book of Silence*, the former by an atheist Anglican, the latter a long-term Anglican recently become Roman Catholic.

no more! Cry out with one hundred thousand tongues. I see that, because of [...] silence, the world is in ruins"![31] In itself silence is multivalent, and needs great care. So I am trying to be more agile in using silence as well as I can, to listen, to make space by not speaking to bolster privilege I already hold in relative abundance and also to speak when silence would give way to more of what is wrong with the *status quo*. Sometimes things need to be said in protest, in refusal, in communication of discontent.

Given its multivalence, the subject-matter can easily become vulnerable to Elaine Graham's critique of certain discussions of power. As she points out with respect to a book by Stephen Sykes on "power in Christian theology," he has not given a full rounded account because he has not paid attention to whose voices have not been heard. His book occludes the basic question of *who* has power, "whose voices, whose perspectives have been incorporated into theology; and by implication, whose voices and experiences are absent."[32] These lessons need to be transferred so that it is clear where silence is a choice and when voice was not invited, about how silence generates space or results from power over one who might otherwise have spoken. Perhaps unsurprisingly, the author of the book on power was one of the aforementioned British-based white male professors, and a bishop to boot.

Silences in the Bible and So On

According to another bishop (later leader of the Three-Self Church), Kuang-hsun Ting, the Bible is a good place to look for silence. Ting argues for giving full heed to what the Bible doesn't say as well as what it does.[33] Sometimes the silence of scriptures is a "blank space" that becomes an invitation to imaginatively fill in, while at other times the silence can shine a "red light," suggesting one should go no further, for beyond that point supposed understanding of "biblical truth" becomes "wildly arrogant." I am not sure how one knows the difference, but for Kuang-hsun Ting, on the one hand the silences of the Bible are open, on the other hand, we might say he says they are a dangerous border.

Zooming in on one aspect of the Bible, the gospels' passion narratives, former Dominican Jacques Pohier (who left his order, as told in *God*

---

31. I am grateful to Cristina Lledo Gomez for this reference in the talanoa towards this publication on December 7, 2019. See https://fauxtations.wordpress.com/2018/09/04/st-catherine-of-siena-the-world-is-rotten-because-of-silence/

32. Graham, *Words Made Flesh*, chap. 16.

33. Ting, "A Chinese Example," 455–56.

in Fragments) hears the silence of Jesus as the sound of mercy—with the "reproaches" of some Good Friday liturgies something Jesus emphatically does not say![34] Drawing on the work of Quaker Rachel Muers, David Ford suggests that silence is "perhaps best understood as God's listening,"[35] an idea that can be turned to the cross, the Bible, and what bothered voices struggle to say.

Yet to me, the most evocative contemporary witness and thinker about silence is not a professional theologian, but a poet: Franz Wright, a person who made an adult commitment to the Roman Catholic tradition, while emerging from multiple addictions, living with terminal disease—and in the midst of all that finding some sort of ministry among, as he puts it, "doomed children,"[36] as volunteer visitor to the dying young at the Children's Hospital in Boston (Massachusetts, USA). His book of poems *God's Silence* begins by citing a Muslim proverb about God being found among the broken-hearted: "I am where you are."[37] Then, many times within the book's pages the poems themselves repeat the strange refrain, "and I have heard God's silence like the sun."[38] At one point he asserts, "I am very afraid but still know You."[39] Daytime warmth (in view of my earlier discussion, I think more subtle than light) on his body is his best take at an image of divine presence, with whatever words towards describing it slow in coming, through which "the long silences need to be loved."[40] But sometimes the poems do depict a voice as, for example, when sitting in the quiet of an empty church building Wright considers that because he has "lived like a monster," his "only hope" is "to die like a child." The voice responds, "I / can do that— / if you ask me, I will do

34. See Pohier, "God is God so God is Not Everything," 148–58. I discuss Pohier's take on the reproaches in Burns, *Liturgy*.

35. Ford, *The Future of Christian Theology*, 83.

36. Wright, *God's Silence*, 37 (From a Line by Reverdy).

37. Wright, *God's Silence*, front matter/no page number. "When Moses conversed with God, he asked, 'Lord, where shall I seek you?' God answered, 'Among the brokenhearted.' Moses continued, 'Lord, no heart could be no more despairing than mine.' And God said, 'Then I am where you are.'" Compare in the Christian tradition, Catherine of Siena: "'My Lord, where were you when my heart was disturbed by all these temptations?' He replies, 'I was in your heart.' She's not satisfied. 'May your truth always be preserved Lord, and all reverence to your Majesty . . . but how can I possibly believe that you were in my heart when it was full of ugly, filthy thoughts?' He helps her to work it out. 'Did those thoughts and temptations bring content or sorrow, delight or displeasure to your heart?' She replies, 'The greatest sorrow and displeasure.' 'Well then,' says the Lord, 'Who was hidden at the centre of your heart?'" See Loades, *Grace and Glory in One Another's Faces*, 136-137.

38. Just some examples: Wright, *God's Silence*, 61, 76, 88.

39. Wright, *God's Silence*, 36 (Arkansas First Light).

40. Wright, *God's Silence*, 8 (East Boston, 1996: II).

it / for you."[41] But the poems also suggest how Wright finds his own voice in response to perception of the presence.

In another poem, another utterance comes to him in the sound of apocryphal gospel, Thomas Saying 28: *"I came in the midst of the world / and in the flesh I appeared to you /* (I seemed to hear this, originless) */ and I found you all / drunk and no one / did I find among you / thirsting."*[42] The "faceless voice" manifest to Franz Wright then asks him a question, "How can you expect energy from above / when you continue to receive it / from below / and are content?" That question evokes Wright's own declaration of intense dis-ease: "I Am Not Content!"[43] As Wright found and tells in these poems, being silent, paying attention, listening, might lead to, stir up, discontent—one reason why for some people (most of us?) silence can be so difficult.

At the Border

Finally, I want to return to a border, and to land my talanoa in the water as it were, by inviting attention to a particular practice that gives powerful expression to discontent, and protest, with large amounts of graced chaos. Also, having engaged above with lessons learned from colleagues, this final part involves a practice about which I am learning because of a former student,[44] and so, I hope, shows something about the multi-directional possibilities of learning.

My former student Sara is now an ordained minister and is involved in an inter-cultural liturgy—in the waters of the Rio Grande. The liturgy is part of a larger "fiesta protesta" at the waters that separate Mexico and the US along north/south-western parts of the borderline, sometimes more narrow and shallow and calm than in other places, but a border nonetheless—and quite likely close to where parents and children have been pulled apart by immigration officials, and looking like the landscape in the background of Latimore's icon of the Latinx holy family. The liturgy, "Vocas de Ambos" ("voices from both sides"), is a picnic, put on by people from a US-based Episcopal Church assembly in Silver City and a Mexican Elim Assemblies of

---

41. Wright, *God's Silence*, 43 (The Heaven).

42. Find the text in another translation in Elliott, *The Apocryphal Jesus*, 55; Lapham, *An Introduction to the New Testament Apocrypha*, 119, is at pains to point out that Thomas' Docetism "must in no way be mistaken for the incarnational teaching of the mainstream Church."

43. Wright, *God's Silence*, 76–77 (The Walk).

44. https://www.episcopalnewsservice.org/2018/05/08/bilingual-eucharist-to-be-celebrated-in-rio-grande-river-at-one-day-texas-border-crossing-party/ In the accompanying photographs Sara Guck is also in the water.

God in Palomas, with some of the fare at the picnic an ecumenical eucharist. I don't know how much silence is involved, but whatever words are used are bilingual. And the presider is waist high in the water, while people wade into the river to stand alongside or sit on the banks nearby. The makeshift table bobs about. And the invitation to become one body in communion with Christ Jesus invites to that same table people from both sides.

Here is an image in which we might glimpse—*glimpse* because this gesture of course needs to be allied with all kinds of other ones, at other times and in other settings[45]—but *glimpse nevertheless* the mystery of divine generosity which promises "energy from above," fills and slakes human hungers and thirsts, and hears all voices.

Works Cited

Althaus-Reid, Marcella. "Gustavo Gutierrez Goes to Disneyland: Theme Park Theologies and the Diaspora of the Discourse of the Popular Theologian in Liberation Theology." In *Interpreting Beyond the Borders*, edited by Fernando Segovia, 36–58. The Bible and Postcolonialism 3. Sheffield: Sheffield Academic, 2000.

Alva, Reginald. *The Spirituality of the Catholic Charismatic Renewal Movement*. New Delhi: Christian World Imprints, 2014.

Barton, Mukti. *Rejection, Resistance and Resurrection: Speaking Out on Racism in the Church*. London: Darton, Longman & Todd, 2005.

Brown Douglas, Kelly. *Stand Your Ground: Black Bodies and the Justice of God*. Maryknoll, NY: Orbis, 2015.

Burns, Stephen. "Forgiveness in Challenging Circumstances." In *Forgiveness in Context: Theology and Psychology in Creative Dialogue*, edited by Fraser Watts and Elizabeth Gulliford, 144–59. London: Continuum, 2004.

———. "A Fragile Future for the Ordo?" In *Worship and Culture: Foreign Country or Homeland?*, edited by Glaucia Vasconcelos Wilkey, 143–61. Grand Rapids: Eerdmans, 2014.

———. "Introduction: Postcolonial Practice of Ministry." In *Postcolonial Practice of Ministry: Leadership, Liturgy, and Interfaith Engagement*, edited by Kwok Pui-lan and Stephen Burns, 1–16. Lanham, MD: Lexington, 2016.

———. *Liturgy*. SCM Studyguide. London: SCM, 2018.

———. *Pastoral Theology for Public Ministry*. New York: Seabury, 2015.

Burns, Stephen, Bryan Cones, and James Tengatenga, eds. *Twentieth-century Anglican Theologians: From Evelyn Underhill to Esther Mombo*. Hoboken, NJ: Wiley-Blackwell, 2020.

Elliott, J. K. *The Apocryphal Jesus: Legends of the Early Church*. Oxford: Oxford University Press, 1996.

Ford, David F. *The Future of Christian Theology*. Oxford: Blackwell, 2011.

Graham, Elaine. *Words Made Flesh: Writings in Pastoral and Practical Theology*. London: SCM, 2009.

Havea, Jione. "The Cons of Contextuality . . . Kontextuality." In *Contextual Theology for the Twenty-first Century*, edited by Steven Bevans and Katalina Tahaafe-Williams,

---

45. In Anglican and other traditions, eucharistic prayer over the gifts of the table often uses the phrase "at all times and in all places . . .".

38–52. Missional Church, Public Theology, World Christianity 1. Eugene, OR: Pickwick Publications, 2011.

———. "Local Lectionary Sites." In *Christian Worship in Australia*, edited by Stephen Burns and Anita Monro, 117–28. Strathfield, NSW: St. Pauls, 2009.

———. "Negotiating with Scripture and Resistance." In *Scripture and Resistance*, edited by Jione Havea, 1–14. Theology in the Age of Empire. Lanham, MD: Fortress Academic, 2019.

———. "Welcome to Talanoa." In *Talanoa Ripples: Across Borders, Cultures, Disciplines*, 11–22. Auckland: Pasifika@Massey, 2010.

Havea, Jione and Clive Pearson, eds. *Out of Place: Doing Theology on the Cross-cultural Brink*. Cross Cultural Theologies. Sheffield: Equinox, 2008.

Jagessar, Michael N., and Stephen Burns. *Christian Worship: Postcolonial Perspectives*. Sheffield: Equinox, 2011.

Lapham, Fred. *An Introduction to the New Testament Apocrypha*. London: Continuum, 2003.

Loades, Ann. *Grace and Glory in One Another's Faces: Worship and Preaching*. Edited by Stephen Burns. Norwich, UK: Canterbury, 2020.

Macculloch, Dairmaid. *Silence: A Christian History*. London: Allen Lane, 2013.

Maitland, Sara. *A Book of Silence*. London: Granta, 2008.

Pohier, Jacques. "God Is God so God Is not Everything." In *Spiritual Classics from the Late Twentieth-century*, edited by Ann Loades, 131–63. London: CHP, 1995.

Reddie, Anthony. *Nobodies to Somebodies: A Practical Theology for Education and Liberation*. Peterborough, UK: Epworth, 2003.

Rosen, Aaron. *Art and Religion in the Twenty-first Century*. London: Thames & Hudson, 2016.

Sedgwick, Peter. "Anglican Theology." In *The Modern Theologians: An Introduction to Christian Theology since 1918*, edited by David F. Ford with Rachel Muers, 178–93. Oxford: Wiley Blackwell, 2005.

Sugirtharajah, R. S. *Postcolonial Reconfigurations: An Alternative Way of Reading the Bible and Doing Theology*. London: SCM, 2003.

Tengatenga, James and Stephen Burns, eds. *Anglican Theology: A Postcolonial Pastiche*. Alameda, CA: Borderless, forthcoming.

Thistlethwaite, Susan B. "Beyond Theological Tourism," in *Beyond Theological Tourism: Mentoring as a Grassroots Approach to Theological Education* edited by Susan B. Thistlethwaite and George F. Cairns, 3–15. Maryknoll, NY: Orbis, 1994.

Ting, T. H. "A Chinese Example: The Silences of the Bible." In *Voices from the Margins: Interpreting the Bible in the Third World*, edited by R. S. Sugirtharajah, 455–56. London: SPCK, 1995.

Vaka'uta, Nasili, ed. *Talanoa Rhythms: Voices from Oceania*. Auckland: Pasifika@Massey, 2011.

Vincent, John. *Hope from the City*. Peterborough, UK: Epworth, 2000.

Wakefield, Gavin. *William Boddy: Anglican Pentecostal*. Milton Keynes, UK: Paternoster, 2007.

Wright, Franz. *God's Silence*. New York: Knopf, 2007.

Yong, Amos. *Renewing Christian Theology: Systematics for a Global Christianity*. Waco, TX: Baylor University Press, 2014.

Part Four

Riotous Bodies

14

Beyond the Symbolic Stripping of Women

Ezekiel 16, Draupadi, and Dalit Women in Juxtaposition

Monica Jyotsna Melanchthon

INDIA IS A LAND of multiple scriptural traditions, cultures, and languages. Anyone growing up in such a culture is exposed to diverse traditions such as the above, through education, media, and interaction with neighbors of other faiths. These traditions, Christian, Hindu, Islamic and others are absorbed and assimilated into our bodies, as a mixture and medley of images, ideas, and expectations. The texts arising from these varied (especially the dominant) religious traditions, fill us with multiple, sometimes competing, vague and impacting details. The experience is akin to that described by Lefkovitz who writes of the "origin stories" in the Hebrew Bible: "reading the original stories has a consolidating effect on this internal textual swirl, bringing to consciousness a relatively coherent narrative, one that is susceptible to scrutiny, critique, wonder."[1] Although the texts under study in this chapter are not "origin stories," their ancientness and their place within literature received as 'Scripture,' uplifts them as important and as authoritative and influential.

---

1. Lefkovitz, *In Scripture*, 1.

The Stripping of Draupadi

One of the main inherited legacies of India in the cultural-religious sphere is the *Mahabharata,* a cultural credential of the so-called Aryan civilization of India,[2] an ancient Sanskrit epic with many variations and revisions extant today. A well-known scene in this epic is that of the disrobing/stripping of the heroine, Draupadi.

The scene occurs in the second book of the *Mahabharata,* narrating the struggle between two clans, the Pandavas and the Kauravas for control of the kingdom. The Pandava brothers have lost all their possessions on few rolls of dice. Gone was their wealth, their gems, their homes, their lands—everything. But Yudhishthira, the oldest of the Pandava brothers could not let the game stop. Much to the concern of the elders in the assembly, he wagers his beautiful and virtuous wife whom he shares with his four brothers describing her as a woman who is exceptional in beauty, compassion, and accomplishment.[3]

He loses and Duryodhana of the Kauravas instructs his minister, Kshatta to bring Draupadi, and says, "Let her sweep the chambers, force her thereto, and let the unfortunate one stay where our serving-women are."[4] Duryodhana is cautioned against such action, but he shouts, "Go *Pratikamin*,[5] and bring thou Draupadi hither. Thou hast no fear from the sons of Pandu."[6] The *Prathikamin* enters the abode of the Pandavas "like a dog in a lion's den," approaches queen Draupadi and says, "Yudhishthira having been intoxicated with dice, Duryodhana, O Draupadi, hath won thee. Come now, therefore, to the abode of Dhritarashtra.[7] I will take thee, O Yajnaseni,[8] and put thee in some menial work."[9]

Draupadi, a Kshatriya woman and a princess, would not normally appear in public. She responds, "Why, O *Pratikamin,* dost thou say so? What prince is there who playeth staking his wife? The king was certainly intoxicated with dice. Else, could he not find any other object to stake?"[10] to

2. Spivak, "Draupadi," 387.
3. *Mahabharata, Sabha Parva,* sec. LXIV, 124.
4. *Mahabharata, Sabha Parva,* sec. LXV, 125.
5. *Pratikamin* was a messenger and a son of a Suta caste (a Suta was a child born to a Brahmin and a Kshatriya—hence of low status)
6 *Mahabharata, Sabha Parva,* sec. LXVI, 126.
7. King of the Kuru Kingdom.
8. "Born from Fire," another name for Draupadi. She came from no mother's womb but out of a sacrificial *yagna* (fire-ritual).
9. *Mahabharata, Sabha Parva,* sec. LXVI, 126.
10. *Mahabharata, Sabha Parva,* sec. LXVI, 126.

which the messenger replies, "When he had nothing else to stake . . . the son of Pandu, staked thee. The king had first staked his brothers, then himself, and then thee, O princess."[11] Draupadi said, "O son of the *Suta* race, go, and ask that gambler present in the assembly, whom he hath lost first, himself, or me. Ascertaining this, come hither, and then take me with thee, O son of the *Suta* race."[12] This is communicated to the Assembly, but he is sent back to bring Draupadi, and no response is given to her query.

The messenger returns to tell her again that she is being summoned. She refuses, appealing to the Kaurava sense of morality saying that if morality is aspired and cherished, it will bring blessing. Frustrated with *Pratikamin* and with Draupadi's obstinance, Duryodhana sends his younger brother Dussasana who enters her chambers, commands her to come since she has been won by them and drags her by the locks of her hair into the presence of the assembly. As he drags her, Draupadi cries, 'Wretch! It will behoveth thee to take me before the assembly. My season hath come, and I am now clad in one piece of attire." But Dussasana, still dragging Draupadi forcibly, says to her, "Whether thy season hath come or not, whether thou art attired in one piece of cloth or entirely naked, when thou hast been won at dice and made our slave, thou art to live amongst our serving-women as thou pleasest." Once in the presence of others, she repeats her question asking if Yudhisthira had a right to stake her if he had already become a slave.[13] Her question is disregarded. Karna on the Kaurava side orders her to be stripped, since he deemed her a "whore" for being married to five men, against custom.[14]

Karna emphasizes that the Pandavas and their wife, Draupadi were fairly won. He orders the Pandava brothers to take off their robes and the attire of Draupadi. On hearing this the Pandava brothers took off their upper garments and sat down. Then Dussasana, "seizing Draupadi's attire before

---

11. *Mahabharata, Sabha Parva*, sec. LXVI, 126.

12. *Mahabharata, Sabha Parva*, sec. LXVI, 126.

13. "The king was summoned to this assembly and though possessing no skill at dice, he was made to play with skillful, wicked, deceitful and desperate gamblers. How can he be said then to have staked voluntarily? The chief of the Pandavas was deprived of his senses by wretches of deceitful conduct and unholy instincts, acting together, and then vanquished. He could not understand their tricks, but he hath now done so." *Mahabharata, Sabha Parva*, sec. LXVII, 129.

14. "O son of the Kuru race, the gods have ordained only one husband for one woman. This Draupadi, however, hath many husbands. Therefore, certain it is that she is an unchaste woman. To bring her, therefore, into this assembly attired though she be in one piece of cloth—even to uncover her is not at all an act that may cause surprise." *Mahabharata, Sabha Parva*, sec. LXVII, 131.

the eyes of all, began to drag it off her person,"[15] while the elders of her family watch in stunned silence. Her emasculated husbands mumble and rumble in anger, but none of them can lift a finger to help her, bound as they are by *dharma*, the *dharma* of their new status as slaves.

Draupadi cries to the gods, covering her face, and thinking of Krishna, of Hari, of the lord of the three worlds.[16] Miraculously, more and more of the sari appears to clothe her, and Dussasana stops exhausted. As the sari was ruthlessly stripped, another appeared in its place. Her garment becomes endless—yards and yards of fabric appear miraculously. The Kaurava brothers were stunned, and then enraged, and Dushasana's lusty intentions are defeated. Draupadi never stands fully naked in that public, fundamentally male space. She opens her eyes, and the pile of clothes vanish in a column of flames. Her husbands stand in shame, while the sky outside went dark and storm clouds burst in thunder and the animals in the field shriek.

The blind and old Dhritarashtra, the Kaurava king cries a halt to this injustice, and he offers Draupadi three boons to console her and compensate her for the insult. She uses these to free her husbands. Dhritarashtra pleads for forgiveness for the dishonorable things done by his sons. In response, Draupadi looks scornfully at everyone and leaves the hall followed by her silent husbands. The Pandavas, in response to Draupadi's rage and her humiliation, vow revenge on the Kauravas. After losing at another gambling match and serving 13 years in exile, they return to wage war against them. The great war is fought, however, not to avenge Draupadi's insult; the righteous war, the occasion of the *Bhagvad Gita*, is fought to settle the long-standing struggle between the clans for political power. Finally, the Kauravas are defeated and killed, the kingdom is restored to the Pandavas and Draupadi is avenged.[17]

The verses about Draupadi praying to Krishna and his divine intervention to salvage her dignity appears outside the main text of the critical edition of the Sanskrit *Mahabharata*.[18] These verses are therefore seen as a later

15. *Mahabharata, Sabha Parva*, sec. LXVII, 132.
16. *Mahabharata, Sabha Parva*, sec. LXVII, 132.
17. Leeming and Page, *Goddess*, 166–67.
18. Sukathankar, *The Mahabharata*. "By this excision of the *deux ex machina* from the scene, Sukhthankar is questioning the validity of a people's engagement with a text, the sacralisation of the epic by Vaishnavism, the consequent transformation in the status of the text, and the religious and political polemics involved in Krishna's succour to Draupadi. In spite of Sukhthankar's rational scissoring of the god, it is difficult for anyone to conceive of the episode without Krishna's timely appearance and so the question remains as to where textual originality lies-in the traditional word to word transmission or in the edited, trimmed texts ... This dilemma around the 'origin' would make us perhaps tentatively conclude that we have only interpretations and that is the strength

insertion. This later insertion or interpolation alludes to a form of cosmic justice. Despite the scholarly discussions that focus on when this interpolation was made, where, and whether she was really stripped,[19] this episode in the epic is perhaps the most well-known among the Indian populace, reproduced in film, theatre, drama, and literature, and it is this version that is most widespread and continues to attract feminist and academic reflection and popular interpretation.

Woman-city (Ezekiel 16)

Ezekiel 16 depicts Jerusalem as God's daughter and wife whose transgression and defilement are foregrounded in language that rouses little sympathy for her. The text is replete with images of exposure—beginning with the infant, still covered in blood, naked, discarded, and abhorred (16:4–5). The next section sees YHWH passing by and seeing her as a young woman, again with her body exposed, naked and bare—flapping in blood, her breasts formed and her pubic hair visible—signs of her having come of age (16:6–7).

In the third section YHWH passes by her again and he realizes that she was "at the age of love," and so YHWH covers her nakedness and enters into a covenant with her (16:8). Now that YHWH wants to make her his wife, YHWH covers her nakedness; YHWH ritually cleanses her, clothes her, adorns her, feeds her and she is beautiful to behold. Her fame is spread among the nations on account of her beauty for it was perfect because of YHWH's splendor bestowed on her. Trusting in her beauty and fame, she turns to whoring in ungratefulness. Using negative language first, the prophet makes her abominations public (16:15–22). She is depicted as deviant (16:30–34), and YHWH speaks the words of punishment:

> [35] Therefore, O harlot, hear the word of the LORD. [36] . . . because of your brazen effrontery, offering your nakedness to your lovers for harlotry . . . [37] I will assuredly assemble all the lovers, along with everybody you accepted and everybody you rejected, I will assemble them against you from every quarter and I expose your nakedness to them, and they shall see all your nakedness. [38] I will inflict upon the punishment of women who commit adultery and murder, and I will direct bloody and impassioned fury against you. [39] I will deliver you into their hands and they shall tear down your eminence and level your mounds; and they shall

---

of the Mahabharata" (Janaky, On the Trail of *the Mahabharata*, 997).

19. See Bhattacharya, "Was Draupadi Ever Disrobed?"

strip you of your clothing and take away your dazzling jewels, leaving you naked and bare. [40] Then they shall assemble a mob against you to pelt you with stones and pierce you with their swords.[41] They shall put your houses to the flames and burn your houses and execute punishment upon you in the sight of many women; thus I will put a stop to your harlotry, and you shall pay no more fees. [42] When I have satisfied My fury upon you, and My rage has departed from you, then I will be tranquil; I will be angry no more. (16:35–42, JPS)

Her punishment is exposure (stripped and exposed) through assault and mutilation, but then restored after a fashion. Ezekiel 16 represents a negative and scathing portrayal of Israel,[20] as a disgraced and forsaken wife, and of God as an "abusive spouse."[21] Her horrific punishment is portrayed as entirely justified by the severity of her violations and extent of her ingratitude to God. Ezekiel chapters 16 and 23 have been identified as "the most lengthily developed and abusive prophet *woman-city* metaphor,"[22] and banned from use in the synagogue.[23]

Reading in Juxtaposition

These two texts have received a fair amount of attention especially from women and feminist interpreters who wrestled with the disturbing issues they raise. Draupadi is recognized as a victim of patriarchal domination, an icon of women's vulnerabilities,[24] and yet an analysis of her character also reveals her strength, pride, wisdom, anger, perseverance, resistance, and vengeance to right the wrong done to her and to her husbands through her speech and her actions. "Draupadi sets a canon of her own for all her beauty, charm, eloquence, intelligence, and personality, besides her unique birth and polyandrous married life."[25] As a wife to five husbands,[26] bestowed upon her by destiny, she is unique. "Within a patriarchal and patronymic context, she is exceptional, indeed 'singular' in the sense of odd, unpaired,

---

20. Shields, "Multiple Exposures," 138.
21. Claassens, "Transforming God-Language." See also L. Day, "Rhetoric and Domestic Violence in Ezekiel 16."
22. Stiebert, *Fathers and Daughters in the Hebrew Bible*, 196 (my italics).
23. Shields, "Multiple Exposures," 138n2.
24. Mankekar, *Screening*, 224.
25. Basak, "Canonizing the Draupadi's in Mahesweta Devi's "Draupadi," 224.
26. Reminiscent of the Samaritan woman in John 4.

uncoupled,"[27] and not condemned for having multiple sexual partners. And yet as Spivak writes, "In the epic, Draupadi's legitimized pluralization (as a wife among husbands) in singularity (as a possible mother or harlot) is used to demonstrate male glory."[28] Sex with "five men is considered her *dharma*, and she is even allowed to have one child with each man."[29] She is depicted as a "symbol of female determination and will," who in response to the humiliation that she endures, refuses to tie up her disheveled hair,[30] until it has been smeared with the blood of Dussasana.[31]

A folk tradition suggests that the great war between the Pandavas and the Kauravas was fought to quench her thirst for blood. She is portrayed as a woman who did not see herself as anything less than the male. She is the "proud and angry heroine," an "enigmatic woman of substance," a subversive character of resilience and power, an early feminist, who also possessed "the austerity of a traditional Hindu wife." The Draupadi narrative is one that has been appropriated by groups at both ends of the "ideological spectrum—from the patriarchal legitimation of the control of women by inflicting punishment upon them, to claims for Draupadi as a proto-feminist cultural heroine."[32]

Ezekiel "is the most problematic of all prophetic books for its sexual and marital metaphorical language, notoriously the most extreme and offensive in the Hebrew Bible."[33] The responses to Ezekiel's very graphic text are also varied, with calls to recognize it as a text that describes the ANE world, and the treatment of enemy soldiers and prostitutes or women accused of adultery. Based on information gathered from Assyrian and Babylonian reliefs, it describes the feminization of enemy soldiers since femininity is "correlated ideologically with passivity and immobility."[34] Jerusalem as *Woman-city* "resembles the feminized conquered male soldiers of the reliefs who are likewise dismembered, stripped and shamed

---

27. Spivak, "Draupadi," 387.

28. Spivak, "Draupadi," 387.

29. Menon, *Infinite Variety*, 199.

30. "When being dragged by her hair, it comes loose, and her hair becomes the marker of her sexual humiliation and the indicator of when that humiliation will end" (Menon, *Infinite Variety*, 201).

31. Chaitanya, "The Willing Woman: On Women and Willpower," 188–89.

32. Sunder Rajan, "The Story of Draupadi's Disrobing," 333.

33. Moughtin-Mumby, *Sexual and Marital Metaphors*, 161.

34. Ann Kessler Guinan, "Auguries of Hegemony: The Sex Omens of Mesopotamia," *Gender and History* 9 (1997): 462–73 as cited in Chapman, "Sculpted Warriors," 13. See also Smith-Christopher, "Ezekiel in Abu-Ghraib."

before their families."[35] The metaphor is violent and extreme and depicts the chaotic experience of the exile in which men were emasculated and treated like women, a type of "gender reversal."[36]

Setting the text within its post-exilic context, Yee[37] (following Patton[38]) suggests that Ezekiel was a witness to the sexual violence to which the women of Judah were subjected under foreign invasion, hence Ezekiel uses the marriage metaphor to project upon the city and its occupants what women have experienced. Yee suggests that Ezekiel takes on an "act of transgendered self-blame," to formulate his and the guilt of the male community, as the guilt of a promiscuous, adulterous women.[39] Ezekiel embodies "'the agony of displacement,' in short, 'of Exile.'"[40]

This treatment of the Woman-city has also been understood to reflect the ANE treatment of prostitutes as opposed to wives. "Prostitutes are not victimized by rape," says Magdalene, and were "righteously subject to sexual humiliation at the hand of God," since they were not seen as "morally responsible women."[41] It mirrors ANE punishment for covenantal/treaty violations[42] and a reminder that Israel has not "lived up to the expectations of covenantal relationship."[43] Peterson writes,

> Judah knew full well about the harsh realities that awaited her as a spiritual prostitute. Even though she understood the horror of war and ANE treaty curses she still chose to remove herself from under the protection of her "Husband." In so doing, she received the due recompense of her error from an ANE perspective—public stripping and abuse . . . Ezekiel is not depicting an *actual* rape but is speaking metaphorically as a means of describing a spiritual reality.[44]

There is consensus that Ezekiel is using a metaphor but there are diverse positions on how one should receive this metaphor. It is an "unambiguous metaphor" depicting a "fictional relationship" between God as

---

35. Chapman, "Sculpted Warriors," 17.
36. Kamionkowski, *Gender Reversal and Cosmic Chaos*, 151–52.
37. Yee, *Poor Banished Children of Eve*, 133.
38. Patton, "Should Our Sister be Treated Like a Whore?," 228.
39. Yee, *Poor Banished Children*, 132; see also, Smith-Christopher, "Ezekiel in Abu-Ghraib," 155.
40. Hornsby, "Ezekiel," 423.
41. Magdalene, "Ancient Near Eastern Treaty-Curses," 340.
42. Peterson, *Ezekiel in Context*, 197, 206, 221, 225.
43. Jacobs, "Ezekiel 16," 205.
44. Peterson, *Ezekiel in Context*, 106.

father and Israel as daughter.⁴⁵ Its harmfulness is thereby "diffused," and it should not be read literally or "transferred onto actual women."⁴⁶ Ezekiel 16 along with other similar prophetic texts are "metaphorized descriptions and representations of imaginary communities and imagined past histories," for "political and ideological propaganda" to "control women and men for ideological purposes."⁴⁷ But some women readers are uncomfortable with the personification of Judah/Israel as errant woman/prostitute, the language, and the "foundational ideology" that suggests that "women's bodies are the property of men."⁴⁸ They note the "sexual violence"⁴⁹ inherent in this text and declare it "aberrant"⁵⁰ and "pornographic,"⁵¹ for it is "a horrifying depiction of spousal abuse, violence and sexual degradation"⁵² that uses a metaphor for "prophetic rape."⁵³

One can, on a purely textual perspective, see the texts as reflections of the times of the authors / editors or simply acknowledge the violence in them with little attention to the manner in which readers or audiences interpret. Such an approach focuses on individual responses and ignores the wider societal discourses that mediate readers' interpretations. The impact and the repercussions that such texts have on women in the real world is recognized by many. In Claassens' words, the metaphors are "shaped by society, but they also have a shaping function."⁵⁴ And as Coogan reminds us: "The punishment of God's unfaithful wife is not just a metaphor but a precedent and warning, so that all women may be instructed not to act promiscuously as you did [Ezek 23:48] or else they too will be punished by their husbands as God punished Jerusalem. Husbands, the implication is, can and should imitate God and wives should learn from the allegory."⁵⁵

These texts resonate with many Indian women on two counts—the experience of spousal abuse⁵⁶ and the practice of stripping and parading.

45. Maier, *Daughter Zion*, 112.
46. Stiebert, *Fathers and Daughters*, 206.
47. Carroll, "Desire Under the Terebinths," 303.
48. L. Day, "Teaching the Prophetic Marriage Metaphor Texts," 175.
49. Exum, "The Ethics of Violence Against Women."
50. Sloane, "Aberrant Textuality?," 55.
51. van Dijk-Hemmes "The Metaphorization of Woman in Prophetic Speech," 168.
52. Seibert, *The Violence of Scripture*, 137.
53. Susane Scholz, *Sacred Witness*, 43.
54. Claassens, "Transforming God-Language," 35.
55. Coogan, *God and Sex*, 186–87.
56. Thirty-one percent of married women have experienced physical, sexual, or emotional violence by their spouses. The most common type of spousal violence is physical violence (27%), followed by emotional violence (13%). ("Every Third Woman

Such texts are mediated through personal experience and by varied visual narratives, societal discourses, including the treatment of Dalit women as the one narrated below.

> Khairlanji, the name of a village in Bhandara district of Maharashtra, evokes the power, brutality and arrogance of India's caste system and the impunity enjoyed by its most cruel practitioners. It was here . . . that Surekha Bhotmange, a Dalit woman farmer, was killed along with her two sons, Roshan and Sudhir, who was visually disabled, and her 17-year-old daughter, Priyanka. Each of them had been subjected to the most horrible violence by members of the dominant . . . caste in this area, who now employ the same upper-caste hegemonic practices and methods against Dalits that they had been victims of, and which they had once fought against.
>
> On September 29, 2006, they stripped the women, paraded, beat, raped and killed them. The dreadful photographs showed there was not an inch of the younger woman's body that was not marked by bruises. The investigation was fixed at every stage to help the accused, from the deliberate delay in the search for the bodies, the destruction of evidence, to the fudged postmortem report and finally to the flawed chargesheet and the biased court proceedings.[57]

Khairlanji has since become a metaphor for all the atrocities committed against Dalits across the country. This is one among hundreds of cases, a cruel expression, of misogyny and caste discrimination in rural India, where being stripped naked and paraded through the village streets is common. It is customary punishment meted out by men in village councils to women found guilty of elopement/marriage with a person of a different caste, illicit relationships, adultery, or other actions seen as contravention of caste boundaries. Many women are labeled witches and treated similarly. Most of these instances when considered consistently turn out to be retribution by dominant caste landlords upon independent, vulnerable Dalit women. These instances reveal the operations of power, desire, and violence in the context of a society hierarchically structured on a system of social stratification of which Dalit and Adivasi women are at the lowest.

My focus here is narrow. Among the many contestations within these texts, I privilege the "stripping and parading of women" that is often

---

in India Suffers Sexual, Physical Violence at Home." https://www.news18.com/news/india/the-elephant-in-the-room-every-third-woman-in-india-faces-domestic-violence-1654193.html).

57. Karat, "Khairanjli, Then and Now."

bolstered by a sanctimonious logic of punishment and attempt to understand the many facets and dimensions of this awful practice. I read in light of a pressing cultural issue arising from the experiences of Dalit women in India, and to bring this pertinent practice into focus. The questions that interest me here is how such texts are received; the impact of references to stripping and parading on women; and more importantly, how such references become materialized in social regulations of gender. I am not suggesting that these texts are necessarily the source for legitimizing these actions but rather, they serve as heuristic, narrative frames for viewing contemporary events. It needs to be borne in mind that texts such as these can be and are often conveniently appropriated to mesh with the requirement of the society, nation, or church to buttress misogyny, especially since they are received as scriptural texts.

Beyond the Symbolic

Verbal Abuse

A first issue that unites these two texts is the label "whore" that is given to the Woman-city and to Draupadi. They are identified as transgressive subjects in order to justify the violent intervention. Draupadi's vulnerability lay in her polyandry,[58] and Jerusalem's lay in her many acts of violating the marriage covenant as described in 16:15–22. Israel behaves as a "lascivious and unfaithful woman,"[59] whose abominations (worship of other gods and alliances with foreign nations) were worse than that of Sodom and Gomorrah (Ezek 16:51). By doing so she has forgotten and disregarded the husband (YHWH) who rescued her. YHWH was therefore going to expose her nakedness to her lovers (other nations) who will punish her—"they shall strip you of your clothing and . . . leave you naked and bare . . . pelt you with stones and pierce you with their swords" (Ezek 16:39–40 JPS). The nations are the instruments that YHWH will use to punish her.

Both Woman-city and Draupadi are branded as "whores," "harlots" (adulterous wives) and thereby permit God and the male community to punish them, although in the case of Draupadi the Divine intervenes and acts contrary to the male community. The punishing action taken says more

---

58. The polyandrous alliance was the result of the word of Kunti, mother to the Pandava brothers who without seeing what he had brought home instructed Arjuna to share it with his brothers.

59. Ganzel, "Ezekiel," 1058.

about the anxieties of men over female sexuality arising out of a heady mix of both sexual arousal, righteous indignation, and anger.[60]

Verbal abuse, verbal assaults, name calling or labelling, and abusive epithets is a prevalent form of violence against Dalit women. Besides contemptuous forms of address that identifies them by their caste of origin,[61] they also reduce the woman to a sexual organ or a prostitute. These abusive terms are "performative words" that enact their own message, unambiguous and therefore do not need to be decoded.[62] The word "whore," "harlot" or *zonah* in the context of the Semitic world, similarly, evokes an entire history of the profession, and the cultural connotations that go with being termed "whore/harlot" and the treatment of prostitutes and adulterous wives.[63] The term has the capacity to evoke shame, pain, and humiliation. Everything that the woman has done—her identity, her body, her social status—now stand exposed and considered insignificant. Such a label is used to deprive the woman of her autonomous subjectivity and to crush her sense of self. By classifying them as "whores," both the Woman-city and Draupadi are deemed deserving of punishment. Such verbal abuse often accompanies other forms of violence as is evident in both texts such as the stripping and the exposing/parading of women.

Stripping and Exposing/Parading in Public

Stripping and exposing/parading naked women as "social behaviour and phenomenon" is taken seriously in contexts such as India where "female chastity and men's honor are major values," and emotions run high when either is transgressed or challenged. Despite moral and legal sensibilities that question such acts, righteous fury and the logic of punishment authorize such social sanction. This "blatant aggression towards the victim" exposes male anxieties over "female sexuality, or female assertion of

---

60. P. Day, "The Bitch Had It Coming to Her," 235.

61. Ezekiel identifies her as the daughter of your mother, a mother who rejected her husband and children, to whom the proverb, "Like mother like daughter" can be applied. She is the daughter of a Hittite mother and an Amorite father, and sister to Samaria and Sodom (Ezek 16:44–54).

62. Delgado and Stefancic. *Understanding Words that Wound*, 207. In Ezekiel, her acts are described in detail in verses 15 and following. In the *Mahabharata*, Draupadi is called a whore because she had five husbands.

63. Prostitution was a regular and accepted feature of ANE society and has been justified as a necessary means to keep the good and chase wife "safe" from men with evil intentions. And yet we cannot ignore the "asymmetrical social consequences of being a prostitute in the Biblical text" (Ipsen, *Sex Working in the Bible*, 37).

superior social status or social mobility, or a combination of these."[64] Such behavior when exhibited in today's world is construed as a "crisis of masculinity," but in fact as suggested by Roy it is the indexing of a spectacle "of the very nature of masculinity."[65]

What these texts demand is the "acknowledgement of the continuum of violence" and the "multiple sites in which sexual violence" takes place, and the realization that the "continuum of violence that women were subjected to went from the home to the streets to the fields and to the borders."[66] These texts also allude to "the culture of impunity that has seeped into every fabric of people's lives," and that such violence is integral to divine, religious, state, cultural "policies of punishing 'recalcitrant' populations" and to "send a message to insurgent populations."[67]

In the context of caste oppression, stripping and being paraded naked requires also "the recognition of the contradiction of untouchability in its relation to physical violence—molestation, stripping and rape—upon the '*untouchable*' sexed/gendered physical body."[68] The woman's nakedness exposes her genitalia to the male gaze, as well as the divine, and are meant to arouse shame and ritual uncleanness.

Nakedness Exposed

One cannot overlook the narrator's preoccupation with the woman's body and her exposed nakedness in the Ezekiel text. The attempt to completely expose Draupadi's body is thwarted by Krishna's intervention. But Draupadi was not dressed for appearance in public and pleads for understanding from Dusassana. At the juxtaposition of these texts, it is not just a (partially) naked body that is exposed but also—a menstruating body (Eze 16:6, 9, 22). The blood of birth and the blood of menstruation are unique to the female gender, bloods that render women unclean, requiring cleansing. "Such references to blood emphasize the woman's body and associate that body with uncleanness,"[69] and thereby render her susceptible to abuse.

Hair too plays a role: the pubic hair of Woman-city and the long black locks of Draupadi's hair—both of which are reference to a woman's maturity, femininity, a potent symbol of desire. YHWH "will uncover/lay bare/

64. Rajan, "The Story of Draupadi's Disrobing," 341.
65. Roy, "A hunt," as cited by Baxi, "Impunity of Law and Custom," 226.
66. Chakravati, "Introduction: The Everyday and the Exceptional," 23.
67. Chakravati, "Introduction," Section 24.
68. Sunder Rajan, "The Story of Draupadi's Disrobing," 344.
69. Shields, "Multiple Exposures," 142.

expose" (from the root *galah*,⁷⁰ Eze 16:36–37; 16:57). Hornsby calls attention to the verb in the Levitical law codes, primarily within sexual codes; the term is significant in that it ties the experience of the exile to the issue of sex and nakedness. YHWH uncovers (sends into exile—vulnerable, open to penetration) so she may be more open to YHWH's saving grace.[71]

These texts attest to how women's bodies are imagined, discussed, and shaped in liminal spaces—the private and the public, home and the world, between wife and whore, and between shame and liberation.[72] The exposure of and disruption of their ritual pollution as menstruating women may be rendered as violation, as intrusion into the "private language of the female body."[73] The usual borders between the public and the private that distinguish the wife from the whore, that offer a semblance of safety, are now blurred. By exposing the naked Woman-city to the nations, or the menstruating and partially dressed Draupadi, the woman becomes "the sole and singular object of the public gaze" and may be "the recipient of both admiration and scorn and neither response is free of the overtones of the other, or of sexual significance."[74]

YHWH as husband becomes brother to the nations (Egypt, Assyria, Chaldea)—a partner of sorts. A major trait of this union, albeit temporary, is that it rests on brutal sexual punishment. As Mehta maintains, "public violence provides one of the most powerful registers of the intimacies between male friends, so much so that it prohibits the democratization of the social body."[75] Ezekiel's Woman-city is unable to defend herself and no one will speak on her behalf. Unlike Draupadi, who is surrounded by men in an assembly of males, the Woman-city will be surrendered to the nations (read: men) and they will punish her in the presence of their women (of Philistia in 16:27, 57; of many women in 16:41; of the daughters of Aram and all her neighbors in 16:57). This mob will do the needful; they are now united, and the differences of race, religion, nation, ethnicity, and gender vane; they are now united, equal, albeit illusory, but their unity is essential for YHWH's plan to work. To quench YHWH's rage, the mob of nations is gathered, and YHWH/husband stands back to watch the punishment of Woman-city, the wife, who is rendered worse than those who traditionally

70. See Hornsby's discussion on this verb in "Ezekiel," 423–425.
71. Hornsby, "Ezekiel," 424–25.
72. Subramanian, "Whom did you Lose First, Yourself or Me?," 77.
73. Janaky, "On the Trail of *the Mahabharata*," 1999.
74. Sunder Rajan, "The Story of Draupadi's Disrobing," 335.
75. Mehta, "Crowd, Cop, Camera: Notes on a Pathological Public Space" (https://www.academia.edu/12124696/Crowd_Cop_Camera_Notes_on_a_pathological_public_sphere; accessed 27 August 2021).

epitomize wickedness and apostasy (Sodom, Samaria). The husband moves between being the initiator of punishment, being the onlooker, and being the punisher—and back again and eventually the savior as well. This movement is unencumbered and relied on incorporating all that were being destroyed—including the stripping and dismembering of the Woman-city's body—all in the name of corrective punishment. This trial of Woman-city does not elicit the speech of the woman who stands accused, except to use her apostasy and foreign liaisons as evidence of culpability.

Shame and Humiliation

Underlying the exposure and the parading of women's nakedness is the intention to humiliate and shame the individual, as well as the family/community to which she belongs. By exposing a "transgressor" to public disapproval (thus requiring an audience), the woman is humiliated and shamed. Neither of these elements remain at the level of abstraction. While there is a distinction between the two, they are also interrelated. These elements acquire definition, meaning, shape and orientation within specific social and cultural contexts and it is this cultural specificity that enables comparison.[76]

Nandy maintains that humiliation is "a form of human relations that can never be a one-way exchange," and that "[n]o humiliation is complete unless the humiliated oblige their tormentors by validating their desire to humiliate."[77] Nandy calls this "Consensual validation," and similarly "consensual shame" from the one who is humiliated and shamed, is essential or else it will remain one sided. Hence, the humiliated also have "some control over their humiliators."[78]

"Exposure is the essence of shaming, and a feeling of exposure is also one of shame's (the emotion) most distinct ingredients and intimately links shame to reputation."[79] An audience is "a pre-requisite for shame, even if the audience is imagined."[80] Such shaming is particularly effective in "Shaming cultures" where "saving face" is culturally important. Shaming techniques and strategies are used in order to regulate and ensure conformation to expected behavior.[81]

---

76. Guru, "Introduction: Theorizing Humiliation," 6.
77. Nandy, "Humiliation: Politics and the Cultural Psychology," 42.
78. Nandy, "Humiliation: Politics and the Cultural Psychology," 6.
79. Jacquet, *Is Shame Necessary?*, 9.
80. Jacquet, *Is Shame Necessary?*, 9.
81. Jacquet, *Is Shame Necessary?*, 11–12, 13.

The attempt to publicly humiliate and shame Draupadi and the Woman-city is clear. If humiliation and shame require consent by the one being humiliated, then Draupadi comes across as one who resists that humiliation through her questioning—although being dragged by one's hair in clothing worn while menstruating, is humiliating enough. Draupadi speaks and she is given ample room to articulate her resistance, anger, intelligence.[82] Her question which is never answered is a sign of her position with, and resistance to, the patriarchal order. The silence of Woman-city is deafening in comparison to the speech of Draupadi. We have no access to the interiority of Woman-city—no protest, no resistance, no voice. Should we therefore construe her humiliation to have been complete? Or are we to assume that she, like many marginalized communities and scores of women, has been numbed by institutionalization, consistent and prolonged humiliation, whose sensitivities have become numb to her own violation and abuse?

The stripping, baring, and parading of women flips all modes by which a woman becomes social. The act of uncovering and stripping needs to be understood both literally and socially. "This spectacle of violence degrades and puts on display a stripped body, in full view of a complicit and voyeuristic spectatorship. It serves a pedagogical function of power—one that teaches a lesson—to subjugated and despised people and communities."[83]

Bordered and Borderless Bodies

What do these scriptural texts of disrobing/stripping and parading tell us about the relationship between contexts, scriptural texts, and lives? Is it likely that the author of Ezekiel 16 was familiar with the stripping and parading of women? Has the Draupadi narrative contributed to the current practice of stripping and parading in the Indian context? How do women react to these texts? These narratives must be treated as "a point of conflation between text and life, a textual testimony, which can penetrate us like actual life."[84] This has been achieved when these texts from the *Mahabharata* and the Hebrew Bible are juxtaposed with the Bhotmange incident.

A scriptural text like the Draupadi story is introduced to every generation. In the recent past, this story has become susceptible to analysis, query, and critique in the light of emancipatory developments and movements

---

82. For a discussion on the meaning and significance of Draupadi's question, see Hitebeital and Erndl, *Is the Goddess a Feminist?*; and Mattilal, *Moral Dilemmas in the 'Mahabarata'*.

83. Baxi, "Impunity of Law and Custom," 247.

84. Felman, "Education and Crisis, or the Vicissitudes of Teaching," 2.

within the culture, with these newer reflections shared through drama, movies, and feminist reflections. Despite this, it is "forever being absorbed and revised," and "plays a significant role in the formation of the self,"[85] making and forming both individuals and collectives, and defining who we are as women within the Indian culture. It continues to exert influence on culture and sway influence on how women are to be viewed and treated by dominant groups or by men in general within the patriarchal framework.

The resonances of the stripping, public exposure and censure of the Woman-city in Ezekiel 16 and the disrobing of Draupadi in the *Mahabharata* in contemporary India are particularly obvious in the context of caste atrocities against women. Scriptures as cultural products cross borders and this is evident in the fact, that Draupadi is an index of the position of all women in Indian society and more fundamentally as a marker of Hindu Indian civilization. Draupadi also represents the creative power and resilience, fire and energy of Indian womanhood. Scriptures cannot be confined to a particular space and time. The borders and boundaries of a text change, and its meaning enhanced, and its influence widened when it is read, appropriated by multiple readers in varied locations. Through the inter-scriptural linkages provided through juxtaposition and attention to the commonality of suffering women that these narratives suggest, camaraderie and a community of women sufferers is created.

The patriarchal agenda and the affirmation of patriarchal privilege is obvious. The woman is constructed as property, and hence can be staked in a game of dice or punished if she is seen to have transgressed either caste, marital or spiritual ties. She is cultural capital, and an object of public viewing. Women's part in these texts embody each cause espoused by the men—pure, virginal, subordinated, and ideologically true to one side and free, autonomous, opinionated and subordinated in other ways. These texts narrate the story of female bodies in threat of injury or extreme suffering, bodies whose integrity has been breached by instruments of shaming, humiliation, torture, or poverty—embodiments of trauma that is at once individual and social.

These texts reveal that torture, abuse, and infliction of pain on the woman's body is the political and social frontier of gendered suffering. How much pain can the woman, even if guilty of transgression, endure? How much abuse and humiliation can the male/the prophet/the Divine inflict to make her believe that she is deserving of this violence? Who will save such women? How can such women defend or save themselves? The index of pain and power is what separates the two bodies. But the woman's

---

85. Lefkovitz, *In Scripture,* 1.

body also stands between the punisher and her community/family. While her body provides border to her 'self,' her pain and suffering are extended beyond the borders of her body to that of other women and marginalized men. The singularity of her pain is taken away and in it rests the implication that other women can also be subject to the same treatment. The inflicting of pain is made imminent, or amplified, to encompass other bodies, thus expanding the frontier.

The stripping and exposing reflect women's susceptibility to abuse and violence in a man's world. Woman-city and Draupadi are icons of women's vulnerability—index of "woman" in Indian society or ancient Israel and more fundamentally,[86] and a marker of (Hindu) Indian/ Israelite "civilization." Krishna's intervention saves Draupadi, and her salvation is often seen to arise from her chastity, devotion, and faith in Krishna. She stands in contrast to the Woman-city who is depicted as a sexual and spiritual ingrate deserving of cruel punishment.[87] Eventually she is saved and liberated by the same God who punishes her.[88] Can a woman ever forget such harsh and brutal treatment even if she was wrong? What does "salvation" mean in this context? Draupadi was a Kshatriya and hence a woman of privilege. But who saves, or will save, the Dalit woman—who lives in the midst and under the threat of countless and similar occurrences that spot the landscape of India today?

Most women (and some men) make connections between the experiences of these textual characters and their own thereby showing that these are more than just symbols. Women readers use the disrobing, the being paraded naked, the rape, and the dismembering in both texts to critique their own lives and to theorize gender relations in the world they inhabit.

These are "moments of rupture, indeed of epiphany" (Mankekar) because they reveal affective interaction with textual worlds, and open spaces and possibilities for social critique. The co-existence of multiple scriptures and their interpretations also offer readers alternative discourses to critique existing systems of power, for interpretation is itself grounded in social, material and historical relationships, conditions and contexts, and across multiple borders.

---

86. Mankekar, *Screening*, 224.

87. What led Woman-city to go after other lovers? What was her experience with her husband until this point?

88. Jacqueline Lapsley, "Ezekiel," 291; see also the interesting reflection on the God image by Mein, "Ezekiel's Awkward God," 261–77.

Works Cited

Basak, Suresh Ranjan. "Canonizing the Draupadi's in Maheshweta Devi's 'Draupadi.'" *Journal of Interdisciplinary Studies in Education* 9.2 (2020) 223–33.

Baxi, Pratiksha. "Impunity of Law and Custom: Stripping and Parading of Women in India." In *Faultlines of History: The India Papers II*, edited by Uma Chakravati, sections 226–58 (Kindle). New Delhi: Zubaan, 2016. Kindle.

Bhattacharya, Pradip. "Was Draupadi Ever Disrobed?" *Annals of the Bhandarkar Oriental Research Institute* 86 (2005) 149–52.

Carvalho, Corrine L. "Sex and the Single Prophet: Marital Status and Gender in Jeremiah and Ezekiel." In *Prophets Male and Female: Gender and Prophecy in the Hebrew Bible, the Eastern Mediterranean and the Ancient Near East*, edited by Jonathan Stökl and Corrine L Carvalho, 237–67. Ancient Israel and Its Literature 15. Atlanta: Society of Biblical Literature, 2013.

Chaitanya, Satya. "The Willing Woman: On Women and Willpower." *Indian Literature* 53.5 (2009) 183–98.

Chakravati, Uma. "Introduction: The Everyday and the Exceptional: Sexual Violence and Impunity in Our Times." In *Faultlines of History: The India Papers II*, edited by Uma Chakravati, secs. 17–40 (Kindle). New Delhi: Zubaan, 2016.

Chapman, Cynthia R. "Sculpted Warriors: Sexuality and the Sacred in the Depiction of Warfare in the Assyrian Palace Reliefs and in Ezekiel 23:14–17." In *The Aesthetics of Violence in the Prophets*, edited by Julia M O'Brien and Chris Franke, 1–17. Library of Hebrew Bible/Old Testament Studies 517. New York: T. & T. Clark, 2019.

Chauddhary, Preeti. "'Frailty! Thy Name Is not Woman' with Reference of Draupadi." *Bhartiya Bhasha, Siksha, Sahitya evam Shodh* 5.3. (2014). www. bhartiyashodh. com.

Claassens, L. Juliana. "God and Violence in the Prophets." In *The Oxford Handbook of the Prophets*, Carolyn J. Sharp, 334–49. Oxford Handbooks. New York: Oxford University Press, 2016.

———. "Transforming God-Language: The Metaphor of God as Abusive Spouse (Ezekiel 16) in Conversation with the Portrayal of God in The Colour Purple." *Scriptura* 11.1 (2014) 1–11.

Coogan, Michael. *God and Sex: What the Bible Really Says*. New York: Twelve, 2011.

Das, Saptorshi. "Vyasa's Draupadi: A Feminist Representation." *International Journal of Gender and Women's Studies* 2.2 (2014) 223–31.

Day, Linda. "Rhetoric and Domestic Violence in Ezekiel 16." *Biblical Interpretation* 8 (2000) 205–29.

———. "Teaching the Prophetic Marriage Metaphor Texts." *Teaching Theology and Religion* 2.3 (2004) 173–79.

Day, Peggy L. "The Bitch Had It Coming to Her: Rhetoric and Interpretation in Ezekiel 16." *Biblical Interpretation* 8.3 (2000) 231–54.

Delgado, Richard, and Jean Stefancic. *Understanding Words that Wound*. New York: Routledge, 2004.

Exum, J. Cheryl. "The Ethics of Violence against Women." In *The Bible in Ethics: The Second Sheffield Colloquium*, edited by John W. Rogerson et al., 248–71. JSOTSup 207. Sheffield: Sheffield Academic, 1995.

Felman, Shoshana. "Education and Crisis, or the Vicissitudes of Teaching." In *Testimony: Crisis of Witnessing in Literature, Psychoanalysis and History*, edited by Shoshana Felman and Dori Laub, 1–56. New York: Routledge, 1992.

Ganzel, Tova. "Ezekiel: Introduction and Annotations." In *The Jewish Study Bible: Jewish Publication Society Tanakh Translation*, edited by Adele Berlin and Marc Zvi Brettler. Oxford: Oxford University Press, 2004.

Guru, Gopal. "Introduction: Theorizing Humiliation." In *Humiliation: Claims and Context*, edited by Gopal Guru, 1–22. New Delhi: Oxford University Press, 2009.

Hitebeital, Alf, and Kathleen M. Erndl. *Is the Goddess a Feminist? The Politics of South Asian Goddesses*. Sheffield: Sheffield Academic, 2001.

Hornsby, Teresa. "Ezekiel." In *The Queer Bible Commentary*, edited by Deryn Guest, 412–26. London: SCM, 2006.

Ipsen, Avaren. *Sex Working and the Bible*. New York: Routledge, 2014.

Jacobs, Mignon R. "Ezekiel 16—Shared Memory of YHWH's Relationship with Jerusalem: A Story of Fraught Expectation." In *Daughter Zion: Her Portrait, Her Response*, edited by Mark J. Boda, Carol J. Dempsey, and LeAnn Snow Flesher, 201–23. Ancient Israel and Its Literature 13. Atlanta: SBL, 2012.

Janaky, "On the Trail of *the Mahabharata*." *Economic and Political Weekly* (September 12, 1992) 1997–99.

Kamionkowski, Tamar S. *Gender Reversal and Cosmic Chaos: A Study on the Book of Ezekiel*. Journal for the Study of the Old Testament Supplements 368. Sheffield: Sheffield Academic, 2003.

Karat, Brinda. "Khairanjli, Then and Now." *The Indian Express* (September 29, 2016; https://indianexpress.com/article/opinion/columns/maharashtra-khairlanji-dalit-rape-murder-una-vemula-caste-system-discrimination-3055056/.

Lapsley, Jacqueline. "Ezekiel." In *Women's Bible Commentary. Twentieth Anniversary Edition. Revised and Updated*, edited by Carol A. Newsom et al., 283–92. Louisville: Westminster John Knox, 2012.

Leeming, David Adams and Jake Page. *Goddess: Myths of the Female Divine*: New York: Oxford University Press, 1994.

Lefkovitz, Lori Hope. *In Scripture: The First Stories of Jewish Sexual Identities*. Plymouth, UK: Rowman & Littlefield, 2010.

Magdalene, F. Rachel. "Ancient Near Eastern Treaty-Curses and the Ultimate texts of Terror: A Study of Divine Sexual Abuse in the Prophetic Literature." In *A Feminist Companion to the Latter Prophets*, edited by Athalya Brenner, 326–52. Sheffield: Sheffield Academic, 1995.

Mahabharata, Sabha Parva. https://www.sacred-texts.com/hin/m02/m02064.htm.

Mankekar, Purnima. *Screening Culture, Viewing Politics: An Ethnography of Television, Womanhood and Nation in Postcolonial India*. Durham: Duke University Press, 1999.

Mattilal, Bimal Krishna. *Moral Dilemmas in the 'Mahabarata'*. Delhi: Motilal Banarsidass, 1989.

Mein, Andrew. "Ezekiel's Awkward God: Atheism, Idolatry and the Via-Negativa." *Scottish Journal of Theology* 66.3 (2013) 261–77.

Menon, Madhavi. *Infinite Variety: A History of Desire in India*. New Delhi: Speaking Tiger, 2018.

Motswapong, Pulane Elizabeth. "Understanding Draupadi as a Paragon of Gender and Resistance." *Stellenbosch Theological Journal* 3.2 (2017) 477–92.

Moughtin-Mumby, Sharon. *Sexual and Marital Metaphors in Hosea, Jeremiah, Isaiah, and Ezekiel*. New York: Oxford University Press, 2008.

Nandy, Ashis. "Humiliation: Politics and the Cultural Psychology of the Limits of Human Degradation." In *Humiliation: Claims and Context*, edited by Gopal Guru, 41–57. New Delhi: Oxford University Press, 2009.

Patton, Corrine L. "'Should Our Sister be Treated Like a Whore?' A Response to feminist Critiques of Ezekiel 23." In *The Book of Ezekiel: Theological and Anthropological Perspectives*, edited by Margaret S. Odell and John T. Strong, 221–39. SBL Symposium Series 9. Atlanta: Society of Biblical Literature, 2000.

Peterson, Brian Neil. *Ezekiel in Context: Ezekiel's Message Understood in Its Historical Setting of Covenant Curses and Ancient Near Eastern Mythological Motifs*. Eugene, OR: Pickwick Publications, 2012.

Roy, Rahul. "A Hunt, the Aftermath, Angry Indian Men and a Tragedy." *Kafila* (4 December 2013). http://kafila.org/2013/12/04/a-hunt-the-aftermath-angry-indian-men-and-a-tragedy-rahul-roy/.

Scholz, Susanne. *Sacred Witness: Rape in the Hebrew Bible*. Minneapolis: Fortress, 2010.

Seibert, Eric A. *The Violence of Scripture: Overcoming the Old Testament's Troubling Legacy*. Minneapolis: Fortress, 2012.

Shields, Mary. "Multiple Exposures: Body Rhetoric and Gender in Ezekiel 16." In *Prophets and Daniel*, edited by Athalya Brenner, 137–53. Feminist Companion to the Bible. Sheffield: Sheffield Academic, 2001.

Sloane, Andrew. "Aberrant Textuality? The case of Ezekiel the (Porno) Prophet." *Tyndale Bulletin* 59.1 (2008) 52–76.

Smith-Christopher, Daniel L. "Ezekiel in Abu-Ghraib: Rereading Ezekiel 16:37–39 in the Context of Imperial Conquest." In *Ezekiel's World: Wrestling with a Tiered Reality*, edited by S. L. Cook and C. L. Patton, 141–57. SBL Symposium Series 31. Atlanta: SBL, 2004.

Spivak, Gayatri Chakravorty. "'Draupadi' by Mahasveta Devi." *Critical Inquiry* 8.2 (1981) 381–402.

Stiebert, Johanna. *Fathers and Daughters in the Hebrew Bible*. Oxford: Oxford University Press, 2013.

Subramanian, Shreerekha. "Whom Did You Lose First, Yourself or Me? The Feminine and the Mythic in Indian Cinema." In *Myth and Violence in the Contemporary Female Text: New Cassandras*, edited by Sanja Bahun-Radunović and V. G. Julie Rajan, 75–96. Surrey, UK: Ashgate, 2011.

Sukathankar, V. S. et al., eds. *The Mahabharata, for the First Time Critically Edited*. Pune: Bhandarkar Oriental Institute, 1933–1971 (1966).

Sunder Rajan, Rajeshhwari. "The Story of Draupadi's Disrobing: Meanings for Our Times." In *Signposts: Gender Issues in Post-Independence India*, edited by Rajeshwari Sunder Rajan, 332–59. New Brunswick, NJ: Rutgers University Press, 2001.

Weems, Renita. *Battered Love: Marriage, Sex and Violence in the Hebrew Prophets*. Overtures to Biblical Theology. Minneapolis: Fortress, 1995.

Yee, Gale. *Poor Banished Children of Eve: Woman as Evil in the Hebrew Bible*. Minneapolis: Fortress, 2003.

15

Mäṉa / Buṉ'manydji Calls for Wounded Theologies

MARATJA DHAMARRAṈDJI
WITH JIONE HAVEA[1]

WAŊARR (CREATIVE POWER) GOES back to the "time"[2] before the first morning. Waŋarr is not captive to linear notions of time, as if it is in the past, divorced from the present or from the future. Waŋarr did not stop when the first morning dawned; it continued into the second and the following dawns, all the way into the present time, providing oversight of and care for ceremonies, customs, stories, arts, and lores.

Waŋarr will continue after the present time because it is interwoven with creation. Creation started before time began, and it continues into and pass the present time. In Yolŋu (for Maratja) and Moana (for Jione) worldviews, creation is not a sequence or cycle of events measurable by time. Creation is

---

1. We register our appreciation to Michelle Cook for her support through the development of this reflection during the difficult days of the COVID pandemic, which prevented us from sitting down and talking properly. We are indebted also to Howard Amery for the careful reading and helpful edits that made this reflection sharper and smarter.

2. Time is not an abstract temporal pattern. Rather, there is a spatial aspect to time because it is experienced in the rhythms of the relationships between people with creation.

neither conceived in nor trapped by human notions of time and space. In and through creation, Waŋarr gives birth to time-and-space. When "we"[3] refer to Yolŋu, Moana and island matters, we understand those in the breathing of creation; and we expect that this way of thinking is understandable to others also. In this way, Waŋarr the creative force is conceived in time-with-space and experienced (rather than timed) in creation.

At the other (unravelling, apocalyptic) end of creation, Waŋarr will not cease when the last evening sets. Darkness might come and human presence might end, but Waŋarr will continue in the land and in the sea, in the underworld and across the sky. The end of time might be far, or it might be near, but Waŋarr will survive.

Waŋarr weaves the ingredients of the (is)land with the rhythms of the sea, together with the energies of the underworld and of the skies. The weavings of Waŋarr are motivations for what some Moana people call *talanoa*—a term that carries three meanings: story, telling of story, and weaving of stories (see chap. 1). Talanoa is a Moana term, but its *event*uation and routines are experienced among First People communities in the cluster of (is)lands now known as Australia. When done well, and this requires a lot of time-with-space, talanoa makes memories and emotions, longings and hopes, come alive and live on (a native form of resurrection). In talanoa, those who have passed come out to dance and the current generation feel their vibrations and appreciate living in the world of the ancestors. In talanoa, the current generation shapes narratives with which they gift coming generations. These gifts are known by many names, in different (is)lands and languages, and we have explained them in another place as *raypirri'*.[4]

Waŋarr is not an abstract phenomenon. It is in us. It is who we are. And when our time runs out, and our memories fade, Waŋarr will survive in the (is)land, in the sea, in the underworld, in the heavens and the skies. The Waŋarr that pass through us (as *raypirri'*) will then wait to be reawaken and embodied in the talanoa of coming generations.

Ancestors

In honor of Yolŋu practice, we acknowledge that the next talanoa relates to a Yolŋu man who recently passed on, to join the circle of the ancestors. He was an accomplished musician whose roots go back to Galiwin'ku, Elcho

---

3. Our "we" refers in the first place to the co-authors; second, our "we" is open to anyone who wishes to journey with us in this reflection without needing to agree with everything that we propose.

4. Dhamarraṉdji with Havea, "Receive, Touch, Feel, and Give *Raypirri'*."

Island, and he *is* ŋapipi (uncle) of Maratja. With respect to Yolŋu practice, we also acknowledge with gratitude the permission given by Djuŋadjuŋa Yunupiŋu, an elder in his family, that we may name him and include a part of his talanoa in this reflection.

We first revisit his talanoa to set up the condition for introducing Maratja's talanoa and our invitation for navigating First People theology, mindful of the place of the ancestors in the Yolŋu worldview.

Gurrumul

Geoffrey Gurrumul Yunupiŋu (22 Jan 1971—25 July 2017), an offspring of the Gälpu (mother) and Gumatj (father) clans, was born blind. Notwithstanding, his exceptional talents testify to the *raypirri'* (gifts that pass through him, to the next generation) that flows from Waŋarr.

Gurrumul taught himself to play multiple musical instruments, and he shyly played and sung with several Indigenous Australian groups including Saltwater Band and Yothu Yindi. His many accomplishments during his short time are discoverable on social media and search engines, but we draw attention to a posthumous 2017 documentary that carries his name—*Gurrumul* (directed by Paul Damien Williams).

The documentary retells his struggles with health and with the whitefella ways, the support and inspirations that he received from his family and his community, several of his ground-breaking achievements, and his local and international tours. He sang with great Western musicians, but in his own Yolŋu way. And according to his own time and rhythm.

One of the revealing characteristics in the documentary is the way that he was amused with requests by interviewers that he introduce and say something about himself. He found the request to introduce himself (as an individual) very difficult, and it became a point of joviality. When he practiced what to say he would start—"Hello, my name is . . ."—and at that point he would bust out laughing.

Why was it difficult for Gurrumul to introduce himself? We assume that he, like other Yolŋu people, found it difficult to think of himself as if he was an individual. He was not on his own, even when he was alone (e.g., overseas), without his family and without his people. To introduce himself properly, he needed to also introduce his patriclan together with his land, his totems, his ocean, and his many neighbors.[5] He was never an individual. We

---

5. At the marae, Māori introduce themselves by naming their river, their mountain, their tribe, their family . . . in this way, their *whakapapa* includes creation and those who have passed. This practice is shared across Pasifika.

thus assume that his laughter was because the individualistic frame of the question was somewhat silly to him as a Yolŋu person. The interviewers were whitefellas who did not understand the Yolŋu worldview in which a person (imagine an artwork here) is like a dot in the canvas that is Waŋarr.

Towards the end of the documentary, he finally, with calmness and confidence, looked through the camera and introduced himself—"I am my ancestors: Maralitja, Bärrupa, Dhukulul, Ŋunbuŋu. That's all!"

From his resting place, Gurrumul continues to affirm with confidence—*I am my ancestors*—and invites we who listen to his recorded voice to hear also the voices of his ancestors. In life and now in death, his voice (in songs and interviews) was the voice of his ancestors. We borrow Gurrumul's *raypirri'* and affirm that, in life and in death, *we always are our ancestors*.

Dhamarrandji

Honour God and respect culture is the policy of Nungalinya College, and it fits well with Maratja's voice and theology: I am a Yolŋu man *and* a Christian man. I am not half this and half that; I am both—Yolŋu *and* Christian—at the same time. In my double (two-paths, two-ways, or bicultural) heritage, I am also body, soul, and spirit. I am connected to the past, the now and the future. I am all of those, at once. I am never alone!

The *wholistic* ministry very much fits in my DNA. After I read the biography of Charles Harris by William Emilsen,[6] I was drawn to his *struggle for justice* based on the passage from Luke 4:18–19: "The Spirit of the Lord is upon me, because he has anointed me to bring good news to the poor. He has sent me to proclaim release to the captives and recovery of sight to the blind, to let the oppressed go free, to proclaim the year of the Lord's favor" (NIV). Jesus's ministry was more than just good news; his ministry was more than a ministry with words. Jesus's ministry also included healing and release from captivity and oppression. Jesus's ministry was a wholistic ministry, a releasing of mind and faith from the trappings of society. It was a ministry not only to the ears and to the minds, but to the bodies as well. In the Foreword to the book, Anne Pattel-Gray explained that this was the epitome of Charles Harris's ministry to his people.

I follow Charles Harris in this way, that ministry is a *struggle for justice*. His story gives me the dream and vision for Aboriginal Theology and for the work of the Uniting Aboriginal and Islander Christian Congress (UAICC)—to enable the wholistic flow from God to Garray (Jesus) to the people, in our already-diverse and complex realities.

6. Emilsen, *Charles Harris.*

Currently I am struggling with my health, and I find that wholistic ministry is very practical and relevant for me. The theology and ministry that appeals to me, and people like me, will be wholistic and relevant to my health as well as to my faith. And most importantly, wholistic ministry and theology are relevant for my people at the same time.

The wholistic theology and ministry must first accept the fact that I am a Yolŋu man, and my worldviews are Yolŋu. Holistic theology and ministry must be appreciative to God-Bäpa, God-Waŋarr the maker of all things.

Echoing my ŋapipi (uncle) Gurrumul, I affirm that in order for me to tell my story and the stories of my people, I must introduce myself in Yolŋu way: I thus first acknowledge from Djambarrpuyŋu (my father's clans): Billy Bapawuṉ Dhamarraṉdji (my father), Galpagalpa Dhamarraṉdji, Bani Gulipawuy, Gämbika Burrminy, Wuṉbaya, Gurwanawuy, Guṉbuku (No. 2), Keith Lapuluŋ and my auntie Dorothy Wanymuli Dhamarraṉdji (Mukul-Bäpa—aunty, Bible translator assistant working with Dianne Buchanan).

From Wangurri clan (my mother's clan): Jean Gundiirrirr Dhurrkay (my mother), George Dayŋumbu Dhurrkay (my uncle), Timothy Buthimaŋ Dhurrkay, Andrew Yotjiŋ Dhurrkay, Kevin Rrurrambu Dhurrkay.

From my Märi clan (my grandmother's clan): Bariya Garrawurra, Djurrpum' Guyula, Geoffrey W Garrawurra. From my other Märi clan: Rev Dr Waṉkal (Djiṉiyiṉi) Goṉḏarra and Kelly Gurruwiwi (deceased).

From my Gäthu clan (my father's grandmother's clan): Rev Rronaŋ Garrawurra, Johnny Djilipa Garrawurra, Richard Gandhuwuy Garrawurra, Rev Walirr Garrawurra.

From my Waku clan: Binydjaḻŋu, Bawuthu Wunuŋmurra, Rev Geluŋ Bukuḻatjpi (wife of Rev Goṉḏarra) and Daymaŋu Bukuḻatjpi.

My Gutharra clan: Bopani Garrawurra and Manydjarri Ganambarr. Also, from my ŋaṉḏi clan (Gupapuyŋu): Djäwa, Djäwa's son Djapani (my wife's father), and my Christian mentor, Bäpa Joe Mawunydjil.

My two grandfathers, Bataŋga Dhurrkay (Bäpa Sheppy's right hand man and a preacher starting his ministry at Miliṉiṉbi working with his brother Harry Makarrwala Dhurrkay as well as Birrinydjawuy and Djäwa) and David Burramarra Bukuḻatjpi (Secretary for Galiwin'ku Village Council), who grew me up in my childhood stage taking me to Sunday School and showing me love and caring for me growing up and my Märi, Läwuk Gurruwiwi and her brothers Gakuba, Monyu', Old Man Willie Walilipa Goṉḏarra, Lawurra, Mathaman and Guṉmaŋa/Djawaḻwuy. Guṉmaŋa/Djawaḻwuy gave me the name of Djawaḻwuy which is given from Märi to Gutharra. I am number two. The name was given to me because of pre-birth signs recognised by Gunmaŋa which placed me from Gurala Binyanbi. Old Man Willie gave me the name Bapuwa when I was born in 1955.

I also acknowledge Howard and Felicity Amery and Nungalinya College for shaping me into the ministry of Deacon in the Uniting Church. Also, key missionary people Bäpa Sheppy and T. T. Webb at Milinįinbi from the Methodist Overseas Mission and Wamuttjan Beulah Lowe (Bible Translator). Lastly, I acknowledge Dorothy Gapany Gumbula (my wife) and my three children—Samantha Raparrk, Theresa Mathayalma and Justin Warrŋgulwuy—and all my grandchildren and great grandchildren.

These people are *Yothu Yindi* (see also next section and the concluding invitation), *märi, gutharra* relationships. I have categorized them to verify the checks and balances for my Yolŋu protocols, for my *madayin'* and for my Djambarrpuyŋu clan.

Put simply, like my ŋapipi (Gurrumul), I am not an individual who can be introduced alone nor think as if he could be alone. No Yolŋu person is ever alone. A Yolŋu is always, and only, in relationship to someone or something else. A Yolŋu is always a "half" of another "set" of Yolŋu. This understanding may be contrasted from the Latin American saying that *it takes two* to tango; in the Yolŋu worldview, it takes *more than one* to be Yolŋu.

Gurrutu / Mälk Culture

One of the means through which the ancestors shape who Yolŋu people are is Gurrutu (kin relationships) culture, within which is Mälk (also known as "skin").[7] The Yolŋu universe is divided into "two halves" (or moieties)—Dhuwa and Yirritja—and the Gurrutu prescribes how the two halves may interweave.[8] The Dhuwa (women ancestral beings) and Yirritja (men ancestral beings) are a bit like the ancient Chinese philosophy of yin and yang—they are "opposites"[9] that shadow each other and fit together. The whole Yolŋu worldview is based on Dhuwa and Yirritja. Waŋarr is the maker of the whole world view—both Yirritja and Dhuwa together. One half cannot be without the other half.

The bedrock story for Dhuwa is that of the Djaŋ'kawu sisters travelling from east to west, and the Wäkilak' sisters travelling from east to west. They travel from east to west, from sunrise to sunset, the former along a northern

---

7. Gurrutu comes from both mother and father; Mälk comes through the mother.

8. We use "two halves" because that is the usual way of speaking about mälk or moieties, but we must qualify: the emphasis is that they are "parts that belong to one another" rather than about numbers (that they are two). We highlight the place of relationships rather than suggest that the moieties are in dualistic or dichotomous relations.

9. This is not about opposition or contradiction, but about relationship—*yin* and *yang* shadow and curve into each other.

line and the latter in a southern one. For Dhuwa, all other stories come from the stories of these sisters.[10]

The Djaŋ'kawu sisters come with the digging sticks, and they find the bore, the water. They bring the dilly bag, the *dhulmu-mulka bathi,* that holds sacred things. At his ordination Maratja had that dilly bag on his chest. It gives the specifications of his clan. It belongs to this clan only. No one can steal that dilly bag. Other Dhuwa clans have their own dilly bag (*dhulmu-mulka*) and coat of arms (*maḏayin' ḻikan*) from the Djaŋ'kawu sisters.

The Djaŋ'kawu sisters give the water to the Dhuwa clans. They also give the *ḻikan* (surname/clan name) to the Dhuwa clans, along with the sacred law—the *maḏayin'*—for the clans.

The Djaŋ'kawu sisters give the law and the *maḏayin'*, while the Wäkilak' sisters give order. The Wäkilak' sisters give the mälk system and marriage system. Law and order come through these two sets of sisters. The Gurruṯu / Mälk culture goes across Dhuwa and Yirritja to create a system of checks and balances.

When Gurruṯu / Mälk functions properly, the Dhuwa and Yirritja clans are in harmony and the Yolŋu world is in balance. If the Yolŋu world is not in balance, Gurruṯu and Mälk undertake the necessary checks and corrections in order to re-establish balance. This is the *struggle for justice* that we find in the ministry of Charles Harris, and which we advocate for Aboriginal theology and ministry.

Yothu-Yindi

Yothu-Yindi is the main system. Yothu is the executor and caretaker for their mother's country and Yindi are the owners or keepers of the law. There are other relationships like *märi-guṯharra* (grandparent and grandchild), *yapa* and *ŋäṉḏi* (sister and mother) that provide checks and balances within the *maḏayin'* (law) which specifies responsibility. The *djuŋgaya* is the caretaker / executor of the law but they are not the owner. The *djuŋgaya* works with the *Liya-Ṉärra'mirr* (the owners / keepers of ceremony) for checks and balances.

No one is a man or woman on his or her own; no one is a law unto himself or herself. There are always checks and balances in all relationships (*gurruṯu*), between moieties (or "halves"). In relationships, "I am to them, and they are to me." Together these relationships, which includes

---

10. The Yirritja clans have their own bedrock stories from which all their other stories come, but that is for them to tell. The following account is limited to Dhuwa because that is what Maratja has responsibility to tell.

relationships with the ancestors and creation, make sure that everything is in order and that everything is kept accountable.

This means that there can be no super-leader, like an emperor over an empire. No-one is a leader all by himself. Likewise, no-one is a leader all by herself. Everyone is accountable to one another through the Yothu-Yindi system of checks and balances.

Wholistic Culture

Gurruṯu applies to all of creation—to all living creatures (including humans) on land and in the waters, the latter being differentiated by saltwater and freshwater bodies (an important distinction for Yolŋu and Moana islanders). Plants and all other living creatures are under the Gurruṯu system. Each member of creation is "a half"[11] of other members of creation with whom they are "paired" by the Gurruṯu culture. The pairing determined by the Gurruṯu and Mälk is according to *raypirri'*. In other words, in Yolŋu way, "the halves" are paired because they are gifts to one another. Or, to borrow another Asian phenomenon, they are the *karma* of each other. Each creature in the Yolŋu universe has the privilege to receive a partner (pair, half), which Gurruṯu and Mälk determine to come from *the other half*.

We quickly explain here that the pairing is not about hierarchy, as if one half is superior to the other. The relationship is not vertical or hierarchical; rather, the pairing is about *raypirri'*—the two halves embody gifts for one another. Gurruṯu and Mälk identify who one might marry, the obligations that one has to one's family and community, as well as give direction in how and with whom one might develop kinship.

Gurruṯu also informs one on how to relate to creation, and how to be in step with the rhythms of *Waŋarr*. Gurruṯu and Mälk are about keeping harmony, and when needed—they enable the carrying out of justice.

Buḻ'manydji

Waŋarr and talanoa keep the ancestors present. Spooky? Yes, but this reflection is shaped by our Yolŋu and Moana worldviews. As Waŋarr continues into our time, the ancestors also continue into our time-with-space. Our ancestors and Waŋarr are not removed from us. It is actually the other way

---

11. "A half" here is about *relations* rather than about *parts* (see also notes 7 and 9). Put it this way: I am related to someone, but that does not mean that there are only two of us who relate. I have many "halves" relating to me.

around—we in the present time live in the time-with-space of our ancestors. The present *is* the world of the ancestors.

It becomes easier for us to understand some of the Christian teachings when we think of those through our ancestral foundations. We will first explain Maratja's *maḏayin'* (sacred law), which intertwines with his *raypirri'*, then explain how that frame of mind helps us understand the idea that Jesus was resurrected.

Mäna / Buḻ'manydji

Related to the Gurruṯu / Mälk culture are maḏayin' (the symbols of law). Whereas Gurruṯu and Mälk refer to an unseen set of guidelines, the maḏayin' on the other hand can be seen, but only by those who are authorized. Maḏayin' represent the *raypirri'* that one generation receives from previous ones. Maḏayin' locates us in the rhythms of Waŋarr and in the breathing of creation, and directs us on how to live and relate, and with whom. For Maratja, this has to do with *Mäna / Buḻ'manydji*, a wounded shark.

During Waŋarr, a hunter of the Yirritja moiety named Murayana went hunting on the beaches of Gurala (Elcho Island, Maratja's home island)[12] with his wives. His wives were collecting oysters, and they jumped when they saw a large shark near the beach. As expected, they were afraid.

Murayana on the other hand was disturbed. He became violently dangerous, a state known as *maḏakarritj*. He entered the water in that state. He bent his spear over his head, as warriors do when they are at full attention, and they want to threaten their opponent; Murayana was so overtaken by maḏakarritj that he broke his spear in two. At that point, he wounded the shark. The wounded shark is known as *Mäna / Buḻ'manydji* (see Figure 15.1). This is represented in Maratja's coat of arms, which belongs to the Dhamarraṉdji Djambarrpuyŋu clan. Buḻ'manydji was butchered at Gurala Binyanbi and segments of his body are sung today by the clan group Dhamarraṉdji, among other Gurala clans (Elcho Is).

---

12. The big name for Maratja's home island is Gurala Binyanbi (the river). One of the significant places on Gurala Binyanbi is Garraṯa, located near Lake Evella Gapuwiyak—the main town, from there the road leads to Garraṯa homeland. Garraṯa is the place where the Yolŋu conflict resolution practice of Makarrata developed.

Figure 15.1 *Mäṉa/Buḻ'manydji*
Used with permission of the Dhamarraṉdji clan

At the top of Maratja's *maḏayin'* (see Figure 15.1) is *gukuk*, the bronze winged pigeon, who is a companion of *mäṉa* (shark).[13] The gukuk lets us know when the tide comes in or goes out. The position of gukuk depends on the ceremony or occasion of the text (or art). The cross hatching represents the waves that the shark makes as it moves through the water.

---

13. The artist is the one who unveils the painting at the right time. The community decides when a person has reached maturity and can have the next ceremony. The *maḏayin* discussed here is the identity of the clan. No one can misuse it or copy it; it belongs to the Dhamarraṉdji.

Figure 15.2: Djambparrpuyngu bible
Photo courtesy: Michelle Cook

The same cross-hatching is shown on the spine of the Djambparrpuyngu bible (Figure 15.2), the coming together of Yirritja and Dhuwa. The Bible is called *God-Waŋarrwu Walŋamirr Dhäruk* (God's life giving story)—something that was sacrificed could be used to feed us. God feeds us, like that wounded shark—Mäṉa / Buḻ'manydji—which feeds Yolŋu.

Underneath the shark is the meat—the liver and belly. The stingray barbs in the full painting (Figure 15.1) tell more of the story.[14] In the Dhamarraṉdji *maḏayin'*, the stingray meat and liver are brought together. This shows that the story is about when the Yirritja and Dhuwa interweave. They had the interaction with the spear in that place—*Garraṯa* (place of war). In the middle of the painting the crosshatches change color. The black comes in to represent the joining of the Dhuwa and Yirritja.

It is from this story that the *djukurr'* (liver fat) and the stingray meat are kneaded together to make them softer. This kneading act is piled up in the cross hatching under the shark. Only *goŋ-manymak yolŋu* (creative Yolŋu

---

14. This is a bit like the synoptic gospels where the stories are told from different perspectives. Some stories may belong to the father's clan, some to the mother's—then they all come together.

hands) can knead that meat together. It is an art. When Yolŋu taste the dish, they will testify that it is *manymak* (very good).

Everything in this story is about raypirri'; the *dhulmu-mulka bathi* (dilly bag) with alternating feathers represent the *djukurr'* (liver) and the *ŋanak* (flesh), which is a favored Yolŋu dish: the meat of the stingray is mixed with the liver fat and kneaded with water and stingray skin then rolled into large balls. We have in this dish Dhuwa (stingray) and Yirritja (shark). The one who cooks well is *goŋ-manymak* (creative and skillful hands). This is a metaphor for God-Bäpa. God is *goŋ-manymak yolŋu* (creative Yolŋu hands).

The story of the wounded shark is *mel-lakaranhamirr* (eye-opening, epiphany) for reflecting on how God works amongst the people. It speaks of the God who created all things. God is a designer and cook who made the way for Yolŋu to receive the story of the wounded shark. The meanings of holy communion can be received in this story.

This story is embedded in the life of Dhamarraṉdji. The story and the totem help our clan remember and think. The story and symbols of law are agents for verifying the Yolŋu community (through the check and balance of Gurruṯu) and for our receiving and gifting of raypirri'.

Calling Every Theology

Whereas the Yothu-Yindi song "Calling every nation" arose out of "mixed emotions at the 2000 [Olympic] games" and challenges listeners with the obliging question "What does it take to win for a nation," this chapter is less patriotic. Our concern is not for winning on behalf of any nation, but in calling every theology to account for wounded subjects like Mäṉa / Buḻ'manydji. This call comes at a time when health and ecological crises are more frequent and more devastating, with annoying debates about the extent of human responsibility for climate change, tsunamis, earthquakes, droughts, rising seas, oil spills, pandemics, and so forth.

Buḻ'manydji Theologies

The talanoa of Mäṉa / Buḻ'manydji comes from Waŋarr, and in the present Yolŋu world it is about *goŋ-manymak yolŋu* cooking. Murayana's wounded shark fed the Yolŋu community, and over time the story gave instructions for how to relate and to cook in Yolŋu way.

In our sublime Yolŋu and Moana ways, we consequently call for theologies that feed both faith and bodies. We are of course not self-centered nor greedy, thinking only for Yolŋu and Moana peoples. Wounded

(*Buḻ'manydji*) theologies are for the healing and feeding of all wounded bodies. In *Eternity in their Hearts* Don Richardson quotes Ecclesiastes 3:11—"He has made everything beautiful in its time. He has also set eternity in the hearts of the human hearts; yet no one can fathom what God has done from beginning to end" (NIV).[15] Richardson's premise is that God who prepared the gospel for people groups also prepared all people groups for the gospel. We imagine the same for *Buḻ'manydji* theologies—they are for all people groups, and for all creatures of creation.

It is easier for us to comprehend the teachings of the resurrection when we reflect with Mäna / Buḻ'manydji. We find in our time a lot of theologies and artworks in which there are no traces of the wounds upon the resurrected Jesus; such theologies leave the wounds and the scars at the cross. The resurrected Christ is cleaned and dressed up; the resurrected Jesus comes out of the tomb in glory and victory. We have found that theologies of a victorious Christ do not know how to relate to wounded bodies in our present world.

Buḻ'manydji (wounded) theologies, on the other hand, seek to relate to wounded bodies of our times. We are referring in the first place to Yolŋu and Moana bodies and minds who were wounded by colonialists and settlers. Buḻ'manydji theologies need to see their wounds and work to heal them, which can happen when theologies are wholistic and *struggle for justice*. We argue that justice needs to be attained in terms of body, mind, and faith because the colonial wounds cut into all three areas.

Second, we also refer to wounded bodies in all human communities. There are many wounded communities, and they are loss without a *gukuk* (bronzed winged pigeon) to give them direction. We imagine the resurrected Christ as *gukuk*, and we moreover imagine the resurrected Christ as still wounded. To be clear—referring to Figure 15.1—we propose that the resurrected Christ is both *gukuk* (bird) and *Mäna / Buḻ'manydji* (wounded shark). In other words, we are calling all theologies to present the resurrected Christ as one with whom fishing, hungry and wounded bodies—due to poverty, racism, illness, gender, orientation, lack of resources and services, and many other causes—could identify.

Third, we also think of creation as a wounded body. Here we think of creation in a wholistic way: earth, sea, underground, and sky. We are concerned for creation because of Waŋarr and our ancestors. The wounding of creation is also the wounding of Waŋarr and of our ancestors. Buḻ'manydji (wounded) theologies, in our thinking, should attend to creation because creation has gifted us (*raypirri'*) and generations to come with Gurruṯu and

---

15. Richardson, *Eternity in the Hearts*.

Mälk and with *maḏayin'* (representations of law), which tell us who we are and how to behave. It is because of creation that we are Yolŋu and Moana people, even with our wounds. So Buḻ'manydji theologies should be responsible for creation. In Yolŋu way: We should be responsible for creation because we are to creation as Dhuwa are to Yirritja. We belong to one another. We are gifts for one another.

A demand for Buḻ'manydji theologies is to *mother* creation. This suggestion supplements conventional thinking, which holds that creation is mother to all living creatures. We do not reject that thinking, but we supplement it (in the way that Dhuwa and Yirritja belong and gift one another) by inviting us all—Yolŋu, Moana natives and everyone—to be mothers for creation. We offer this invitation on the basis of the basic meaning of Yothu-Yindi (described above as the "main system" of the Yolŋu world)—in Yolŋu, "Yothu-Yindi" means "mother and child." Waŋarr and creation have mothered us; and in Buḻ'manydji theologies, we also mother creation. Buḻ'manydji theologies are theologies that mother to the wounded, including dear wounded creation. In this mothering function, Buḻ'manydji theologies also perform the role of *gukuk*—calling all fisher peoples, calling all nations, calling all theologies, calling all wounded bodies, calling all bothered voices, calling all . . .

Works Cited

Dhamarraṉdji, Maratja with Jione Havea, "Receive, Touch, Feel, and Give *Raypirri*'." In *Indigenous Australia and the Unfinished Business of Theology: Cross-cultural Engagement*, edited by Jione Havea, 9–15. Postcolonialism and Religions. New York: Palgrave, 2014.

Emilsen, William W. *Charles Harris: A Struggle for Justice*. Unley: MediaCom Education, 2019.

Richardson, Don. *Eternity in the Hearts*. Ada, MI: Baker, 2006.

Index

abuse, xx, xxi, 13, 62, 119, 130, 147, 162–71, 210, 211, 213–15, 218, 219, 220
acculturation, 140–45
adultery, 207, 209, 212
afterlife, 112, 113
aitaumalele, 179–84
ancestors, 8, 43, 59, 120, 131, 132, 133, 225–26, 227, 231, 236
apology, 63, 193, 194
art, xxii, 3, 10, 42, 54, 58, 67, 188–91, 233, 235
asylum seekers, 84, 119
Atua, xvii, 13, 38–48

babaylan, xix, 122, 128–32, 134, 135
badass, 5
baptism, 25, 28, 32–35
belonging(ness), 73, 85, 90, 116, 125
black, 60, 121, 128, 133, 163, 187, 189, 193, 194, 215, 234
Black Lives Matter, 187, 189
blessing(s), 12, 44, 182, 205
borderline, 188, 197
brown, 133, 186, 187

capital(ism, ist), 4, 24, 25, 31, 35, 145, 165, 219

captivity, 159, 227
caste, 29, 30, 130, 212, 214, 215, 219
catalyst, 193
ceremony, ceremonies, 6, 41, 130, 224, 230, 233
chaos, 56, 57, 59, 60, 197
chrysalis, xx, 155
cis-gender(ed), 144, 165
climate, 120, 181, 192, 235
colonial mentality, 34, 122–26, 127
colonial power, 27, 30, 31, 72, 86
coloniality, xviii, 96, 97
comfort zone, 71, 74, 94
complicity, xxi, xxii, 97, 143, 148, 149, 171
consent, 162, 167, 218
consumerism, 31, 34
contest(ed), xviii, 23, 87, 88
conversion, 95, 109, 113, 115
converts, 31
counter(cultural), 75, 182
covenant, 10, 40, 41, 63, 120, 213
creation, 42, 43, 60, 61, 67, 68, 69, 74, 75–77, 78, 134, 135, 224, 225, 231, 232, 236–37

Dao(ist), xix, 103, 110
defilement, 15, 207

239

dharma, 206, 209
diaspora, xvii, 38, 39, 47, 48, 54, 55, 56, 97, 122, 124, 139, 144, 147, 181, 182, 183
discipleship, 70
disease, 165, 193, 196
dispossession, 62, 143, 148
dissent, 62
dissonance, 121, 182
doctrine of discovery, 86
domination, 24, 26, 27, 31, 51, 52, 86, 96, 135, 165, 166, 208

empathy, 75, 116, 120, 163
empowerment, 8, 163
epiphany, 220, 235
erasure, xix, 112, 113, 116, 127
ethnoautobiography, xix, 122
ethnobiological, xx, 149
exile, 52, 60, 83, 84, 88, 206, 210, 216

fa'afāfine, xxi, 173, 174, 176, 177, 178, 181, 184
faith seeking understanding, 3
fragility, 72
freedom, xxi, 41, 42, 59, 60, 66, 74, 78, 121, 155, 157, 158, 159, 161, 188

glossolalia, 25, 28, 33
good intentions, 58, 192, 193–95
grief, 55, 56, 57, 59, 60
Gurrumul, 226–27

harlot(ry), 129, 207, 208, 209, 213, 214
healing, 57, 59, 131, 163, 164, 170, 171, 227, 236
hermeneutics, xiii, xix, 4, 97, 103, 136
heteropatriarchy, 140, 144, 147, 150
historiography, 141
holy communion, 17, 235
home, xix, 9, 13, 38, 52, 57, 59, 60, 66, 68, 70, 71, 74, 86, 93, 103, 107, 126, 131, 132, 133, 179, 180, 215, 216
homogeneity, 33, 83, 89, 90
hospitality, xviii, xix, 57, 61, 66–79, 96, 101–17
humanization, humanize, 188, 190

humiliation, 206, 209, 210, 214, 217–19
hundun, xix, 110–11, 115
hybridity, 74

inclusivity, 34
independence, xvii, 24, 38, 40, 41, 64
individualism, 34, 35
intelligence, 3, 208, 218
interrogating, 3, 7
interstitial space, 67, 68, 71, 75, 77
invasion, 84, 88, 90, 102, 109, 143, 210

justice, xxi, 2, 40, 69, 131, 149, 163, 64, 168, 207, 227, 230, 231, 236

kairos, 61
kapwa, xix, 122, 134–35
kenosis, 67, 75, 77

liberation, 3, 4–5, 128, 216
liminal space, 67, 70, 71, 74–78
liturgical, 31, 32, 54, 192, 193
liturgy, 33, 197

mainlandisation, 101, 102, 114
marginality, 68, 74, 77, 79
memory, 112, 114, 116, 117, 131, 141
menstruation, 215
mestizaje, 71, 74, 78, 79
#MeToo, xxi, 163–64, 167, 169
mimicry, 32
misogyny, 212, 213
mission Dei, 149
morality, 205
mother, 18, 44, 54, 112, 122, 123, 189, 209, 226, 228, 230, 237

Nafanua, 44–45, 46, 47, 48
naked, 72, 205, 206, 207, 208, 212, 213, 214, 215, 220
nativism, xix, 101, 103–6, 108, 109, 115–17
negative space, 67, 68, 73, 78
negotiation, 27, 38, 39, 48, 148
NextGen, 140, 150

occupation, 84

oppression, xix, 97, 113, 122–29, 133, 135, 165, 176, 215, 227
orality, 2, 3, 6, 10, 13, 14
oratory, 2, 13–14, 47
organicism, 26
orthodoxy, 182, 183

patriarchy, 164–66, 168, 170, 171, 177
pedagogy, 97
permission, 42, 136, 143, 226
perseverance, 208
polyandry, 213
pride, 53, 208
proselytization, 69

queer, 7

race, 4, 32, 57, 60, 62, 71, 84, 90, 125, 126, 127, 143, 148, 205, 216
racialization, xxii, 148
rape, 144, 165, 166, 169, 210, 211, 215, 220
reciprocity, 105, 107, 109, 110, 111
reclamation, 24, 122, 129, 131, 132
refugee(s), xviii, 46, 84, 105, 189
relocate, xviii, 94
resistance, xix, xxii, 5, 40, 69, 86, 103, 113–16, 160, 163, 208, 218
respect, 4, 48, 53, 61, 62, 109, 115, 120, 121, 131, 134, 173, 176, 183, 195, 226, 227
(re)storying, 6, 10
resurrection, 225, 236
retribution, 182, 212
revival, 23, 24, 28
roots, 8, 29, 38, 47, 53, 54, 59, 60, 84, 95, 123, 132, 170, 225

sacred, 42, 53, 54, 55, 56, 59, 116, 156, 160, 161, 163, 166, 169, 171, 183, 230, 232
sacrifice, 15, 70, 111
secular, 94, 158
settler, xx, 85, 140, 142–44, 147–50, 155
sexual conquest, 166
shame, 62, 124, 206, 214, 215, 216, 217–18

shitstem(s), xx, 4
silent exodus, 139 145–46
sin, 192, 193
skin, 39, 52, 71, 73, 123, 127, 133, 191, 193, 229, 235
slave(s), slavery, 10, 29, 31, 135, 166, 167, 169, 205, 206
somatechnics, 125–27
sorry, 12, 194
sovereign(ty), 11, 12, 13, 24, 58, 59, 62, 63, 107, 121
stolen generation, 11, 12, 13, 62, 73
subaltern(s, ity), 4, 24, 52, 96

talanoa, xix, 6–7, 11, 13, 39, 54, 58, 59, 120, 121, 127, 163, 186, 191, 197, 225, 226, 231, 235
Tagaloaalagi, xvii, 38, 39, 42–44, 45, 46, 48
temple, 59, 156, 157, 158, 159, 161
terra nullius, 86
terrorism, 90, 164
tether, 157, 161
token(ism), 134, 163, 190, 193
totem(s), 226, 235
toxic masculinity, xx, xxi, 165, 166, 173–84
transformation(s), xxi, 12, 96, 102
transgress(ed, ing, ion, ive), 25, 31, 192, 207, 213, 214, 217, 219
truth, 9, 10, 12, 51, 52, 60, 69, 195

Ubuntu, 67, 69 73, 75, 76

voiceless, 60, 183, 184

Waŋarr, 224–37
whiteness, 89, 91, 125, 126, 127, 128
wholeness, xix, 122
wholistic, 227, 228, 231, 236
whore, 11, 205, 213, 214, 216
woking, xxii

yin, yang, 129, 229
yothu yindi, 226, 229, 230–31, 237

zonah, 214

www.ingramcontent.com/pod-product-compliance
Lightning Source LLC
Chambersburg PA
CBHW050348230426
43663CB00010B/2036